CONTRIBUTORY FAULT AND INVESTOR MISCONDUCT IN INVESTMENT ARBITRATION

Investors must be held to account for their faultworthy contributions or otherwise wrongful conduct, but exactly what 'holding to account' means remains an enigma. Opinions vary on whether such circumstances are relevant to admissibility, jurisdiction, liability, or remedies. Reasoning from certain proposed axioms, this book suggests that such circumstances are generally relevant to liability, meaning that the legal concepts that they activate, contributory fault and illegality, are defences. Three defences are identified: mismanagement, investment reprisal, and post-establishment illegality. While they might lack formal recognition, arbitral tribunals have implicitly applied them in multiple investment arbitrations. In detailing their legal content, special attention is paid to resolving the problems that they raise relating to causation, apportionment of liability, distinguishing these defences from their conceptual cousins, and arbitral tribunals' jurisdiction over pleas based on investor misconduct. The result is a restatement of the rules on contributory fault and investor misconduct applicable in investment arbitrations.

Martin Jarrett is a Senior Lecturer in the Department of Law, University of Mannheim. He holds a BA and LLB (with first class honours) from the University of Newcastle, Australia. After qualifying and practising as a lawyer, he entered academia and was awarded his doctorate (summa cum laude) at the University of Mannheim.

Contributory Fault and Investor Misconduct in Investment Arbitration

MARTIN JARRETT

University of Mannheim

CAMBRIDGE
UNIVERSITY PRESS

CAMBRIDGE
UNIVERSITY PRESS

University Printing House, Cambridge CB2 8BS, United Kingdom

One Liberty Plaza, 20th Floor, New York, NY 10006, USA

477 Williamstown Road, Port Melbourne, VIC 3207, Australia

314–321, 3rd Floor, Plot 3, Splendor Forum, Jasola District Centre, New Delhi – 110025, India

79 Anson Road, #06-04/06, Singapore 079906

Cambridge University Press is part of the University of Cambridge.

It furthers the University's mission by disseminating knowledge in the pursuit of education, learning, and research at the highest international levels of excellence.

www.cambridge.org
Information on this title: www.cambridge.org/9781108481403
DOI: 10.1017/9781108630511

© Martin Jarrett 2019

First published 2019

Printed and bound in Great Britain by Clays Ltd, Elcograf S.p.A.

A catalogue record for this publication is available from the British Library.

Library of Congress Cataloging-in-Publication Data

ISBN 978-1-108-48140-3 Hardback

Contents

Foreword

The asymmetrical nature of investment treaties is one of their features that engenders discussion as to whether such treaties are beneficial for host states. This asymmetry is manifested in various forms: for instance, such treaties usually only impose obligations on states, but confer rights on investors, including the right to initiate a claim in investor-state dispute settlement against the host state. In this respect, investment treaties reflect the traditional conception of international investment law as affording protection for foreign investors and disciplining the conduct of states, which is consistent with public international law rules on diplomatic protection and the protection of aliens. In contrast, investment treaties are usually silent on the relevance for the determination of investor-state claims of allegations of investor misconduct. In the absence of treaty provisions, arbitral tribunals have grappled with such allegations with some difficulty. Is investor misconduct relevant to the jurisdiction of the tribunal, the admissibility of the claim, the liability of the state, or the question of reparation? And do the consequences (if any) depend on the precise nature of the conduct in question?

The author of the present monograph, Dr Martin Jarrett, seeks to answer these questions, and he digs deep in so doing; he does not content himself with the recitation of (and reliance on) decisions and awards of arbitral tribunals. This would be self-defeating, as the decisions and awards in question lack consistency in their treatment of these issues. Instead, in a search for general principles, he conducts an analysis of municipal law defences to civil wrongs, concepts of causation, contributory negligence, and notions of apportionment. This foundational work is important, for such concepts are comparatively underdeveloped in public international law. In this regard, the International Law Commission's Articles on State Responsibility restrict their consideration of such issues to Article 39, which concerns the obligation to make reparation. As another commentator has put it, 'the doctrine and the case law suggest that it is necessary to consider the conduct of the victim, [but] there is disagreement as to the function of that conduct and its effect on the obligations of the respondent State'.[1]

Dr Jarrett develops a classification of three situations in which the 'faultworthy' conduct of the investor can have an effect on the investor's assertion of state responsibility. These are 'mismanagement' by the investor, which refers to a situation where the investor can foresee the host state's impending breach, but invests nonetheless; 'investment reprisals', where the host state's breach of an investment treaty obligation is provoked by conduct of the investor which amounts to an affront to the host state's sovereignty; and 'post-establishment illegality'. Following this analysis, Dr Jarrett offers a series of rules which explain the content and consequences of these concepts. He concludes that such instances of misconduct provide the host state with a defence to any breach of investment treaty obligations, with provision being made for the apportionment of liability.

This volume is the result of Dr Jarrett's labour and represents a fresh approach to conceptualising this area of international investment law. His research and conclusions are not characterised by a slavish adherence to perceived authority, but rather constitute a principled search to explain the law and provide analytical rigour in an area which remains unsettled. Dr Jarrett is to be warmly commended for this publication, which will undoubtedly be widely consulted by counsel, arbitrators, states, scholars, and other stakeholders in the international investment law regime.

PROFESSOR CHESTER BROWN
THE UNIVERSITY OF SYDNEY LAW SCHOOL

---

[1]   See Moutier-Lopet, 'Contribution to the Injury', 639.

Acknowledgements

This book is based on a dissertation that was awarded a doctor of laws degree by the University of Mannheim on 5 July 2018. It is the fruit of work that could not have been produced without the generous support of the Department of Law at the University of Mannheim. In this regard, Dr Katrin Schoppa and Professor Andreas Engert, who also acted as the second grader, deserve special recognition. For all of their help, I am very grateful.

I also extend my sincerest thanks to Professor Oliver Brand, my doctoral supervisor. As any doctoral candidate can attest, a doctoral supervisor who is constantly willing to practically assist in creating the opportunities for undertaking the requisite research is invaluable. For all of his (significant) efforts in this regard, I count myself as particularly fortunate.

Contrary to the conventional wisdom on the adverse mental health consequences that are brought on by writing a significant and original research piece, the writing of this book did not induce any kind of despondency. Barring the occasional issue (particularly on causation in the law) that threw me back in my chair with my hands tied around the back of my head, the writing process was a very enjoyable experience! No doubt much of this enjoyment came from the fact that the jurisprudence on the topics of contributory fault and investor misconduct is in its developmental stage and there remain many outstanding questions. I have offered my version of what doctrine should apply to resolve these questions. In creating that doctrine, I have had the great fortune of throwing my (good and bad) ideas at some of the brightest minds in the field of international investment law. Naturally, the usual qualifier applies that any errors in this book remain my own.

Foremost, I wish to thank Professor Chester Brown. During 2017, I was the beneficiary of research funding from the German Academic Exchange Service. This funding took me to the Sydney Centre for International Law at the University of Sydney. There, I took advantage of Professor Brown's generous nature by posing a multitude of impromptu questions at him, all of which were expertly answered despite the very considerable time constraints that he was labouring under. For all of his patience and advice, I have incurred a considerable debt to him. I also wish to acknowledge and thank Irene Baghoomians for the wonderful welcome that she extended to me.

Additionally, in 2018, the University of Mannheim funded my research visits to Helsinki and Washington, DC. This generous funding let me undertake research at the law libraries of Georgetown University Law Center, the George Washington University Law School, and the University of Helsinki (Erik Castrén Institute). Being in Helsinki and Washington, DC also gave me access to a host of academics and practitioners who were willing to dig deep into some of the doctrinal questions that this book covers, including Arif Ali, Professor Rosa Celorio, Professor Jan Klabbers, Professor Martti Koskenniemi, Ian Laird, Dr Aloysius Llamzon, Dr Borzu Sabahi, Mallory Silberman, and Professor Don Wallace. All of them have helped me to sharpen my thinking on contributory fault and investor misconduct.

I could not have dealt with a more competent commissioning editor than Tom Randall. On more than one occasion, Tom was very willing and able to work with me to satisfy the various regulations that apply to the publication of German doctorates, notwithstanding the hassle that this involved. It made working with him an absolute pleasure.

Finally, I want to pay tribute to my (extended) family. Without their love and support over many years, this book would have remained an idea. Most particularly, I thank my wife, Katharina. For all of her love, and encouragement and understanding on what was required to produce this book, I am very deeply indebted to her.

Table of Arbitral Awards and Case Reports

Arbitral Awards (Investment Arbitrations)

Case Reports (Domestic)

Case Reports (International)

Other Arbitral Documents

Table of Statutes, Treaties, and Other Documents

Statutes

Treaties

Other Documents

1

A Schematic of International Investment Law

1 RESTATING CONTRIBUTORY FAULT AND INVESTOR MISCONDUCT IN INTERNATIONAL INVESTMENT LAW

Whatever their merits, the attacks that have been launched against the regime of international investment law have created a legitimacy crisis. The crisis is not the existential threat that the aggressors have made it out to be. The best evidence for this is the continual accession of states to the ICSID Convention[1] and the proliferation of large multilateral treaties with investment chapters.[2] But there is no doubt that these attacks have changed international investment law. Most prominently, these new investment treaties afford host states more regulatory freedom than what was previously perceived to be available[3] and, on the procedural front, transparency has come to the fore[4] and the idea of an investment court has been mooted.[5] Surprisingly, one of the most frequently cited defects of international investment law, its asymmetry in favour of investors, has escaped drafters' attention. The problem of asymmetry is that investment treaties bestow a bevy of rights on investors, without any reciprocal

---

[1] Since the withdrawal of Bolivia, Ecuador, and Venezuela, eight states (South Sudan, Montenegro, Sao Tome and Principe, Canada, San Marino, Iraq, Nauru, and Mexico) have acceded to the ICSID Convention.

[2] The most prominent of which are the Comprehensive Economic and Trade Agreement (European Union-Canada), the Comprehensive and Progressive Agreement for Trans-Pacific Partnership (Australia, Brunei, Canada, Chile, Japan, Malaysia, Mexico, New Zealand, Peru, Singapore, and Vietnam), and the Intra-MERCOSUR Investment Facilitation Protocol (Argentina, Brazil, Paraguay, Uruguay, and Venezuela).

[3] See, for example, the 2012 US Model Bilateral Investment Treaty, Arts. 12 and 13. This perceived lack of regulatory freedom has habitually been invoked as one of the most negative aspects of international investment law; see Schultz and Dupont, 'Investment Arbitration', 1152.

[4] Maupin, 'Transparency', 142.

[5] For the background to this proposal and the issues that it potentially faces, see Howse, 'Designing a Multilateral Investment Court', 209.

obligations that would serve as rights for host states. Restoring some balance to international investment law by restating the rules on contributory fault and investor misconduct is this monograph's objective.

The term 'restating' is used very deliberately.[6] It indicates that there is an existing body of jurisprudence on contributory fault and investor misconduct, which is the probable explanation for the absence of any rules on these topics in the new generation of investment treaties. It also suggests that this jurisprudence is disorganised and underdeveloped. The task that beckons is organising the concepts into coherent rules and clarifying their legal content, but that task cannot be achieved if contributory fault and investor misconduct remain blighted by some basic misconceptions. The first of these misconceptions concerns the legal functions of these concepts, specifically whether they are relevant to jurisdiction, admissibility, liability, or remedies.[7] The second misconception relates to their legal content, with the pervasive belief being that contributory fault is a single legal concept.

Dispelling these misconceptions will not be achieved by hand waving. An entrenched wall of jurisprudence stands behind them, but this wall is not as imposing as it might seem. Like many walls of jurisprudence, it is ultimately a house of cards built on appeals to authority.[8] But as appealing to authority is the default mode of reasoning in law, this wall will stand as long as its foundations are not rocked. That being the case, the approach of this chapter and all the following chapters is to return to the fundamentals and, from the foundations built there, create a new paradigm for contributory fault and investor misconduct.

Following this approach, this monograph begins by figuratively drawing a schematic of international investment law. This is not an overview of the legal content of the rules that make up this area of law, but an exposition of their legal functions. A rule's legal function refers to its operative role in the process of adjudicating a dispute. As an example, take the rule that a claimant invoking an investor-state dispute settlement clause in an investment treaty must be an investor, the legal function of which is to determine the arbitral tribunal's jurisdiction. Because of this, it can be definitively said that the circumstance of the investor's nationality relates to the jurisdiction question. The same is not the case for the circumstance of investor misconduct, which has been variously described as relating to jurisdiction, admissibility, and liability.[9] Equally,

---

[6] Borrowing from Martha Minow's definition of 'restating'; see Minow, 'Archetypal Legal Scholarship', 66.

[7] See Moutier-Lopet, 'Contribution to the Injury', 639.

[8] An observation that has been made in respect of other topics of international investment law; see Roberts, 'Power and Persuasion', 179.

[9] Newcombe, 'Investor Misconduct', 189.

drawing this schematic will partially solve the riddle of whether contributory fault as a legal concept belongs to the province of liability or remedies. Moreover, the classification of a rule is of general importance in international investment law because of the limited grounds of appeal available against arbitral awards. The usual option of bringing a merits-based appeal is excluded,[10] but an appeal claiming that the arbitral tribunal exceeded its jurisdiction is possible.[11] On account of this, it might be expected that there would be sharp divisions between the rules of jurisdiction, admissibility, liability, and remedies, yet there is a jurisprudential void here. This schematic seeks to fill that void and place the plank in the argument that circumstances of contributory fault and investor misconduct generally relate to liability.

2 CAUSES OF ACTION AND DEFENCES – JURISDICTION

The first point of reference in this schematic is the question of jurisdiction: does the arbitral tribunal have the power to adjudicate on the cause of action or defence? This question could be divided into two parts, with one part looking at jurisdiction in respect of causes of action and the other examining defences, but this separate treatment would lead to unnecessary duplication as the rules that inform their answers are much the same. The ultimate explanation for this is that the arbitral tribunal's jurisdiction to adjudicate on a cause of action or a defence emanates from the same source in investment arbitration: the disputants' consent. By contrast, domestic courts source their jurisdiction from sovereignty.

Most obviously, this means that the core requirement for jurisdiction with respect to both causes of action and defences is that the disputants must have consented to the arbitral tribunal's adjudication of them.[12] A necessary incidental of this rule is that the relevant cause of action or defence must be real, as opposed to a cause of action or a defence that is based on hypothetical

---

[10] Article 52(1)(e) is often seen as a provision through which a surreptitious merits-based challenge can be lodged, but it should not be used for this purpose; see Schreuer and others, *ICSID Convention*, 997–998. This might be changing, however. CETA affords a right to launch a merits-based challenge; see CETA, Art. 8.28.

[11] For ICSID arbitration the challenge could be based on ICSID Convention, Art. 52(1)(b), while for non-ICSID arbitration the challenge could be based on New York Convention, Art. 5(1)(c).

[12] *Bureau Veritas, Inspection, Valuation, Assessment and Control, BIVAC BV v. Republic of Paraguay*, ICSID Case No. ARB/07/9, Further Decision on Objections to Jurisdiction (9 October 2012) § 292.

facts.[13] But consent is rarely given out without conditions attached, and any such conditions will give rise to additional rules on jurisdiction. Identifying these conditions is the challenging part at this stage in the schematic's design.

2.1 *The Conditions of the Host State's Consent*

To decipher what the host state's conditions of consent are, it must be understood that, with its consent to arbitrate, the state gives up one of its sovereign immunities. States generally enjoy immunity from legal claims at both the domestic and international levels.[14] A state does not give up this immunity gratuitously, but with a single objective in mind: to promote its economic development by attracting investment into its territory from persons connected to other parties to the investment treaty.[15] From this, the core conditions of host states' consent can be extracted: the investment requirement, the locality requirement ('into its territory'), and the investor requirement.

That these requirements are relevant to the arbitral tribunal's jurisdiction is not in question. What are more controversial are the conditions that supplement these core conditions. Part of the controversy seemingly stems from the need to interpret each investor-state dispute settlement clause individually, with the theory being that these supplementary conditions differ according to the terms of the applicable clause. This theory, however, should not cloud the reality that, although the wording of the clauses might differ, these supplementary conditions are virtually uniform because they arise by necessary implication; in other words, the omnipresent core conditions would be ineffectual without them. An example is the requirement on timing of investment ownership,[16] a necessary derivative of the requirement that the investor own the investment. Similarly, it would make little sense if the

---

[13] *Siemens A.G. v. The Argentine Republic*, ICSID Case No. ARB/02/8, Decision on Jurisdiction (3 August 2004) § 158.

[14] Kaushal, 'Revisiting History', 510. This is recognised as a legal right of states under customary international law; see Crawford, *Brownlie's Principles*, 487.

[15] What informs this view is that modern international investment law grew out of President Kennedy's idea of declaring that the 1960s would be the 'decade of development'; see Kennedy, 'JFK Address', part VII. In the UN resolution adopting this idea, it was provided: 'To adopt measures which will stimulate the flow of private investment capital for the economic development of the developing countries, on terms that are satisfactory both to the capital-exporting countries and the capital-importing countries'; United Nations, Resolution 1710, § 2(d). For an overview of the history, see Parra, *History of ICSID*, 11–26.

[16] *Philip Morris Asia Limited v. The Commonwealth of Australia*, PCA Case No. 2012-12, Award on Jurisdiction and Admissibility (17 December 2015) ('*Philip Morris v. Australia*, Award on Jurisdiction and Admissibility') § 586.

investor's cause of action could relate to anything other than this investment, thus giving rise to the relation to the investment requirement.

A final supplementary condition of universal application is the requirement that the investor lawfully establish its investment, although it has been powerfully argued that the circumstance of the investment's lawful establishment bears no relation to the arbitral tribunal's jurisdiction. As the answer to this controversy determines the scope of the proposed defence of post-establishment illegality, it is comprehensively addressed chapter 5.[17] In summary, it is argued that lawful establishment is a necessary variable in the equation of the arbitral tribunal's jurisdiction because an unlawfully established investment, properly defined, acts as a negative force on the host state's economic development, thereby defeating the host state's purpose of consenting to investment arbitration. This legality requirement should not be confused with a similar requirement that the designated investment must have been approved by the host state for it to benefit from the host state's offer to arbitrate. Whereas the legality requirement looks at whether the conduct leading to the investment's establishment is legal, the approval requirement looks at whether the specific investment has passed through the host state's various laws that limit foreign ownership of certain assets on, for example, national security grounds.[18]

In addition to these supplementary conditions of the host state's consent, there are, for lack of a better expression, definitional conditions. While the supplemental conditions support the application of the core conditions, the definitional conditions refine the core conditions. The most prominent example is the ubiquitous 'denial of benefits' clause:[19]

ARTICLE XII

Each Party reserves the right to deny to a company of the other Party the benefits of this Treaty if nationals of a third country own or control the company and:

(a) the denying Party does not maintain normal economic relations with the third country; or
(b) the company has no substantial business activities in the territory of the Party under whose laws it is constituted or organized.

---

[17] See section 1.2.2 of chapter 5.
[18] See section 1.2.2.1 of chapter 5.
[19] Bolivia-United States BIT, Art. XII.

This article's operative effect is to delimit the wide definitional scope of investor for the purposes of jurisdiction.[20] There is, however, a pervasive view that denial of benefits clauses contain rules determining a claim's admissibility.[21] The idea of connecting denial of benefits clauses to the admissibility of claims can be summarily dismissed because, as explained in section 3 below, admissibility examines a claim's maturity for adjudication. But the idea that Article XII and its ilk are defences is plausible if the relevant provision indicates that it defines investor as the word 'investor' appears in a liability rule,[22] as opposed to defining investor for the purposes of the investor-state dispute settlement clause.

2.2 *The Conditions of the Investor's Consent*

While the conditions of the host state's consent act as the jurisdictional rules determining the arbitral tribunal's jurisdiction to decide on the investor's cause of action, the conditions of the investor's consent perform the same role in respect of the host state's defence pleas.[23] As the frequency with which host states advance such pleas has increased, the issue of the investor's consent has come into the spotlight.

Again, this is another issue that falls more squarely within the domain of chapter 5 and a more comprehensive analysis is undertaken there. To avoid any repetition, this section will focus on the principle that informs the approach taken in respect of this issue. This is conveniently referred to as the mirroring conditions approach; in other words, the conditions of the investor's consent mirror those of the host state's consent. This contradicts the position espoused in the current jurisprudence.[24] That jurisprudence holds that the investor must specifically consent to the arbitral tribunal's jurisdiction to decide a defence plea, particularly those alleging illegality on the part of the investor, presumably meaning that it can choose its conditions of consent. The approach proposed here opposes that idea. It argues that an investor consents by making its investment and submitting its cause of action to investment arbitration. The primary reason for preferring this proposed approach

---

[20] For an example of how the usual elements of the denial of benefits clause can be incorporated into the definition of 'investor', see China-Colombia BIT, Art. 2.1(b).

[21] But see *Liman Caspian Oil BV and NCL Dutch Investment BV v. Republic of Kazakhstan*, ICSID Case No. ARB/07/14, Excerpts of the Award (22 June 2010) § 258, where the question was described as 'irrelevant'. For an illumination of the distinction between jurisdiction and admissibility, see Paulsson, 'Jurisdiction and Admissibility'.

[22] For an explanation of how this classification works, see section 1.4 of chapter 2.

[23] On the distinction between pleas of defences and counterclaims, see section 4.1 of chapter 5.

[24] See section 3.1 of chapter 5.

is that it makes investment arbitration more efficacious because it gives the arbitral tribunal the opportunity to decide on the dispute as a whole. What this implies is that the facts that give rise to the host state's defence plea must form part of the dispute for the investor's consent to cover it.

This reasoning explains why the investor's conditions of consent for the arbitral tribunal's jurisdiction to entertain defence pleas mirror those of the host state: they form part of the same subject matter, namely the dispute from which the cause of action arises. What this means for counterclaims, as opposed to defence pleas, is that the investor must specifically consent to the arbitral tribunal's jurisdiction and it can designate its own conditions for that consent. The fulfilment of the conditions for defences will usually never be in question if the arbitral tribunal has jurisdiction to decide on the investor's cause of action, with the exception of the jurisdictional requirement that the defence plea must relate to the investment at the centre of the dispute. As explained in section 3.2 of chapter 5, certain pleas of investment reprisal and post-establishment illegality might not satisfy this requirement because, for example, the relevant offensive conduct concerns the personal life of one of the investor's directors.

2.3 *The Jurisdictional Questions – Answers and Their Consequences*

Having identified the rules determining the arbitral tribunal's jurisdiction over causes of action and defences as the consent of the investor and the host state and the conditions attached thereto, the question arises as to what their satisfaction or non-satisfaction entails. In the case of their complete satisfaction, the next major destination in the schematic – the admissibility of the cause of action or the defence – is reached.[25] Failure to satisfy one requirement means that the arbitral tribunal lacks jurisdiction over the cause of action or defence. In theory, this means that the cause of action or the defence can still be brought before another adjudicative body, including potentially another arbitral tribunal established under the applicable investor-state dispute resolution clause,[26] but practically such failure will signal the death of the cause

---

[25] Reinisch, 'Jurisdiction and Admissibility', 24.

[26] In *Murphy v. Ecuador*, the arbitral tribunal originally ruled that it lacked jurisdiction because the investor failed to attempt to negotiate with the host state; see *Murphy Exploration and Production Company International v. Republic of Ecuador*, ICSID Case No. ARB/08/4, Award on Jurisdiction (15 December 2010) § 157. This obligation was held to relate to jurisdiction, although, as explained in section 3.1, it is better viewed as a requirement for admissibility. After fulfilling this requirement, the investor again initiated arbitration, and the other arbitral tribunal ruled that it had jurisdiction, notwithstanding the earlier decision; see *Murphy Exploration and Production Company International v. The Republic of Ecuador*, PCA Case No. 2012-16, Partial Award on Jurisdiction (13 November 2013) §§ 203–204.

of action, particularly if advanced by the investor. This is because the adjudicative body most likely to have jurisdiction over the affected cause of action is a court in the host state[27] – a court that, for any number of legitimate or illegitimate reasons, is unlikely to find in favour of the investor. If the arbitral tribunal hands down a negative decision on jurisdiction, the investor's usual course of action is to challenge that decision – an option also open to the host state if the arbitral tribunal finds that it has jurisdiction.

3   CAUSES OF ACTION AND DEFENCES – ADMISSIBILITY

A concept with a special place in international law,[28] admissibility is the metaphorical equivalent of the maturity of a merlot, with the merlot being the cause of action or the defence, and its consumption being the adjudication. Fundamentally, the admissibility question asks: is the cause of action or defence ready for adjudication?[29] Habitually confused with jurisdiction,[30] admissibility examines the claim itself,[31] as opposed to the adjudicative power of the arbitral tribunal.[32] The distinction is critical in international investment law, and disputes decided by arbitration more generally,[33] because while decisions on jurisdiction can be appealed,[34] decisions on admissibility cannot.

3.1 *Rules of Admissibility for Causes of Action and Defences*

The applicable admissibility rules differ from investment treaty to investment treaty, but the following are the usual suspects, starting with the rule on 'no prior binding resolution'. This rule is reflected in the choice that investment

---

[27] Reinisch and Malintoppi, 'Methods of Dispute Resolution', 694.
[28] See Fitzmaurice, *Law and Procedure*, 438–439. For a discussion of its importance in international investment law, see Douglas, *International Law*, 146–148. For a panorama of recent scholarship on admissibility, see Reinisch, 'Jurisdiction and Admissibility', fn. 4.
[29] Waibel, 'Investment Arbitration', 1213; Douglas, *International Law*, 148 ('Admissibility deals with the *suitability* of the claim for adjudication').
[30] For example, in *Telefónica v. Argentina*, the arbitral tribunal held that the compulsory local litigation requirement related to a claim's inadmissibility, but then went on to note that 'inadmissibility of the claim would result in the Tribunal's temporary lack of jurisdiction'; see *Telefónica S.A. v. The Argentine Republic*, ICSID Case No. ARB/03/20, Decision of the Tribunal on Objections to Jurisdiction (25 May 2006) § 93.
[31] *Waste Management, Inc. v. United Mexican States*, ICSID Case No. ARB(AF)/98/2, Dissenting Opinion (8 May 2000) § 58.
[32] Crawford, *Brownlie's Principles*, 697.
[33] See generally Paulsson, 'Jurisdiction and Admissibility'.
[34] For arbitration conducted under the ICSID Convention, see ICSID Convention, Art. 52(1)(b); and for non-ICSID arbitration, see New York Convention, Art. V(1)(c).

treaties offer investors between litigation in the host state or arbitration. Pursuit of one necessarily excludes the other. No investment treaties contain such a rule with respect to defences, but it is undoubtedly the case that there is a similar rule, sourced from the general principles of law, that excludes an arbitral tribunal from deciding on the merits of a defence if a court has already entertained the defence in the form of a cause of action; for example, if the host state previously prosecuted the investor for some wrongful conduct before its own courts, it cannot use the same facts to launch a plea of post-establishment illegality in investment arbitration. Returning to the merlot metaphor, the 'no prior binding resolution' rule for causes of action and defences effectively means that the merlot has already been consumed.

By contrast, some investment treaties do not offer a choice between litigation or arbitration, but mandate that litigation precede any arbitration. In many cases, this will simply delay the submission of the cause of action to arbitration, but, like some merlots, these causes of action need more time to mature.[35] This is the local litigation rule. It does not apply in respect of defences, nor does the next admissibility rule – compulsory negotiation.[36] A standard provision in investment treaties, this rule requires that the investor and the host state should attempt to negotiate a settlement within a designated time period.[37] Some arbitral tribunals have ruled that this 'requirement' may be dispensed with,[38] although others have held otherwise.[39] The first approach

---

[35] In *Kiliç v. Turkmenistan*, the claimant advanced the argument that this requirement should not be given effect to because it would be wasteful, but the argument was rejected by the arbitral tribunal; see *Kiliç İnşaat İthalat İhracat Sanayi Ve Ticaret Anonim Şirketi v. Turkmenistan*, ICSID Case No. ARB/10/1, Award (2 July 2013) § 8.1.21. In this case, however, the arbitral tribunal classified this requirement as a requirement for jurisdiction, a classification that was implicitly confirmed in the annulment proceedings; see *Kiliç İnşaat İthalat İhracat Sanayi Ve Ticaret Anonim Şirketi v. Turkmenistan*, ICSID Case No. ARB/10/1, Decision on Annulment (14 July 2015) §§ 95–128.

[36] This circumstance is habitually (and incorrectly) described as a jurisdictional requirement. An example of this can be seen in *Guaracachi v. Bolivia*, where the arbitral tribunal held: 'The explicit wording requiring a written notification and the expiry of a period of six months from that notification [until initiating arbitration] leads the Tribunal to consider that the "cooling off period" *narrows the consent* given by the Contracting Parties to international arbitration'; see *Guaracachi America Inc. and Rurelec PLC v. Plurinational State of Bolivia*, PCA Case No. 2011-17, Award (31 January 2014) § 388 (emphasis added).

[37] Usually six months; see, for example, Israel-Romania BIT, Art. 7(2).

[38] *SGS Société Générale de Surveillance S.A. v. Islamic Republic of Pakistan*, ICSID Case No. ARB/01/13, Decision of the Tribunal on Objections on Jurisdiction (6 August 2003) § 184.

[39] *Murphy Exploration and Production Company International v. Republic of Ecuador*, ICSID Case No. ARB/08/4, Award on Jurisdiction (15 December 2010) § 157, although in this dispute it was classified as a requirement for jurisdiction, as opposed to a requirement for admissibility.

is justified on the ground that negotiations would be futile.[40] This pragmatic reasoning, however, strips this requirement of any legal effect, and thereby offends the presumption against ineffectiveness.[41]

A less frequent[42] requirement found in investment treaties is the limitation period.[43] It stipulates that a cause of action must be submitted to arbitration within a designated period of time after its crystallisation.[44] The corresponding rule for defences comes from the general principles of law. It would likely operate, for example, if the host state's plea of post-establishment illegality was based on facts that occurred many years in the past relative to the facts that found the correlative cause of action. When the limitation rule applies, the arbitral tribunal effectively finds that the merlot has 'gone bad'. This introduces the final admissibility rule, one that is unique to defences: the correlative rule. It stipulates that the defence must be one that can be pleaded against the investor's cause of action, for example:

> Consistent with the right of states to regulate and the customary international law principles on police powers, bona fide regulatory measures taken by a Member State that are designed and applied to protect or enhance legitimate public welfare objectives, such as public health, safety and the environment, shall not constitute an *indirect expropriation* under this Article.[45]

Accordingly, for this defence to be invoked, the investor must have proven an indirect expropriation, as opposed to any other cause of action.

3.2 *The Admissibility Questions – Answers and Their Consequences*

Other than respecting the conceptual difference between them, the main reason for distinguishing admissibility rules from jurisdictional rules is the different consequences they yield. For the admissibility questions, there are three possible answers. The positive answer, which follows when all the

---

[40] See, for example, *Abaclat and others v. The Argentine Republic*, ICSID Case No. ARB/07/5, Decision on Jurisdiction and Admissibility (4 August 2011) § 564.

[41] Scalia and Garner, *Reading Law*, 63.

[42] *William Nagel v. The Czech Republic*, SCC Case No. 049/2002, Award (9 September 2003) § 258.

[43] In international investment law, they are sometimes referred to as 'prescription periods'; see Salomon, 'Prescription Periods'. In general international law, the expression 'extinctive prescription' has greater currency; see Wouters and Verhoeven, 'Prescription', § 2.

[44] See, for example, Austria-Kazakhstan BIT, Art. 13(3) (a period of five years from the date of the investor's constructive knowledge of the cause of action).

[45] COMESA Investment Agreement, Art. 20(8) (emphasis added). This is usually referred to as the 'police powers defence'.

applicable admissibility rules for the cause of action or defence are fulfilled, leads to the liability station, while there are two varieties of negative answers. One type follows if the cause of action fails to satisfy an admissibility rule that can be subsequently satisfied, such as the rules on compulsory negotiation or local litigation. This negative answer means that the relevant cause of action or defence is still alive and may yet be admitted if the required reparatory acts are undertaken. By contrast, the second type of negative answer renders a cause of action or defence dead. This second negative answer arises if there is a failure on either of the 'no prior binding resolution' or 'limitation period' rules.

4 CAUSES OF ACTION AND DEFENCES – LIABILITY

Frequently referred to as the merits phase, the liability question fundamentally asks: has conduct been performed that is wrongful according to the applicable standards? This question examines the quality of certain conduct, hence explaining why liability is synonymous with merits. It divides between two parts, the first of which is the cause of action part. In this part, the question is: has conduct, attributable to the host state, been performed that is in breach of an applicable liability-creating rule? This is not the occasion to identify those rules because they are well known, but the chance will be taken to argue that they necessarily contain a consequence (harm) legal element.

This is a controversial submission because, one, harm is not a prerequisite to creating liability under international law[46] and, two, the standard formulations of these rules do not specify a harm legal element. The commentary attaching to the ILC Articles on State Responsibility, however, recognises that if harm is the gist of a rule,[47] then a harm legal element can be read into it.[48] Considering that these rules aim to 'protect' investments, it can be reasoned that this principle applies. The confirmation of its application can be seen in the preposterousness of the investor bringing, for example, a claim based on a breach of the fair and equitable treatment standard without being able to prove that the relevant offensive conduct failed to cause any investment loss, which reveals the significance of this submission: all liability-creating rules of international investment law must contain cause legal elements. Accepting this conclusion,

---

[46] International law has abandoned the notion that legal liability arises if there is unlawful conduct, some harm, and a causal connection between them; see Stern, 'Obligation to Make Reparation', 194.

[47] ILC Articles on State Responsibility (with commentaries), Art. 2 (cmt 9).

[48] However, this abandonment does not mean that a liability rule without an explicit consequence legal element does not contain one by implication; see Crawford, *First Report on State Responsibility*, § 117.

its significance is that pleas of contributory fault relate to the liability question, rather than to the question of what remedies the investor can obtain.[49]

The second part of the liability question is the defences part, which asks: is there conduct that, one, falls within the scope of one of the applicable defences and, two, is attributable to the subject of that defence? Again, this is not the occasion to detail the legal content of those defences. What is more important is understanding how they impact on the liability question. If a defence is established, it will either eliminate the host state's liability or reduce it. How this reduction is calculated depends on the nature of the partial defence in question. For many partial defences, the reduction comes about through dividing the disputants' liability according to, for example, the extent to which they could have foreseen the relevant loss or helped to cause it.[50] Another approach is to divide liability according to the losses each disputant is responsible for, which is the approach adopted in respect of the defence of mismanagement.[51] Following this approach, each loss caused by the breach is identified and then, applying the relevant rules, pinned to either the claimant or the respondent. If there is no applicable defence and a breach can be established, then the respondent's liability stands at 100 per cent.

Regardless of whether the respondent is fully liable or a complete or partial defence applies, the legal consequence for the cause of action and any pleaded defence is its inadmissibility in any later adjudicative proceedings pursuant to the rule on 'no prior binding resolution'.[52] Accordingly, if the investor successfully argues a breach of an investment treaty and the host state raises the defence of post-establishment illegality to counter that cause of action, then, pursuant to the admissibility rule on 'no prior binding resolution', the host state should be subsequently barred from dressing up the same defence as a cause of action and arguing it before its domestic courts. If the corresponding rule in the host state's domestic law was not applied by its courts, this should constitute a denial of justice.

5 REMEDIES – JURISDICTION, AVAILABILITY, AND MEASUREMENT

If after the application of a partial defence there is complete or residual liability, then the remedies for that liability may be considered. In the remedies

---

[49] On the distinction between liability rules and remedy rules, see sections 1.6.1 and 1.6.2 in chapter 2.

[50] This is the default approach in international law in cases involving contributory fault; see Moutier-Lopet, 'Contribution to the Injury', 644.

[51] See sections 2.3.1.1, 2.3.1.2, and 2.3.1.3 in chapter 4.

[52] See section 3.1 above.

phase, there are three questions to answer, starting with the arbitral tribunal's jurisdiction in respect of remedies. Although the jurisdiction question is often overlooked because there are typically no explicit rules on this matter, arbitral tribunals can be limited in the types of remedies that they can order. Some investment treaties do provide for such limitations,[53] but most do not,[54] meaning that arbitral tribunals theoretically have power to order any remedy recognised under international law. These remedies are authoritatively stated in the ILC Articles on State Responsibility.

The next question asks:[55] what remedies are available for the breach in question and how is the extent of the chosen remedy measured? Many liability-creating rules designate the remedy that follows their breach, but this is not true of international investment law, except in respect of the rule on lawful expropriations where compensation is the sole remedy available. Accordingly, a breach of the fair and equitable treatment standard could be remedied with an order of restitution, which is the default remedy in international law.[56] In practice, however, arbitral tribunals seldom order performance-based remedies,[57] presumably because they feel that they lack the legitimacy[58] to order, for example, a state not to apply certain legislation to the investor held to be in breach of the applicable investment treaty.[59] What this means is that the actual default remedy in international investment law is compensation.[60] It is awarded to cover the main investment loss and any reasonably related consequential losses.

After identifying the compensable losses, the final task is the calculation of the compensation.[61] For the main investment loss, the objective is to ascertain

---

[53] Although under NAFTA arbitral tribunals are limited to monetary-based remedies; see NAFTA, Art. 1135.

[54] Sabahi, *Compensation and Restitution*, 63.

[55] Gray, *Judicial Remedies*, 1.

[56] ILC Articles on State Responsibility (with commentaries), Art. 35 (cmt 3).

[57] For an example of a case where such a remedy was awarded, see *Bernhard von Pezold and others v. Republic of Zimbabwe*, ICSID Case No. ARB/10/15, Award (28 July 2015) § 1020. Similarly, in *ATA v. Jordan*, the arbitral tribunal ordered the immediate termination of litigation in Jordan; see *ATA Construction, Industrial and Trading Company v. The Hashemite Kingdom of Jordan*, ICSID Case No. ARB/08/2, Award (18 May 2010) § 133(4).

[58] Van Aaken, 'Primary and Secondary Remedies', 725. See also *Occidental Petroleum Corporation and Occidental Exploration and Production Company v. The Republic of Ecuador*, ICSID Case No. ARB/06/11, Decision on Provisional Measures (17 August 2007) § 84.

[59] This was the remedy that the investor in *Philip Morris v. Australia* sought; see *Philip Morris Asia Limited v. The Commonwealth of Australia*, PCA Case No. 2012-12, Notice of Claim (15 July 2011) § 49.

[60] As it also is in international law more generally; see ILC Articles on State Responsibility (with commentaries), Art. 36 (cmt 2).

[61] Gray, *Judicial Remedies*, 1.

the fair market value of the investment immediately before the breach. There are three valuation options for ascertaining fair market value,[62] beginning first with the hypothetical bargain option.[63] This option ascertains value from the amount that the hypothetical seller and the hypothetical buyer would agree to in an arm's length transaction.[64] To utilise this valuation technique, however, arbitral tribunals have required that there be an active market for the investment.[65] The second option is to apply an income capitalisation valuation method. In international investment law, the discounted cash flow method has become the principal method in this regard.[66] The third option is an asset-based approach.

The more pressing question is: which option is applicable? There is limited jurisprudence on this question, but it appears that there is an order of priority beginning with the hypothetical bargain.[67] If there is an inactive market for the investment, the income capitalisation option is used, although this similarly reaches its limitations if the investment has not and will not generate income.[68] In this case, the asset-based approach is used. The jurisprudence from arbitral awards shows that this effectively means that the investment is valued at the same price that the investor paid for it.[69] As regards the esoteric topiç[70] of the valuation of the reasonably related losses, the limited jurisprudence indicates that the investor's incidental losses will be valued on a costs basis.[71]

---

[62] Kantor, *Valuation*, 7.

[63] Ripinsky and Williams, *Damages*, 186. It is also called the 'actual transaction price'; see Kantor, *Valuation*, 17.

[64] *Venezuela Holdings, B.V. and others v. The Bolivarian Republic of Venezuela*, ICSID Case No. ARB/07/27, Award (9 October 2014) ('*Venezuela Holdings v. Venezuela*') § 385.

[65] In *Yukos v. Russia*, the arbitral tribunal found that an active market for the investor's investments, being shareholdings in an upstream oil and gas company, existed when there were nine other similar companies; see *Yukos Universal Limited (Isle of Man) v. The Russian Federation*, PCA Case No. AA 227, Final Award (18 July 2014) ('*Yukos v. Russia*') § 1788. Similarly, in *Enron v. Argentina*, the arbitral tribunal commented: 'the Tribunal accepts Claimants' point that when markets are illiquid or the volume of transactions is limited, market capitalization might provide distorted valuation indications'; see *Enron Corporation and Ponderosa Assets, L.P. v. Argentine Republic*, ICSID Case No. ARB/01/3, Award (22 May 2007) § 383.

[66] Marboe, *Calculation of Compensation and Damages*, § 5.02.

[67] Ibid.

[68] *Venezuela Holdings v. Venezuela* § 382.

[69] See, for example, *MTD Equity Sdn. Bhd. and MTD Chile S.A. v. Republic of Chile*, ICSID Case No. ARB/01/7, Award (25 May 2004) ('*MTD v. Chile*, Award') § 240.

[70] Ripinsky and Williams, *Damages*, 299.

[71] See, for example, *Metalclad Corporation v. The United Mexican States*, ICSID Case No. ARB(AF)/97/1, Award (30 August 2000) § 123.

6 CONCLUSION

What this schematic shows is that each rule of international investment law can be categorised according to the relevant legal question to which it relates. The factor guiding this categorisation is the nature of the question; for example, as the admissibility questions specifically examine the readiness of the cause of action or any pleaded defence, only rules performing that examination can be categorised as admissibility rules, to the exclusion of all others. Categorising a rule as a jurisdictional rule, admissibility rule, liability rule, or remedy rule signals its legal function. Upon their satisfaction, defences can have one of two legal functions, either completely eliminating or partially reducing liability. These legal functions are unique to defences, making them distinct from other types of rules. What is not apparent, however, is how a rule earns the classification of defence – a task that is the business of the next chapter.

2

A Definition of Defence

1 DEFINING DEFENCE

On account of the juristic compulsion to define words and the fundamental importance of the concept, it is surprising[1] that a commonly accepted definition cannot be ascribed to 'defence'. Worse, it is habitually used in a 'slap-dash'[2] and 'sloppy'[3] way.[4] Robinson[5] and Goudkamp[6] identify, in the context of Anglo-American criminal and tort law, respectively, five different uses for defence. The jurisprudence from international law is equally unhelpful.[7]

The lack of a commonly accepted definition of defence gives rise to the need to create one.[8] In law, the task of definition is aided by rules of interpretation.[9] This aid, however, is not applicable for present purposes because the task is to define a transjurisdictional concept,[10] as opposed to a legal element

---

[1] Although it is generally acknowledged that the more fundamental a concept, the more diffi-cult it is to find a commonly accepted definition; see Hart, 'Definition and Theory', 23.

[2] Goudkamp, *Tort Law Defences*, 64.

[3] Campbell, 'Offence and Defence', 75.

[4] For a list of the various synonyms of defence in international law, see Szurek, 'Notion of Circumstances Precluding Wrongfulness', 427 and 432–433.

[5] Robinson, 'Criminal Law Defenses', 204–232.

[6] Goudkamp, *Tort Law Defences*, 1–5.

[7] Crawford, *State Responsibility*, 275; Szurek, 'Notion of Circumstances Precluding Wrongfulness', 427.

[8] In the words of John Locke: 'it is not enough that men have ideas, for which they make these signs stand; but they must also take care to apply their words as near as may be to such ideas as common use has annexed them to'; see Locke, *Essay Concerning Human Understanding*, Book III, chap. 11, § 11.

[9] In international investment law, these rules are found in Articles 31 to 33 of the Vienna Convention on the Law of Treaties and apply regardless of whether the host state has signed this treaty, as the rules of interpretation are part of customary international law; see Gardiner, *Treaty Interpretation*, 7.

[10] See Bar, *Common European Law of Torts*, 502.

in a particular rule. This is actually a blessing because it is a licence to propose a new definition of defence, namely:

> A rule that relates to the liability question and has a correlative relationship with a liability rule, but contains either, one, an external legal element compared to that rule or, two, restricts the definitional scope of any legal element in that rule. If proven by a respondent, it operates to eliminate or reduce the liability of that respondent.

This definition only imparts sufficient information to offer a basic understanding. It requires significant amplification of six concepts, all of which are addressed in the sections below.

1.1 *Relation to Liability Question*

As discussed in chapter 1, the liability question assesses the quality of the conduct that gives rise to a dispute. If defences are the second half of the liability walnut,[11] then they must equally evaluate conduct. Depending on the defence, this might be the claimant's conduct, as is the case with the contributory fault defences. Alternatively, the same conduct that constitutes the breach might be re-evaluated in light of other circumstances, such as grave and imminent peril in the host state.[12]

The conduct founding a defence cannot be any conduct, but must form part of the factual matrix that constitutes the dispute. Evaluating conduct that is distinct from the dispute between the investor and host state is problematic because the arbitral tribunal risks straying beyond its jurisdiction.[13]

Once this is accepted, the following question arises: what conduct and circumstances form part of a dispute? A simple example can help to illustrate the answer. Imagine that the parents have a strict rule for their child: on Saturday evenings the child must be home before 22:00 hours, otherwise the child is banned from going out of the home on the next Saturday evening. On one Saturday evening the child arrives home at 22:45. When asked for an explanation, the child cites his or her prior good record. Assuming that the parents are not overwhelmed by feelings of sympathy for the child, they should not accept this answer as it bears no relation to whether the conduct

---

[11] Referring to the idea of the tripartite division in international law; see Condorelli and Kress, 'Rules of Attribution', 224.

[12] Grave and imminent peril is one of the legal elements that must be established to make out the defence of necessity; see ILC Articles on State Responsibility, Art. 25(1)(a).

[13] See sections 3.1.1 and 4.1 of chapter 5 for a discussion of how the determination of counterclaims by arbitral tribunals in investment disputes is usually outside their jurisdiction.

in question is wrongful. By contrast, if the explanation was that the child was stuck in a traffic jam that blocked the road leading home, then this would be relevant. The reason for this relevance is that this circumstance bears a causal relation to the child's breach, which is one factor that can link a fact to a dispute. The other factor that can achieve this link is one that has a beneficial relationship to the subject matter at the dispute's core. For the rule under consideration, that subject matter is presumed to be the child's safety. Because of this, if the child's explanation was that he or she was visiting a trusted family member or friend, such as a grandparent, and that person escorted the child back home, then this circumstance might also be accepted as an answer to his or her lateness.

1.2 *Correlative Relationship to a Liability Rule*

Liability rules and their applicable defences are in correlative relationships. They are correlatives because a defence's invocation is dependent on proof of the applicable liability rule's breach – a factor that distinguishes the plea of a defence from a counterclaim. Counterclaims are independent because their invocation is not dependent on a prior breach of a liability rule. But because the facts underlying a plea of a defence and a counterclaim are seemingly the same, some confusion has arisen as to how they should be distinguished – an issue addressed in section 4.1 of chapter 5.

1.3 *External Legal Element*

Typically, a defence's foundational fact is an external legal element. An external legal element is a legal element that does not have to be proven by the claimant to establish a breach of the relevant liability rule.[14] As a legal element is a fact in a liability rule's predicate, this means that an external legal element is a fact that does not have to be proven by the claimant to establish its claim.

Identifying a fact as independent from another fact is usually unproblematic. The task becomes more complicated if the two facts are of a causal nature[15] – a problem that is necessarily encountered if the liability rule contains a cause legal element. Exemplifying the distinction between causal facts is a task undertaken in sections 5.1.1 and 5.1.2 below and, to avoid any duplication, that exemplification is not repeated here.

---

[14] Virgo, 'Justifying Necessity', 139.
[15] See Youngs, *English, French & German Comparative Law*, 451.

1.4 *Restriction of Definitional Scope*

If a putative defence does not contain any external legal elements, it may nonetheless constitute a defence by restricting the usual definitional scope of any legal element in the relevant liability rule. Consider the following liability rule:

(1) A passenger must not talk while travelling in Carriage A of the train (the 'no talking rule').

This liability rule is subject to two defences, and they read:

(2) It is a complete defence to a breach of the no talking rule if the:
   (a) passenger asks another person for information relating to the train's next stop; or
   (b) passenger's talking does not disturb any other person.

These rules are apocryphal, but they are instructive. The first defence ((2) (a)) is an example of a defence that restricts the definitional scope of a legal element in the no talking rule. The relevant legal element is 'talk'. Asking another person for information about the train's next stop would fall within the usual definition of talk, but this rule effectively carves out this conduct from the definition of talk.

This should be compared to the second defence ((2)(b)). It does not carve out an exception to the legal element's usual definition, but adds a new legal element: disturbance of another person. This is an example of an external legal element.

1.5 *Respondent's Burden of Proof*

If a legal element is classified as part of a defence, what consequence does this entail? The definition of defence proposed here adopts the traditional answer[16] to this question: if a legal element forms part of a defence, then the respondent assumes the burden of proof in respect of that legal element.[17] Concisely, this means that the respondent must produce sufficient evidence to prove a fact

---

[16] Fletcher, *Rethinking Criminal Law*, 524. In English law, this traditional answer finds its roots in the writings of William Blackstone: 'And all these circumstances of justification, excuse, or alleviation, it is incumbent on the prisoner to make out, to the satisfaction of the court and jury'; see Blackstone, *Commentaries*, 201.

[17] This is a well-recognised principle of international law; see Crawford, *Brownlie's Principles*, 563.

and develop legal arguments to show that that fact falls inside the definitional scope of the relevant legal element.[18]

Most jurists accept the traditional answer,[19] but, among some prominent jurists who have developed theories on defences, it has been the subject of sustained attack. This challenge finds its origins in the work of George Fletcher. Fletcher claims that 'prosecutorial burdens across the board' have developed,[20] and, with this development, the allocation of burdens of proof between legal elements belonging to liability rules and defences has evaporated. Two comments can be made in respect of this observation.

First, the observation should be limited to Anglo-American criminal law. Fletcher implicitly acknowledged this limitation when he lamented that judges have a tendency to wrongfully allocate the burden of proof in criminal cases[21] as they adopt the civil law rule that it alternates between the claimant and the respondent.[22] Moreover, the supporters of this challenge, Gardner[23] and Glanville,[24] also restrict their analyses to Anglo-American criminal law.[25] By contrast, the jurisprudence of international investment law displays a healthy respect for the idea of shifting burdens.[26] Second, if a claimant or prosecutor always carried the burden of proof, then this would simply mean that the legal elements of the relevant 'defence' would migrate over to their correlative liability rule. This would extinguish the independent existence of any such defence.

A second challenge, which has been raised in the context of private law, can be traced back to John Wigmore. In an article on American tort law, Wigmore commented:

> Sometimes, however, the principles of pleading cannot be relied upon to show in this way the line of distinction. For instance, in actions for malicious prosecution, these tertiary limitations vindicate or exempt the defendant, if he brought the suit upon reasonable or probable ground and without malice;

[18] Phelps and Lehman (eds.), *West's Encyclopedia*, 166 (definition of 'burden of proof'). This principle is also reflected in procedural rules that are applicable in most investment arbitrations; see, for example, UNCITRAL Arbitration Rules (2013), Art. 27(1).
[19] Moore, *Act and Crime*, 179. For international investment law, see Pauwelyn, 'Defenses and the Burden of Proof'.
[20] Fletcher, *Rethinking Criminal Law*, 553.
[21] Ibid., 530.
[22] Ibid., 531.
[23] Gardner, 'Fletcher on Offences and Defences', 818.
[24] Williams, 'Offences and Defences', 236.
[25] Williams also supports the interpretation of Fletcher's work adopted in this paper; see ibid., 235.
[26] Sourgens and others, *Evidence*, § 3.14.

nevertheless, it is the plaintiff who is required to show that this reasonable or probable ground did not exist, a sensible requirement which we must not allow to obscure the true nature of this element.[27]

This statement captures the core of this challenge: there are some rules that are substantially classified as defences, but for which the claimant carries the burden of proof. Effectively, the claimant has the obligation to disprove the existence of these defences' legal elements. Wigmore did not elaborate on how these substantive defences could be distinguished from other defences. More recently, Goudkamp has endorsed this challenge.[28] To substantiate his claim, a citation[29] is made to a report of the Law Commission (England and Wales) where it is noted that if a respondent raises the 'limitation defence', it falls to the claimant to disprove the application of this 'defence'.

With respect, it is considered that the reasons Wigmore and Goudkamp marshal in support of their challenge lend it no validity. Aside from citing no authority, Wigmore's difficulty is the Restatement (First) of Torts, the most authoritative statement of the law on malicious prosecution following his article. There, 'without reasonable or probable ground' is included as a legal element of the rule on malicious prosecution.[30] The applicable defences to a breach of the rule on malicious prosecution are signified as such by their structural separation from this rule.[31]

For Goudkamp, the difficulty lies in the fact that the 'limitation defence' is not a defence at all.[32] The limitation defence is a rule that goes to the question of the claim's admissibility, as opposed to the liability question. This is a conclusion that holds not only in respect of international investment law, but all areas of law.[33] As discussed above,[34] whatever conduct constitutes the founding fact of a defence, it must be a constitutive element of the dispute from which the claim arises. The conduct regarding the timing of a claim's submission

---

[27] Wigmore, 'Tripartite Division of Torts', 207–208.

[28] Goudkamp, *Tort Law Defences*, 4 and 47.

[29] Ibid., 4.

[30] Restatement (First) of Torts, § 653(1)(a)(i).

[31] While the tort of malicious prosecution is contained in Division Seven, the applicable defences are contained in Division Twelve.

[32] See sections 5.3.1 and 5.3.2 below for a discussion of the distinction between defences and claim admissibility rules.

[33] For a similar view, see Duarte d'Almeida, 'Defining "Defences"', 51–52. Most jurists, however, hold that claim limitation periods are defences; see Dyson and others, 'Thinking in Terms of Contract Defences', 3.

[34] See section 1.1 above.

cannot be described as one of these facts as it is a circumstance relating to the claim itself.

1.6 Legal Function of Defences: Elimination or Reduction of Liability

Defences operate to either eliminate or reduce the respondent's liability. While defences that eliminate liability are complete defences, defences that reduce liability are partial defences. Partial defences enjoy wide recognition in domestic criminal law,[35] but are more controversial in domestic private law[36] and international law.[37]

In international investment law, however, partial defences have been implicitly, albeit unconsciously, recognised as 'limitations on compensation'.[38] *Yukos v. Russia* offers an example. There, after having determined that the investors made a faultworthy contribution to their losses[39] in the form of investment reprisal,[40] the arbitral tribunal concluded that:

> the Claimants contributed to the extent of 25 percent to the prejudice they suffered at the hands of the [respondent]. As a consequence, the amount of damages to be paid by Respondent to Claimants will be *reduced by 25 percent.*[41]

The reference to reducing damages is unfortunate because it suggests that investment reprisal acts as a reduction on remedies, as opposed to liability. This is a mere terminological error induced by the ILC Articles on State Responsibility.[42] What is important is that this 25 per cent reduction was

---

[35] The most recognisable is the defence of provocation or, in English law, 'loss of control', which reduces the defendant's potential punishment from the punishment for murder to the punishment for manslaughter; see Coroners and Justice Act 2009 (England and Wales) s. 54.

[36] See Goudkamp, *Tort Law Defences*, 17–18.

[37] There is limited authority on the issue in international law, but the following statement from Crawford indicates that international law only recognises complete defences: 'So circumstances can have the effect of precluding wrongfulness and therefore responsibility if they mean that there is *no breach*'; see Crawford, *State Responsibility*, 275 (emphasis added).

[38] Ripinsky and Williams, *Damages*, 313.

[39] *Yukos v. Russia* § 1633.

[40] The arbitral tribunal did not explicitly make a finding of investment reprisal, but rather 'contributory fault'. As explained in section 1 of chapter 5, the arbitral tribunal's finding is best described as a finding of investment reprisal because this expression most accurately reflects the nature of the investor's conduct which gives rise to the defence.

[41] *Yukos v. Russia* § 1827 (emphasis added).

[42] Although, originally, contributory fault was classified as a defence in the ILC Articles on State Responsibility; see section 1 of chapter 6.

actually applied to Russia's liability for the investor's loss.[43] The other cases involving faultworthy contributions by the investor in international investment law have made the same application.[44]

1.6.1 The Province of the Law of Remedies

Presumably, an objection will be raised that this theory misclassifies legal concepts involving faultworthy contributions[45] from the claimant as defences; rather, these concepts are remedy rules. This objection, however, misconceives the factors that determine residency in the province of the law of remedies. Remedies are concerned with the following two questions:[46]

- What are the possible legal consequences (remedies)[47] attaching to the liability created by the breach of the liability rule?
- What is the measurement of the selected legal consequence (remedy)?

An objectionist would assert that the claimant's faultworthy contribution relates to the second question. The rules that actually relate to this question, however, are rules that *define*, as opposed to rules that *evaluative* conduct. For example, if the selected remedy is compensation, then its measurement looks at the valuation of the qualifying losses. For this purpose, the definition of 'fair market value' is critical. Similarly, if the selected remedy is an apology,[48] then the rules on measurement are those that define its nature and extent; for example, it must be proportionate to the claimant's harm and not humiliating.[49]

Yet, how can this theory be reconciled with the outcome that a claimant's faultworthy conduct practically reduces its remedies? Concisely, this finding acts as a cap on the respondent's liability, and the remedies are calculated with

---

[43] *Yukos v. Russia* § 1888. In this paragraph, the arbitral tribunal clarifies that the reduction applies to the loss that the host state is liable for, and then proceeds to calculate the interest due on that amount.

[44] *MTD v. Chile*, Award § 253; *Occidental Petroleum Corporation and Occidental Exploration and Production Company v. The Republic of Ecuador*, ICSID Case No. ARB/06/11, Award (5 October 2012) ('*Occidental v. Ecuador*, Award') § 876.

[45] This is meant to be a broad reference to the many varieties of contributory fault across different jurisdictions, specifically including the Anglo-American law concepts of 'contributory negligence' and 'comparative negligence', the French law concept of 'faute de la victime', and the German law concept of 'Mitverschulden'.

[46] Gray, *Judicial Remedies*, 1; Dobbs, *Law on Remedies*, 1.

[47] At least in private law cases these legal consequences are called remedies, but in criminal law cases they are referred to as punishments or sentences, see York and Bauman, *Remedies*, 1–2.

[48] A remedy provided for under customary international law; see ILC Articles on State Responsibility, Art. 37(2).

[49] Ibid., Art. 37(3).

reference to that cap. For example, if the respondent's liability is 75 per cent for a breach, then the compensation attaching to any loss caused by this breach is capped at 75 per cent. The same result will follow if the claimant's faultworthy contribution of 25 per cent is reduced from the compensation for this loss, but this method risks undercompensating the claimant. This would be the case where there are two breaches with multiple losses attaching thereto, but the claimant has made a faultworthy contribution in respect of only one breach. The reduction approach is prone to reduce the claimant's compensation by 25 per cent for both breaches.

1.6.2 The Province of the Law of Liability

In contrast to the law of remedies, the law of liability evaluates the conduct of legal subjects as acceptable or not acceptable, with liability attaching to the latter finding. The two principal types of rules in the law of liability are liability rules and defences. An example of a liability rule would be:

A person must not litter in a public place (the 'littering rule');

and a corresponding defence:

It is a defence to a breach of the littering rule if the person leaves a newspaper in a public place with the intention of donating it to another person.

What is important to appreciate is that both of these rules regulate and evaluative human conduct. Equally, any rule on a claimant's faultworthy contribution evaluates human conduct because, one, the claimant's contribution must necessarily take the form of human conduct and, two, its faultworthy nature means that it should attract condemnation. This is the fundamental reason for classifying rules on a claimant's faultworthy contribution into the law of liability.

2 CLASSIFICATION OF LEGAL ELEMENTS

Liability rules and defences are made up of various legal elements. Take the rule on fair and equitable treatment:[50]

A host state must not unfairly and inequitably cause the devaluation of an investment, and any reasonably related incidental loss, belonging to an investor and within its territory.

---

[50] Formulated in accordance with the principles of plain legal English.

It is possible to relocate a legal element from this rule, such as the legal element 'unfairly and inequitably', to create a defence. The new rule on fair and equitable treatment (the 'rule on investment devaluation') would remove the words 'unfairly and inequitably', and a new corresponding defence would read:

> It is a defence to a breach of the rule on investment devaluation if the host state's conduct was fair and equitable.

The point is that legal elements of correlative liability rules and defences are transposable;[51] in other words, they may be included in the liability rule or the defence.[52] On account of this, it needs to be asked: what determines whether a legal element should be part of a liability rule or a defence?

This is a question that has preoccupied jurists who have considered the nature of defences,[53] with most attention being given to whether consent should be viewed as a defence.[54] What is most important to appreciate is the nature of the question. Whether a legal element forms part of a liability rule or a defence is not a matter of logical necessity because potentially any legal element can be transposed.[55] For example, the legal element of the investment's locality in the rule on fair and equitable treatment, seemingly an entrenched legal element,[56] could be extracted to create the following defence:

> It is a defence to a breach of the rule on fair and equitable treatment if the investment is not within the host state's territory.

Accordingly, the decision on where a legal element belongs, either in a liability rule or a defence, is a normative matter.[57] In turn, this raises the question: what are the relevant factors that should influence the exercise of this discretion?

---

[51] Goudkamp, *Tort Law Defences*, 34.

[52] In the context of international investment law, this problem was also alluded to in *CMS v. Argentina*, where the arbitral tribunal, when considering the necessity defence, commented: 'One could wonder whether state of necessity in customary international law goes to the issue of wrongfulness [liability rule] or that of responsibility [defence]'; see *CMS Gas Transmission Company v. The Republic of Argentina*, ICSID Case No. ARB/01/8, Decision of the Ad Hoc Committee on the Application for Annulment of the Argentine Republic (25 September 2007) § 132.

[53] Szurek, 'Notion of Circumstances Precluding Wrongfulness', 427 and 429.

[54] For domestic law, see Fletcher, *Rethinking Criminal Law*, 698–707; Williams, 'Offences and Defences', 254. For international law, see Crawford, *Second Report on State Responsibility* § 241.

[55] Campbell, 'Offence and Defence', 73.

[56] But see Viñuales, 'Seven Ways of Escaping a Rule'.

[57] Fletcher, *Rethinking Criminal Law*, 566; Jeffries and Stephan, 'Defenses, Presumptions, and Burden of Proof', 1332.

2.1 *Identifying the Minimum Legal Elements for Liability Rules*

To begin with, consideration will be given to which legal elements should form part of liability rules as, deductively, these legal elements cannot be included within defences. These are called the minimum legal elements. What are the minimum legal elements for a particular liability rule? The answer ultimately depends on which theory of ethics is subscribed to. The minimum legal elements for a liability rule guided by deontological ethics will differ from those in a liability rule motivated by consequentialism. At this juncture, the temptation to launch a review into these philosophical questions should be resisted. Not only is this beyond the scope of this monograph; it is also submitted that consequentialism, particularly its branch of utilitarianism, usually guides the creation of most liability rules.[58] This is particularly true in respect of international investment law because it aims to *protect* investments. However, as explained in section 2.2, where the occurrence of the relevant harm,[59] which a liability rule seeks to avoid, is insufficiently harmful to justify the creation of a liability rule, deontological factors come into play to explain a particular liability rule's legal elements.

Once that premise is accepted, it can be concluded that the minimum legal elements for most liability rules are those facts which are necessary and minimally sufficient in number to either, one, prevent or limit the harm or, two, create the benefit that the liability rule is concerned with. Take, for example, the following liability rule:

> A person must clear of debris every Sunday morning the street area which is adjacent to his or her residence (the 'street cleaning rule').

With these minimum legal elements, this rule achieves its desired benefit of clean and orderly streets. It could be imagined that there might be some other relevant facts impacting on whether a person must perform this obligation, such as the person's health, but these facts are, for present purposes, superfluous. Such facts, however, could be used to create a defence, such as:

> It is a defence to the street cleaning rule if the person was on holiday on a Sunday.

---

[58] Wasserstrom, *Judicial Decision*, 10.
[59] See, for example, Malone, 'Ruminations on Cause-in-Fact', 73: "All rules of conduct … exist for purposes. They are designed to protect *some* persons under *some* circumstances against *some* risks."

The difficulty is that 'harms' and 'benefits' are vague because they differ between societies. While one society might appreciate clean streets, another might think nothing of it. This is aptly demonstrated by Kenneth Campbell with his example of what this monograph calls a liability rule on 'radio operation'.[60] In summary, Campbell proposes a rule that would make it an offence to operate a radio in a private residence without a licence. The question is whether the rule should be drafted to make 'without a licence' a legal element of the liability rule, or to carve it out and create a defence from it. For the former scenario, the rule would read as follows:

A person must not operate a radio in a private residence without a licence.

Campbell opines that this formulation would be acceptable in a society where the liability rule is designed to generate revenue for the state. This is because merely operating a radio is not sufficiently offensive, but operating a radio without a licence reaches the requisite degree of harm as the relevant licence fee would not have been paid. Interestingly, there is a similar,[61] although popularly much maligned, rule in Germany, the 'Rundfunkbeitrag'.

Alternatively, the rule could be formulated by carving out the 'without a licence' legal element, and constructing the following defence:

It is a defence to the rule on operating a radio if the person held a licence to operate a radio in a private residence.

In what type of society would it be sufficiently harmful to merely operate a radio in a private residence? Campbell suggests that in fundamentalist societies that reject Western technology such a rule would be acceptable. The defence above would only apply in very limited cases where the state deemed it necessary for a particular person, such as an intelligence officer, to have regular access to a radio.

2.2 Minimum Legal Elements for Liability Rules in International Investment Law

To illuminate the question of which legal elements should belong in a defence, it is worth considering the minimum legal elements for the liability rules in international investment law. If international investment law's sole

---

[60] Campbell, 'Offence and Defence', 80–81.

[61] It does not operate to prohibit the use of radios and other similar devices, but mandates the payment of a fee from private residences and other places used for non-private purposes for the financing of certain media outlets; see *Rundfunkbeitragsstaatsvertrag* § 2(1) (for private residences) and § 5(1) (for non-private residences).

purpose is providing a stringent level of protection for investments,[62] then the basic liability rule of international investment law should read:

> A host state must not cause a deprivation or any devaluation of an investment, within its territory, belonging to an investor (the 'deprivation/devaluation rule').

A myriad of defences could be created around this liability rule, for example:

> It is a defence to a breach of the deprivation/devaluation rule if the host state's conduct was:
> (i) neither arbitrary nor discriminatory; or
> (ii) fair and equitable.

The legal framework of international investment law does not work according to this method, thus indicating that there must be other factors relevant to the question of whether a legal element forms part of a liability rule or a defence.

This is where deontological factors must be considered. The reason why the legal elements of 'arbitrary and discriminatory' and 'fair and equitable' are transposed from the defences above into the rules on arbitrary and discriminatory measures and fair and equitable treatment is because the mere devaluation of an investment is an insufficient harm to ground the creation of a liability rule. International investment law not only looks at the harm, but also at the nature of the conduct causing that harm, except in respect of the rule on expropriation. The foundation of this distinction is that its harm is either a *complete* or *substantial* deprivation or devaluation of the investment.[63] Accordingly, the harm that the rule on expropriation is concerned with is of a greater magnitude in comparison to the other liability rules.

---

[62] Schneiderman, *Constitutionalizing Economic Globalization*, 4.

[63] In *El Paso v. Argentina*, the arbitral tribunal expressed its doubts as to whether a substantial devaluation could be a harm giving rise to a breach of the rule on expropriation; see *El Paso Energy International Company v. The Argentine Republic*, ICSID Case No. ARB/03/15, Award (31 October 2011) ('*El Paso v. Argentina*') § 249. The weight of authority, however, indicates that a substantial devaluation is sufficient; see, for example, *LG&E Energy Corp., LG&E Capital Corp., and LG&E International, Inc. v. Argentine Republic*, ICSID Case No. ARB/02/1, Decision on Liability (3 October 2006) § 191; *Archer Daniels Midland Company and Tate & Lyle Ingredients Americas, Inc. v. The United Mexican States*, ICSID Case No. ARB (AF)/04/5, Award (21 November 2007) § 240; *Philip Morris Brands Sàrl, Philip Morris Products S.A., and Abal Hermanos S.A. v. Oriental Republic of Uruguay*, ICSID Case No. ARB/10/7, Award (8 July 2016) § 286.

2.3 Access to Evidence

Logically, any relevant legal elements which are not minimum legal elements for the purpose of the particular liability rule are candidates for inclusion in a defence. A pragmatic factor to consider when deciding whether those residual legal elements should find their way into a liability rule or a defence is access to evidence.[64] As noted above in section 1.5, the principal consequence of demarcating a rule as a defence is to effect a shifting of the burden of proof from the claimant to the respondent. With respect to many legal elements that make up defences, this shift is appropriate considering that the respondent is best able to access the evidence that is relevant to proving that legal element.[65]

Consider the defence of force majeure. One of the legal elements of this defence is that compliance with the liability rule[66] which has been breached was materially impossible. As it might be supposed the respondent has the most information regarding what conduct was possible or impossible in the circumstances, it can legitimately be expected to be in the best position, relative to the claimant, to obtain the relevant evidence on this legal element.

3 IDENTIFYING DEFENCES

The questions of, one, what constitutes a defence and, two, what legal elements they should contain are theoretical in nature. This section examines a more practical question:[67] in a large body of rules, how is a defence distinguished from other rules? In some cases, the process of identification is unproblematic. Take, for example, the following provision:

> It is a defence to the publication of defamatory matter if the defendant proves that the defamatory imputations carried by the matter of which the plaintiff complains are substantially true.[68]

---

[64] Fletcher, *Rethinking Criminal Law*, 524; Goudkamp, *Tort Law Defences*, 47.

[65] Fletcher, *Rethinking Criminal Law*, 524.

[66] This liability rule should be a mandate, as opposed to a prohibition. This conclusion is also informed by the wording of the rule, which provides that it must be 'materially impossible in the circumstances to *perform the obligation*'; see ILC Articles on State Responsibility, Art. 23(1). See also Bjorklund, 'Emergency Exceptions', 465.

[67] In Anglo-American law, the relevance of this question was rejected by Glanville Williams when he asked: 'Is there any reason why rules of substantive law should hinge upon a draftsman's convenience?'; see Williams, 'Offences and Defences', 256.

[68] Defamation Act 2005 (New South Wales) s. 25.

Not all rules are so diligently drafted. One key demarcator is the burden of proof. If the rule explicitly places the burden of proof on the respondent, then the rule is a defence, as the defence of saving a slave illustrates:

(3) A person who engages in any conduct with the intention of securing the release of a person from slavery does not commit an offence against this section.

(4) The defendant bears a legal burden of proving the matter mentioned in subsection (3).[69]

In many cases, however, the rule is silent as to whether the claimant or respondent carries the burden of proof. In this circumstance, the factors below should be considered.

The first factor to assess is whether the proposed defence is structurally distinct from the liability rule to which it relates. By 'structurally distinct', it is meant that the two rules are physically separated in the document in which they appear. This will usually be achieved by placing the two rules in separate sections. Consider the following rules from the COMESA Investment Agreement:[70]

ARTICLE 20 Expropriation

1. Member States shall not nationalize or expropriate investments in their territory or adopt any other measures tantamount to expropriation of investments ...

6. This Article shall not apply to the issuance of compulsory licences granted in relation to intellectual property rights, or to the revocation, limitation or creation of intellectual property rights, to the extent that such issuance, revocation, limitation or creation is consistent with applicable international agreements on intellectual property.

Aside from appearing in a provision separate from the liability rule to which it relates, what is noticeable about this defence is that it restricts the usual definitional scope of the cause legal element. The cause legal element provides that there must be causality between the host state's conduct and the investor's loss. Effectively, the liability rule provides that this can be any conduct, but Article 20(6) restricts this by carving out an exception in respect of the types of conduct mentioned. This is an example of a defence that restricts the definitional scope of one of the liability rule's legal elements.[71]

---

[69] Criminal Code Act 1995 (Australia) s. 270.3(4) and (5).
[70] COMESA Investment Agreement, Art. 20.
[71] See section 1.4 above.

Another factor is the general applicability of the proposed defence. If the rule is of general application to all liability rules, then it usually indicates that it should be classified as a defence. The Canada-China bilateral investment treaty provides:

> Except as provided in this Article nothing in this Agreement shall apply to taxation measures.[72]

If the legal element in this rule – taxation measure – were a legal element in every liability rule in this investment treaty,[73] it would mean that the rule on fair and equitable treatment would be awkwardly formulated as follows:

> A host state must not unfairly and inequitably cause, excluding conduct that constitutes a taxation measure, the devaluation of an investment, and any related incidental loss, belonging to an investor and within its territory.

Finally, there are some words that indicate that the relevant rule is a defence. There are a plethora of expressions for the concept of defence, but it seems that the most frequently encountered is the word 'exception' and its derivatives. Take, for example, the following formulation of the rule on expropriation:

ARTICLE 5 Expropriation and Compensation

(1) A Contracting Party shall not expropriate or nationalise directly or indirectly an investment … *except*:
   (a) for a purpose which is in the public interest,
   (b) on a non-discriminatory basis,
   (c) in accordance with due process of law, and
   (d) accompanied by payment of prompt, adequate and effective compensation.[74]

When conjunctions such as 'except' and 'unless'[75] are used after a liability rule to introduce new legal elements, this will generally indicate that those new legal elements cumulatively constitute a defence to that liability rule.[76]

---

[72] Canada-China BIT, Art. 14(1).

[73] These types of legal elements have been referred to in the jurisprudence of international law as 'negative rule-elements'; see Paddeu, 'Clarifying the Concept of Circumstances Precluding Wrongfulness'.

[74] Austria-Yemen BIT, Art. 5(1) (emphasis added).

[75] Some investment treaties use 'unless' to introduce the lawful expropriation defence; see, for example, Norway-Sri Lanka BIT, Art. 6(1).

[76] This linguistic approach was the approach originally adopted by English criminal law; see *R v. Edwards* [1974] 2 All ER 1085. It was later amended, however, to factor in other considerations such as the purpose of the liability rule; see *R v. Hunt* [1987] 1 All ER 1.

4 EXCUSES AND JUSTIFICATIONS

Among criminal law[77] and international law[78] theorists, much scholarship has been devoted to categorising defences as excuses or justifications. An excuse may be thought of as an explanation for a wrongful act that casts a favourable moral light on the conduct of the respondent.[79] The prototypal example is the defence of mistake.[80] Meanwhile, a justification is an explanation that the act of the respondent, although constituting a breach of a liability rule, is rightful[81] because it avoids some greater harm than the harm caused by the relevant act.[82] The most cited example is self-defence.[83]

Although the excuse/justification dichotomy might be philosophically stimulating,[84] it is not important in international investment law.[85] For any theory of defences, the fundamental tasks are ascribing a meaning to the concept of 'defence', deciphering the legal content and legal functions of the defences under consideration, and offering a methodology for their identification. The excuse/justification dichotomy only distracts from these tasks.

5 DISTINGUISHING DEFENCES FROM OTHER LEGAL CONCEPTS

A more pressing task is distinguishing defences from other legal concepts with which they are habitually confused. This is the business of the following sections, starting with the legal concept that is most frequently confused with defences:[86] denials.

---

[77] See generally Fletcher, *Rethinking Criminal Law*, 759–875. This tendency has its genesis in John Austin's work in the field of the philosophy of language; see Austin, 'A Plea for Excuses', 1.

[78] See Lowe, 'Precluding Wrongfulness or Responsibility', 405; Christakis, 'Les circonstances excluant l'illicéité', 223; Crawford, *State Responsibility*, 274 and 279; and Paddeu, *Justification and Excuse*, 23.

[79] Horder, *Excusing Crime*, 8–9.

[80] Fletcher, *Rethinking Criminal Law*, 760.

[81] Ibid., 759.

[82] Robinson, 'Criminal Law Defenses', 213.

[83] Fletcher, *Rethinking Criminal Law*, 763.

[84] For an overview, see Greenawalt, 'Perplexing Borders', 1897.

[85] As Frederica Paddeu acknowledges: 'in principle, there is no distinction between justification and excuse in respect of the [reparation] consequences [for the host state]'; see Paddeu, *Justification and Excuse*, 64. The same contention has also been made in respect of Anglo-American criminal law; see Duff, *Answering for Crime*, 263–264, where he comments that 'needless confusion has been bred by attempts to fit all defences into a simple two-part schema of "justification" and "excuse"'; Colvin, 'Exculpatory Defences', 382.

[86] Goudkamp, *Tort Law Defences*, 46.

5.1 Defences and Denials

Referred to by Robinson as 'failure of proof defences',[87] denials are the respondent's legal or evidentiary arguments that a legal element of the relevant liability rule cannot be established.[88] Consider a dispute[89] where the investor's claim is founded on a breach of the rule on expropriation. To prove the 'complete or substantial deprivation or devaluation' legal element, it adduces evidence that its investment was worth USD 5,000,000 before the host state's allegedly wrongful conduct, and USD 1,000,000 thereafter. To effect a denial, the host state could either challenge this assertion (an evidentiary argument) or argue that this devaluation is not a substantial devaluation[90] (a legal argument). These two pleas are paradigm examples of denials.

It should be apparent that, conceptually, there is a distinction between defences and denials,[91] but practically, these two concepts have proved difficult to distinguish.[92] This is particularly true with respect to denials of a cause legal element in a liability rule and cause-related defences, such as contributory fault. Goudkamp submits that any plea of contributory fault is a denial of the cause legal element,[93] thereby suggesting that each consequence in law has one dominant or operative cause – a position that reflects the general approach in Anglo-American tort law and (unfortunately) international law. In chapter 3, it is argued that, at least for international investment law, the notion that there is one particularly dominant cause should be abandoned. This monograph emphasises the pluralistic nature of causation.[94] A consequence always has various causes, and the cause legal element in a liability rule only requires that the respondent be responsible for one of those causes.

---

[87] Robinson, 'Criminal Law Defenses', 204.

[88] Campbell, 'Offence and Defence', 75.

[89] This example is based on the facts and the decision in *Burlington Resources Inc. v. Republic of Ecuador*, ICSID Case No. ARB/08/5 (*'Burlington v. Ecuador'*).

[90] An argument which would probably succeed on the current understanding of what constitutes a substantial devaluation; see particularly *Burlington v. Ecuador*, Decision on Liability § 457, where it was held that even though the investor's 'windfall profits' were subject to a tax rate of 99 per cent, the investor's business was still viable.

[91] The distinction is well recognised in continental European private law; see Bar, Clive, and Schulte-Nölke (eds.), *Principles, Definitions and Model Rules*, 331 (definition of 'defence'). For an example of the distinction in American civil procedure law, see Code of Civil Procedure (California) § 431.30(f) and (g).

[92] See generally Goudkamp, *Tort Law Defences*, 46–74 for a discussion of the application of denials in Anglo-American tort law.

[93] Ibid., 60.

[94] Mackie, *Cement of the Universe*, 38.

With a plea of contributory fault, there is an allegation that the claimant is responsible for another cause of this consequence.

5.1.1 Possible Denials of a Cause Legal Element

If a respondent denies a cause legal element, what it argues is that *it* did not cause the relevant consequence.[95] There are three reasons that could underpin this denial. First, it could be argued that the respondent's conduct which is alleged to be a cause bears no causal relationship to the consequence. Second, there is another cause that necessarily excludes the respondent's act or omission as a cause. Third, the respondent had no opportunity to cause the consequence; in other words, the respondent advances an alibi. For example, imagine that the investor's investment is a shareholding in a restaurant chain called 'Big and Greasy Grill'. As the name suggests, this restaurant chain specialises in serving fast food with high fat content. After the host state launched its 'Active Nation' campaign, which encourages its citizens to do more physical exercise, the investor alleges that its shareholding was completely devalued.[96]

To deny that the 'Active Nation' campaign caused the devaluation, the host state might adduce evidence from other jurisdictions demonstrating that after similar campaigns were launched there, similar restaurant chains did not suffer a loss of business. This is an example of the first denial. For the second denial, the host state might point to an alternative cause that necessarily excludes the 'Active Nation' campaign as a cause. For example, some weeks before the 'Active Nation' campaign was launched, media reports surfaced of an incident at a 'Big and Greasy Grill' restaurant where a customer suffered a fatal cardiac arrest while eating a 'Mega Grease' burger. To prove that these media reports were the cause of the devaluation, the host state adduces evidence of a significant downturn in customer numbers occurring immediately after their publication.

5.1.2 Comparison of 'Denials of Cause' Legal Element to Contributory Fault Defences

These denial arguments are of a different nature, however, to a plea of contributory fault. Whenever a host state raises contributory fault, its conduct has already

---

[95] Virgo, 'Justifying Necessity', 139.

[96] Patently, this example is for illustrative purposes only. If a dispute did arise out of these facts, the host state could invoke the police powers defence to defeat it. For a discussion of the police powers defence in customary international law, see *Philip Morris Brands Sàrl, Philip Morris Products S.A. and Abal Hermanos S.A. v. Oriental Republic of Uruguay*, ICSID Case No. ARB/10/7, Award (8 July 2016) §§ 287–307.

been proven as a cause. The question that a plea of a contributory fault defence asks is: did the investor *also* cause the investment's devaluation?

With reference to the example above, suppose that the host state had evidence that the investor knew, before investing, that it would launch the 'Active Nation' campaign. With this evidence, the host state could argue that the investor recklessly contributed to the loss, which is essentially a plea of mismanagement.[97] This is comparable to the driver who hits a jay-walking pedestrian while driving in excess of the speed limit, but argues that the pedestrian knew of the risk of being hit; in other words, if the investor and pedestrian had not positioned the object of their losses – being the purchasing of its shareholding and walking its person onto the road – at the time and place of the host state's or driver's performance of its or his or her cause, then no loss would have occurred.

5.2 *Defences and Exceptions*

No legal concept is used as a synonym for defence as frequently as exception.[98] Colloquially, an exception is any deviation from 'the rule',[99] but this definition lacks precision. More precisely, an exception is a rule that limits the definitional scope of a legal element in another rule.[100] To understand this definition, amplification of two attributes, 'limitation of definitional scope' and 'another rule', is required.

Each legal element has a definitional scope. This definition scope can be either, one, the attributes of the usual definition attaching to the legal element or, two, the attributes of a stipulative definition for the legal element. For example, consider the following liability rule:

A student must not arrive late to class.

Looking at the legal element of 'late', there is the option of giving its usual definition, such as 'any time after the beginning of the class'. Alternatively, a stipulative definition might be attached to it, such as 'any time five minutes

---

[97] How this conduct can become the foundation of a plea of contributory fault is discussed in section 2.1 of chapter 4.

[98] This is particularly evident in international investment law as both arbitral tribunals – see *Sempra Energy International v. The Argentine Republic*, ICSID Case No. ARB/02/16, Award (28 September 2007) § 372 (referring to the necessity defence as an exception) – and scholars refer to defences as exceptions. See, for example, Bjorklund, 'Emergency Exceptions', 459; Vandevelde, 'Rebalancing through Exceptions', 449; Newcombe, 'General Exceptions', 355.

[99] Viñuales, 'Seven Ways of Escaping a Rule'; Williams, 'Logic of "Exceptions"', 262.

[100] It seems that Paul Robinson had a similar definition in mind for his concept of 'offense modification', although he did not clarify the meaning of this concept; see Robinson, 'Criminal Law Defenses', 208–210.

after the beginning of the class'. While a legal element's usual definition or stipulative definition give it definitional scope, an exception restricts that definitional scope, as the following rule illustrates:

> Investments in cultural industries are exempt from the provisions of this Agreement.[101]

Accordingly, under the Canada-Czechia bilateral investment treaty, an investment in a cultural industry[102] – an investment that would otherwise fall under the stipulative definition of investment – is excluded.

For an exception to operate as a defence, it is not enough that it restrict the definitional scope of a legal element. In addition, that legal element must originate from a liability rule. For this reason, the exception extracted above on cultural industries is arguably not a defence. It refines the definition of investment, and investment is a legal element relating to the jurisdiction question.[103] An example of an exception taking the form of a defence can be seen in section 1.4 above. As discussed there, that exception operates if the host state's conduct can be described as the issuance of a compulsory license in respect of intellectual property, thereby carving out part of the usual definition of conduct amounting to an expropriation.

It follows that while some exceptions are properly described as defences, others are not. Only exceptions that refine the definitional scope of a legal element in a liability rule are defences. The reason for this exclusiveness is informed by the idea that defences must relate to the liability question and its evaluative function. As these exceptions change the quality of otherwise wrongful conduct, they relate to the liability question and thus must be viewed as defences.

5.3 *Defences and Claim Admissibility Rules*

In international investment law,[104] Anglo-American tort law,[105] and Anglo-American criminal law,[106] the conviction among scholars is that defences and certain claim admissibility rules are one and the same. It is accepted that

---

[101] Canada-Czechia BIT, Art. IX(7).
[102] A term extensively defined to cover most investments in the media sector; see ibid., Art. IX(7) (a)–(e).
[103] See section 2 of chapter 1 for a discussion of jurisdiction.
[104] *Marvin Roy Feldman Karpa v. United Mexican States*, ICSID Case No. ARB(AF)/99/1, Award (16 December 2002) ('*Feldman v. Mexico*') § 63 (claim limitation period); *CME Czech Republic B.V. v. The Czech Republic*, Ad Hoc Arbitration (UNCITRAL Arbitration Rules), Final Award (14 March 2003) ('*CME v. Czechia*, Final Award') § 431 (no prior binding resolution).
[105] Goudkamp, *Tort Law Defences*, 130–131.
[106] Robinson, 'Criminal Law Defenses', 229–230; Campbell, 'Offence and Defence', 77.

there can be confusion between defences and exceptions given that some of the latter are defences, but there is no such excuse in respect of defences and claim admissibility rules or, as they are sometimes called, 'claim bars'.[107] Claim admissibility rules were examined in section 3.1 of chapter 1. That examination will not be repeated here, other than to emphasise that these rules cover the topic of the maturity of the claimant's cause of action for adjudication. In this way, they focus on the cause of action itself, as opposed to the conduct which gave rise to that cause of action. In light of this, the working definition of 'claim admissibility rule' adopted in this monograph is:[108]

> Any rule stipulating that some procedural performance must be undertaken to make a claim ready for adjudication.

This is a theoretical distinction, but it also has practical significance in at least two respects, both are of which are explored in the sections below.

5.3.1 First Practical Distinction: Different Consequences

The claim admissibility rule that is misclassified most frequently[109] is the rule on limitation periods.[110] The confusion is presumably induced[111] by the perception that the application of a defence or a claim limitation period yields the same outcome: the defeat of the claim. The meaning of defeat differs greatly, however, between the admissibility question and the liability question.

As discussed in section 3.2 of chapter 1, the admissibility question can yield one of two negative answers. Both negative answers mean that the cause of action cannot be entertained, but whereas one negative answer can be overcome by perfecting the relevant defect, this option is not available for the second negative answer. This second negative answer appears to be the same as an answer to the liability question that refutes the respondent's liability on account of a successful plea of a defence.

---

[107] Scott, 'Collateral Estoppel by Judgment', 2.
[108] For alternative definitions, see Fitzmaurice, *Law and Procedure*, 439; Douglas, *International Law*, 148.
[109] The other admissibility rule liable to misclassification is the rule on no prior adjudication or the res judicata defence; see, for example, *CME v. Czechia*, Final Award § 431; *Eli Lilly and Company v. The Government of Canada*, ICSID Case No. UNCT/14/2, Final Award (16 March 2017) §§ 111–113.
[110] In international investment law, see *Feldman v. Mexico* § 63; in Anglo-American criminal law, see Robinson, 'Criminal Law Defenses', 229–230; and in Anglo-American tort law, see Goudkamp, *Tort Law Defences*, 130–131.
[111] Although another explanation might be that it was included as a defence in many of the early Restatements of the Law produced by the American Law Institute; see, for example, Restatement (First) and (Second) of Torts (1934 and 1979) § 899 (for both restatements).

A decision on the liability question, however, has a much broader scope by application of the rules on finality of judgments.[112] Rules on finality differ from jurisdiction to jurisdiction.[113] In civil law jurisdictions, their scope tends to be narrower compared to common law jurisdictions.[114] For example, in German law, a claim of compensation for loss resulting from property damage can be entertained after the dismissal of a claim of compensation for loss resulting from personal injury caused by the same incident.[115]

Meanwhile, Anglo-American law[116] prevents the adjudication of subsequent claims arising out of the same dispute. This is because it adopts a broad definition of 'claim' to include all claims that could have been filed by the claimant with its original claim.[117] With reference to the example above illustrating claim preclusion in German law,[118] this second claim would be the same as the first claim under Anglo-American law, and thus precluded.[119] Although international investment law initially adopted a narrow conception of finality in the much criticised[120] *CME v. Czechia* case,[121] it has since embraced the wide notion encapsulated in Anglo-American law,[122] including collateral estoppel.[123]

---

[112] Article 60 of the Statute of the International Court of Justice is recognised as the codification of the finality principle in international law; see Dodge, 'Res Judicata', § A(1).

[113] For a comparative overview, see Clermont, 'Res Judicata as Requisite for Justice', 1067.

[114] Sinai, 'Reconsidering *Res Judicata*', 384.

[115] Murray and Stürner, *German Civil Justice*, 357.

[116] Although American law is slightly broader than English law, the rules on finality in English law are broader than the same rules in continental European jurisdictions; see Clermont, 'Res Judicata as Requisite for Justice', 1095–1096 and 1103.

[117] In American law, see Restatement (Second) of Judgments § 25. Although this expanded definition of 'same cause of action' was only developed in the nineteenth century after the abandonment of the strict writ system; see Silberman and others, *Civil Procedure*, 826–827.

[118] ZPO § 322(1).

[119] The American Law Institute also used the same example in its commentary on the Restatement (Second) of Judgments to illustrate that this second claim would be barred under American law; see Restatement (Second) of Judgments, § 24 (cmt (c)). For a case with the same facts, see *Rush v. City of Maple Heights* (1958) 167 Ohio St. 21. Under English law, this second claim would also be precluded; see Zuckerman, *Zuckerman on Civil Procedure*, § 25.87.

[120] Described by August Reinisch as the 'ultimate fiasco'; see Reinisch, 'Proliferation of International Dispute Settlement Mechanisms', 117.

[121] *CME v. Czechia*, Final Award §§ 432–433.

[122] In *Apotex Holdings Inc. and Apotex Inc. v. United States of America*, ICSID Case No. ARB(AF)/12/1, Award (25 August 2014) ('*Apotex v. USA*') § 7.58, the arbitral tribunal noted that the practice of 'claim-splitting' – filing one claim from one dispute, and then attempting to file a second claim from the same dispute after the first claim fails – is prohibited under international investment law.

[123] *Rachel S. Grynberg, Stephen M. Grynberg, Miriam Z. Grynberg and RSM Production Company v. Grenada*, ICSID Case No. ARB/10/6, Award (10 December 2010) § 7.1.2. Although, as noted by the arbitral tribunal in *Apotex v. USA*, this conception of collateral estoppel is not as expansive as the American conception because it applies only to parties who were involved in the original case; see *Apotex v. USA* § 7.18 (fn. 26).

By contrast, a negative answer, of the non-remediable variety, to the admissibility question is more limited in scope as it bars, rather than extinguishes, a cause of action.[124] Potentially, a claimant can refer back to the same dispute, but change its cause of action to overcome a claim limitation period. Admittedly, this option is not currently open in international investment law[125] because a claim limitation period in an investment treaty usually applies generally to all causes of action based on that investment treaty.[126] The situation is different in domestic law,[127] however, where there are differing time limitation periods; for example, in English law, if a claim is based on any cause of action where the harm is death or personal injury, the limitation period is three years, whereas for most other causes of action that period is six years.[128] These differing time periods demonstrate the potential of overcoming a negative determination in respect of a claim's admissibility.

5.3.2 Second Practical Distinction: Potential Disregard of Claim Admissibility Rule

The second practical distinction between defences and claim admissibility rules is that an adjudicative body has greater liberty to disregard the application of the latter. Again, this principle is provided for both in Anglo-American law, particularly in respect of claim limitation periods,[129] and in international investment law.[130]

---

[124] Scott, 'Collateral Estoppel by Judgment', 3.

[125] Seemingly, this could occur in international investment law if an investor's cause of action is inadmissible on the application of the rule of no prior adjudication and the investor later turns that cause of action into a breach of the rule on fair and equitable treatment (denial of justice) on account of procedural irregularities in the host state's court when it decided on the investor's original claim. However, these are two separate causes of action because they arise out of two different sets of facts. For a discussion of this, see *Pantechniki S.A. Contractors & Engineers v. The Republic of Albania*, ICSID Case No. ARB/07/21, Award (30 July 2009) ('*Pantechniki v. Albania*') §§ 50–68.

[126] The following provision is indicative of this trend: 'A dispute may be submitted for resolution pursuant to [this investment treaty], but not later than five years from the date the investor first acquired or should have acquired knowledge of the events which gave rise to the dispute'; see Austria-Tajikistan BIT, Art. 14(2).

[127] See, for example, *Commonwealth of Australia v. Cornwell* [2007] HCA 16, where the claimant's claim based on breach of contract was time-barred, but its claim based on tort of negligence was not time-barred. In this instance, the claimant benefitted from the fact that the limitation period for the tort-based claim ran from the occurrence of the damage, whereas for the contract-based claim it ran from the date of the breach of contract.

[128] Limitation Act 1980 (England and Wales) s. 11(4) and (5).

[129] See, for example, ibid., ss. 32A and 33; Limitation Act 2010 (New Zealand) s. 50. Those provisions give courts a discretion to disregard the claim limitation period in respect of certain causes of action. But Californian law explicitly states that there are no exceptions to the limitation periods; see Code of Civil Procedure (California) § 312.

[130] On numerous occasions, arbitral tribunals have waived the requirement for compulsory negotiation, although this is controversial. For an overview, see McLachlan and others, *International Investment Arbitration*, §§ 3.23–3.31.

The idea that an adjudicative body would refuse to give effect to a defence as defined in this monograph is unthinkable. The host state would be rightly aggrieved if it established a defence, but, on unspecified grounds of equity,[131] the arbitral tribunal refused to eliminate or reduce its liability. Most probably, such a refusal would give rise to a challenge of the arbitral award on the grounds that the arbitral tribunal failed to provide reasons[132] or did not respect fundamental procedure.[133]

5.4 Defences and Jurisdictional Rules

As their name suggests, jurisdictional rules relate to the jurisdiction question: does the adjudicative body have the power to decide the dispute? They take the form of requirements that, if fulfilled, bestow jurisdiction on the adjudicative body. Their content varies, but they generally stipulate that, one, the cause of action must relate to a certain subject matter, two, the claimant must have an interest in the subject matter, and, three, the subject matter must be situated in a particular locality. In international investment law, the first stipulation is embodied in the requirement that there be an investment. The requirements that the claimant must be, one, an investor and, two, own the investment are representative of the second stipulation. The third stipulation finds expression in the requirement that the investment be located within the host state's borders.

These requirements also have domestic law equivalents. For example, a specialist family court will require that any cause of action relate to a family law matter.[134] In most cases, the second stipulation is unproblematic as the claimant will have a clear interest in the subject matter; for example, in a case where the claimant's cause of action is the tort of negligence, then the relevant harm must accrue to the claimant. The question can be controversial, however, in constitutional law cases.[135] The Brussels I Regulation contains many

---

[131] See, for example, Limitation Act 1980 (England and Wales) s. 33(1).

[132] For ICSID arbitration, the challenge could be based on ICSID Convention, Art. 52(1)(e), while for non-ICSID arbitration, the challenge could be based on New York Convention, Art. 5(1)(c).

[133] For ICSID arbitration, the challenge could be based on ICSID Convention, Art. 52(1)(d), while for non-ICSID arbitration, the challenge could be based on New York Convention, Art. 5(1)(d).

[134] See, for example, Family Law Act 1975 (Australia) s. 31(1)(a)–(d).

[135] See, for example, Canadian law, where the claimant must establish a genuine interest and no other effective or reasonable way to pursue the case; *The Canadian Council of Churches v. Canada* [1992] 1 S.C.R. 254 per Cory J.

examples of the third stipulation.[136] For example, Article 7(1)(a) provides that where the subject matter is a contract, the respondent can be sued in the place of performance.

Defences and jurisdictional rules relate to two different legal questions, but they are routinely misclassified. An example is the rule on what is commonly called 'sovereign immunity'.[137] This rule is codified under American federal law as follows:

> Subject to existing international agreements to which the United States is a party at the time of enactment of this Act a foreign state shall be immune from the *jurisdiction* of the courts of the United States and of the States except as provided in sections 1605 to 1607 of this chapter.[138]

As with a finding of claim inadmissibility, a finding of lack of jurisdiction ostensibly defeats a claim. Again, clarification is needed on what defeat means. A lack of jurisdiction merely entails that the particular adjudicative body has no jurisdiction, although this conclusion does not exclude the jurisdiction of another adjudicative body. A determination that the respondent is not liable should, at a minimum, permanently extinguish the claimant's actual cause of action and potentially other potential causes of action arising out of the dispute.

5.5 Defences and Remedy Rules

The distinction between defences and remedy rules has been considered in sections 1.6.1 and 1.6.2 above, so it will only be briefly dealt with here. In those sections, it was reasoned that remedy rules take one of two forms: either they provide for a certain remedy or they define how that remedy should be measured. By contrast, defences evaluate conduct, with contributory fault offering a paradigm. Effectively, a finding of contributory fault signals that the claimant has performed risky conduct and, on account of that, must completely accept or share liability.

---

[136] Regulation on Jurisdiction and the Recognition and Enforcement of Judgments in Civil and Commercial Matters (recast) (European Union) Art. 7(1)–(7).

[137] John Gardner, James Goudkamp, and Paul Robinson all classify sovereignty immunity as a defence; see Gardner, *Offences and Defences*, 89; Goudkamp, *Tort Law Defences*, 124; Robinson, 'Criminal Law Defenses', 231.

[138] 28 United States Code § 1604 (2012) (emphasis added). See also Crawford, *Brownlie's Principles*, 487. For an illuminating overview of the same rule as it applies to the states making up the United States, see the judgment of Associate Justice Clarence Thomas in *Federal Maritime Commission v. South Carolina State Ports Authority et al.* (2002) 535 U.S. 751–753.

6 CONCLUSION

Putting the theory of this chapter and chapter 1 together, the question of the legal function of the rules (the contents of which are detailed in chapters 4 and 5) that this monograph derives from the concepts of contributory fault and investor misconduct has been resolved. As the circumstances that enliven them must come from the facts that make up the relevant dispute, the starting point is that they relate to the liability question. Further confirmation of this classification is provided by the nature of contributory fault and investor misconduct as they both evaluate conduct of the investor, which is the thrust of the liability question. That evaluation can be performed by liability rules or defences, and these circumstances can become legal elements in either. Their inclusion in defences follows from the fact that the minimum legal elements in international investment law's liability rules are settled and they are not part of those minimum legal elements, a fact attested by the practice of arbitral tribunals to look to the host state to prove them. Accordingly, the rules derived from contributory fault and investor misconduct are defences, meaning that their legal function is to either eliminate or reduce the host state's liability. With that problem resolved, the journey to elucidate the legal content of these defences can begin. Given that contributory fault is an allegation that the investor also caused the relevant loss, that process begins by looking at what it means in law to cause a consequence.

3

A Theory of Causation for International Investment Law

1 THE SIGNIFICANCE OF CAUSATION FOR CONTRIBUTORY FAULT

Contributory fault is saturated with causation[1] because, at its core, lies one essential ingredient: the claimant also causes the relevant loss. It follows that to acquire an understanding of contributory fault, an understanding of causation is a prerequisite. This is where the problems begin. Presumably acting on a belief that causation is a primitive topic[2] incapable of meaningful analysis,[3] many jurists are happy to be guided by their common sense in the resolution of causal questions.[4] If that view holds sway, there is little to understand. But at least officially,[5] the jurisprudence of international investment law subscribes to the alternative view – that these questions can be resolved by a coherent theory on causation.

2 THE FACTUAL-LEGAL CAUSE THEORY IN INTERNATIONAL INVESTMENT LAW

That theory, which is also the dominant theory in law more generally, is what is called the factual-legal cause theory,[6] although it goes by any number of

---

[1] Youngs, *English, French & German Comparative Law*, 451.
[2] Fair, 'Causation and the Flow of Energy', 219.
[3] Although not a jurist, Bertrand Russell is the flag-bearer: 'To me it seems that philosophy ought not to assume such legislative functions [the discovery of causes], and that the reason why physics has ceased to look for causes is that, in fact, *there are no such things*. The law of causality, I believe, like much that passes muster among philosophers, is a relic of a bygone age, surviving, like the monarchy, only because it is erroneously supposed to do no harm'; see Russell, 'On the Notion of Cause', 1 (emphasis added).
[4] In Anglo-American law, Herbert Hart and Tony Honoré are the most recognised proponents of using 'common-sense principles' to guide the resolution of causal questions; see Wright and Puppe, 'Causation', 482–483.
[5] But see Plakokefalos, 'Causation in the Law of State Responsibility', 473.
[6] Bishop and others, *Foreign Investment Disputes*, § 7.02[A][2]; Ripinsky and Williams, *Damages*, 138–140.

other descriptors. As its name suggests, this theory consists of two parts. How each part applies is described in the sections below, with an emphasis on showing how arbitral tribunals in investment arbitrations have (implicitly) applied them. In the absence of such jurisprudence, reference will be made to general international law and domestic law, drawing primarily on Anglo-American law and German law.

2.1 Factual Causation

Often referred to as the 'but for' test, factual causation requires that there must be a necessary connection between the antecedent and the consequence. To establish that connection, it asks the following counterfactual:[7]

> If the antecedent (the conduct in question) had not been performed, would the consequence (the investment loss) have occurred?

With a negative answer, the antecedent counts as a factual cause. Technically, reference should be made to causal laws to inform the answer, but adjudicative bodies in their reasoning rarely specify them, unless the causal law is beyond common knowledge. This is often the case where the causal connection between the antecedent and the consequence is non-perceptible, as in chemical interactions. In these cases, adjudicative bodies can have recourse to expert evidence or rules of evidence that presume causality upon proof of some basic fact, with such rules usually existing if the same non-perceptible problem arises recurrently. For example, in cases involving gross medical negligence, there is a presumption in German law that the claimant's subsequent injuries are causally linked to the medical professional's negligence.[8] As international investment law does not incorporate an established[9] body of rules on evidence,[10] it contains no rules similar to those that help overcome problems of causal proof.

---

[7] Steel, *Proof of Causation in Tort Law*, 16. Factual causation is principally inspired by David Hume's regularity theory of causation; see Wright and Puppe, 'Causation', 464–465.

[8] German Federal Supreme Court (1 February 1994) VersR (1994) 562.

[9] In the sense of being authoritatively stated in a recognised legal instrument, as opposed to the belief in the existence of a single rule authorising arbitral tribunals to decide wholly on matters of evidence, which is false; see Sourgens and others, *Evidence*, §§ 1.01–1.09.

[10] It is arguable that such a body of rules exists in customary international law, but the consensus view holds otherwise; see Brown, *Common Law of International Adjudication*, 84.

2.2 *Legal Causation*

Because factual causation theoretically[11] identifies an infinite number of causes,[12] it is supplemented by legal causation. Legal causation delimits factual causation by requiring that any factual cause is legally relevant to the consequence. This legal relevance is established if the factual cause is not eliminated by one of the rules that test for legal causality. If a factual cause passes these tests, arbitral tribunals in investment arbitrations have variously referred to it as an 'adequate cause',[13] 'direct cause',[14] 'operative cause',[15] 'prevailing cause',[16] 'proximate cause',[17] or 'sufficient cause'.[18] There is limited commentary on what any of these notions mean, but some clues can be taken from the following extract in *Blusun v. Italy*:[19]

> In the Tribunal's view, the Claimants have not discharged the onus of proof of establishing that the Italian state's measures were the operative cause of the Puglia Project's failure. Of far greater weight was the continued dependence on project financing.

What this indicates is that an operative cause[20] is one that, relative to the other factual causes, has particular causal potency. But how does a cause become

---

[11] In practice, the difficulties of proof mean that it is not as troublesome as it seems – see Honoré, 'Causation in the Law', § 3 – although some scholars take the possibility seriously; see Keeton and others, *Prosser and Keeton on the Law of Torts*, 264.

[12] Wright and Puppe, 'Causation', 502. See, for example, James and Perry, 'Legal Cause', 761, where it was commented: 'Obviously the legal test includes a requirement that the wrongful conduct must be a *cause in fact* of the harm; but if this stood alone the scope of liability would be vast indeed, for "the causes of causes [are] infinite"–"the fatal trespass done by Eve was cause of all our woe".'

[13] *Feldman v. Mexico* § 194.

[14] *Link-Trading Joint Stock Company v. Department for Customs Control of the Republic of Moldova*, Ad Hoc Arbitration (UNCITRAL Arbitration Rules), Final Award (18 April 2002) § 91.

[15] *Blusun S.A., Jean-Pierre Lecorcier and Michael Stein v. Italian Republic*, ICSID Case No. ARB/14/3, Award (27 December 2016) ('*Blusun v. Italy*') § 394.

[16] *El Paso v. Argentina* § 488.

[17] *LG&E Energy Corp., LG&E Capital Corp., and LG&E International, Inc. v. Argentine Republic*, ICSID Case No. ARB/02/1, Award (25 July 2007) § 50; *S.D. Myers, Inc. v. Government of Canada*, Ad Hoc Arbitration (UNCITRAL Arbitration Rules), Second Partial Award (21 October 2002) ('*S.D. Myers v. Canada*') § 140.

[18] *Victor Pey Casado and President Allende Foundation v. Republic of Chile*, ICSID Case No. ARB/98/2, Award (13 September 2016) § 218; *S.D. Myers v. Canada* § 140.

[19] *Blusun v. Italy* § 394.

[20] Although earlier in the arbitral award the arbitral tribunal referred to the 'operative cause' as the 'effective cause'; see ibid. § 310.

particularly potent? In the absence of a developed body of jurisprudence in international investment law, reference can first be made to the corresponding jurisprudence in domestic law. This monograph cannot comprehensively summarise the full extent of that jurisprudence. Rather, an outline is offered of the two dominant principles that have emerged from it.

2.2.1 Legal Causation in Domestic Law

The first principle holds that a factual cause's consequence must be foreseeable for it to become legally relevant.[21] The only question that this principle raises is whose knowledge is used to draw the requisite conclusion that the consequence was foreseeable at the time of the factual cause's performance. The original position was that all knowledge could be consulted,[22] although it was later settled that the applicable knowledge was that of a reasonable person[23] or an optimal observer.[24]

The second principle is the harm within the risk principle.[25] It provides[26] that a factual cause is legally relevant if, one, its consequence was one that the rule sought to avoid and, two, it occurred in the manner that the rule envisioned. As an example[27] of the first criterion, suppose that a rule stipulates that sheep must be placed in pens during their transportation by ship. The respondent fails to perform this duty, leading to the sheep falling overboard. If the rule sought to avoid the transmission of diseases between the sheep, the respondent's factual cause would not be legally relevant because that consequence differs from the actual consequence of the sheep being lost overboard.

---

[21]   In American law, 'foreseeability' is preferred, while for English law 'remoteness' has greater currency. In German law, the relevant expression is 'Adäquanztheorie'.

[22]   The leading case in English law was *Re Polemis and Furness, Withy & Co. Ltd* [1921] 3 KB 560, while in German law the main proponent of this position was Max von Rümelin; see Markesinis and Unberath, *German Law of Torts*, 107.

[23]   This is the standard in English law. The leading case is *Overseas Tankship (UK) Ltd v. The Miller Steamship Co (Wagon Mound (No. 2))* [1967] 1 AC 617.

[24]   'Optimal observer' is the standard in German law; see Markesinis and Unberath, *German Law of Torts*, 108. Such a person perceives 'all the circumstances that a very perceptible observer would have noticed'; see Hart and Honoré, *Causation in the Law*, 472.

[25]   This American law expression finds its origins in Keeton, *Legal Cause in the Law of Torts*, 4. For a critique, see Moore, *Causation and Responsibility*, chaps. 8–10. In German law, it is known as 'Schutzzweck der Norm'. As regards English law, this second principle is usually informed by Hart and Honoré's 'common sense principles'; see, for example, Jones (ed.), *Clerk and Lindsell on Torts*; Deakin and others, *Markesinis and Deakin's Tort Law*.

[26]   This conception borrows most heavily from the jurisprudence of German law; see generally Markesinis and Unberath, *German Law of Torts*, 108.

[27]   Example taken from *Gorris v. Scott* [1874] LR 9 Exch 125 as described in Markesinis and Unberath, *German Law of Torts*, 108.

As for the second criterion,[28] suppose that the rule prohibited a licensed gun owner from providing any other person with a gun.[29] The respondent breaches this rule by handing the claimant his gun, after which the claimant injures her foot by dropping the gun on it. Although bodily harm is a consequence that this rule seeks to avoid, the factual cause is not a legal cause because the rule does not envision this consequence occurring by means of dropping a gun.

2.2.2 Legal Causation for Factual Cause of Claimants in International Law

In addition to this jurisprudence from domestic law, there is also jurisprudence from general international law specifically on the question of legal causation for factual causes attributable to claimants. The leading source[30] is Brigitte Stern's work on 'the intervention of an external cause of the injured person'. She posits[31] that a claimant's factual cause becomes legally relevant if it is an exclusive intervention,[32] cumulative intervention,[33] or complementary intervention.[34] *Cowper's Case*[35] offers an example of the first kind. There, Great Britain took the claimant's slaves, but the latter's failure to secure other labour sources over a ten-year period was held to be the sole cause of the lost harvests during that time.[36] Cumulative interventions occur if the claimant provokes the respondent. If the respondent's response is proportionate, the claimant's conduct is the sole cause, while disproportionate responses throw causal responsibility back on the respondent.[37] With complementary interventions, the claimant and the respondent share the liability.[38] An example[39] comes from the *Naulilaa Arbitration*.[40] There, after a serious of

---

[28] Example inspired by a similar example in Restatement (Third) of Torts: Liability for Physical and Emotional Harm § 29 (cmt d.).

[29] *Firearms Act 1996* (New South Wales) s. 39.

[30] See Moutier-Lopet, 'Contribution to the Injury', 642.

[31] Stern also introduces a fourth type of causative contribution of the injured party, a 'parallel intervention', but it is submitted that this is not a specific type of contribution but rather an instance where the injured party cannot prove that the other party's conduct caused its injury; Bollecker-Stern, *Le préjudice*, 343.

[32] Ibid., 293.

[33] Ibid., 270.

[34] Ibid., 281.

[35] *Cowper's Case (United States of America v. Great Britain)* (see Lapradelle and Politis, *Recueil*, vol 1, 348–349). For an English language summary, see Gray, *Judicial Remedies*, 23.

[36] Lapradelle and Politis, *Recueil*, 349.

[37] Moutier-Lopet, 'Contribution to the Injury', 642.

[38] Bollecker-Stern, *Le préjudice*, 285.

[39] Ibid., 331.

[40] *Naulilaa Arbitration (Portugal v. Germany)*, Reports of International Arbitral Awards (Volume II) (31 July 1928) 1013. For an English language summary, see Pfeil, 'Naulilaa Arbitration'.

misunderstandings, Portugal (the claimant) fired upon German governmental officials who were visiting Angola (at the time a Portuguese colony). In response, Germany destroyed a Portuguese fort in Angola. After both Germany and Portugal retreated, the Angolan indigenous population began looting the area around the fort and general chaos ensued. For the damage caused by the looting, Portugal and Germany were both liable because their actions had jointly created the environment for the looting to commence.[41] Unfortunately, the arbitral tribunal did not reveal how liability would be apportioned and simply commented that it would 'fairly determine the figure taking into account all the circumstances'.[42]

3 CRITIQUE OF THE FACTUAL-LEGAL CAUSE THEORY

The above outline was necessarily cursory, but it serves its two purposes: conveying an idea of how the factual-legal cause theory operates, and setting the scene for the demonstration of its complete inadequacy and inapplicability for the purposes of international investment law. The terms 'inadequacy' and 'inapplicability' are chosen very deliberately. Like most theories, the factual-legal cause theory has some shortcomings, most particularly the confusion that it has created among adjudicators on how to distinguish factual causation from legal causation.[43] With some perseverance, these shortcomings might be overcome. But the theory has bigger problems that make it unworkable, and this critique focuses on those problems.

3.1 The Fault Aspect as the Antecedent

The first problem is the choice of the antecedent for testing factual causation. The factual-legal cause theory stipulates that this antecedent is the conduct in question. For example, if the host state's conduct is enacting legislation that mandates the drab presentation of tobacco products, then the question is:

> If the host state had not enacted this law, would the investment loss have occurred?

---

[41] Pfeil, 'Naulilaa Arbitration', § 14.

[42] *Naulilaa Arbitration (Portugal v. Germany)*, Reports of International Arbitral Awards (Volume II) (31 July 1928) 1032.

[43] Stapleton, 'Factual Causation', 468; Wright, 'Causation, Responsibility, Risk', 1011; Bar, *Common European Law of Torts*, 457.

At least for antecedents that are most likely to be seen in legal disputes, the answer to this question will invariably be negative,[44] thereby entailing that this antecedent is a factual cause. But if this test operates to identify virtually all antecedents as factual causes, then this indicates that something is missing[45] – any test that is invariably passed has minimal value.

That missing something is what might be called fault causation. Fault causation seeks to establish whether the fault aspect of the conduct in question caused the consequence.[46] With reference to the tobacco case and assuming that the cause of action is a breach of the fair and equitable treatment standard, the question is:

> If the host state had enacted the fair and equitable version of the relevant law, would the investment loss have occurred?

If the answer is 'no' and the answer to the question on factual causation is yes, then it follows that the faultworthy aspect of host state's conduct caused the consequence.[47] The challenge in this context is to correctly designate the non-faultworthy version of the host state's conduct. If that conduct is an omission, this will require some adjudicative imagination[48] because the arbitral tribunal will have to determine what non-faultworthy action the host state should have performed. But even when this problem arises, which will be infrequently because the only liability rule in international investment law that is premised on the host state's performance of an omission is the rule on full protection and security, it will not present a significant hurdle. What ultimately guides this reformulation is a profound knowledge of the relevant fault legal element – knowledge that all arbitral tribunals can be presumed to possess.

3.2 *Causal Overdetermination*

If the absence of a test for fault causation was the only problem afflicting the factual-legal cause theory, it could survive in an amended form. But it is encumbered by another, more serious, problem: the absurd answers that it delivers in cases of causal duplication and causal pre-emption.[49]

---

[44] Wright, 'Duty, Causal Contribution', 1082–1084.
[45] The commentaries on causation in international law fail to mention the relevance of fault causation; see, for example, ILC Articles on State Responsibility (with commentaries), Art. 31 (cmt 10).
[46] Steel, *Proof of Causation in Tort Law*, 17.
[47] Steel, 'Defining Causal Counterfactuals', 564.
[48] Wright, 'Causation, Responsibility, Risk', 1040–1041.
[49] For an overview, see Wright, 'Causation in Tort Law', 1775–1777.

3.2.1 The Problems of Causal Duplication and Causal Pre-emption

Causal duplication occurs when two or more antecedents spatio-temporally converge, with each being sufficient to produce the relevant consequence.[50] As an example, suppose that the investor has a shareholding in a company that manufactures and distributes energy drinks in the host state. Alarmed by research showing that teenagers routinely binge on energy drinks and the risks that bingeing gives rise to,[51] the host state enacts two new laws to counteract this. The first law imposes a 90 per cent consumption tax on energy drinks, while the second law bans the supply of energy drinks to persons under 23 years. Both these laws come into force at the same time. Empirical evidence demonstrates that either of these two measures could have substantially devalued the investor's shareholding. Yet the but for test cannot identify any measure as a cause for the reason that, on account of the operative effect of the other measure, the measure that is subjected to the test cannot logically prove its necessity. For example, if it is asked:

> If the consumption tax had not been imposed, would the shareholding have been substantially devalued?

Because the evidence establishes that the prohibition on supply would have caused the substantial devaluation, the answer has to be yes, meaning that the imposition of the consumption tax is not a factual cause.

The same is true for cases of causal pre-emption. Causal pre-emption[52] occurs where one antecedent is performed which is sufficient to produce the consequence, but, before that consequence is realised via that first antecedent, a second antecedent is performed which produces the same consequence first in time.[53] A typical example is where one person consumes a poisoned drink, but is fatally shot before the poison causes death.[54] Referencing the energy drinks example above, a case of causal pre-emption would arise where the consumption tax takes effect immediately and, three months after its imposition, the prohibition on supply comes into effect. Because most consumers of the energy drink are under 23 years, the prohibition on supply causes the investment's substantial devaluation before the consumption tax can have the same effect.

---

[50] Hart and Honoré, *Causation in the Law*, 123.

[51] Particularly regarding cardiac arrests, see Gray and others, 'Cardiovascular Effects of Energy Drinks', 150; and subsequent drug use, see Arria and others, 'Trajectories of Energy Drink Consumption', 424.

[52] In German, the concept is known as 'Ersatzursache'; see Puppe, 'Concept of Causation', 70.

[53] Wright and Puppe, 'Causation', 474.

[54] Hart and Honoré, *Causation in the Law*, 123 and Wright, 'Causation in Tort Law', 1775.

3.2.2 The Solutions for Cases of Causal Duplication and Causal Pre-emption

To overcome these problems, jurists usually press the common-sense button to seek out the 'substantial cause' among the competing factual causes.[55] A more scientific approach is to describe the consequence more precisely so as to make it more unique, usually by adding details on the time or the place of the consequence,[56] but two difficulties rule out this approach. First,[57] without a theory guiding the determination of what descriptive details should be added, it is likely that arbitrariness will serve as the guide; and second,[58] if details can be added, it is unclear what relevance these details have to the causal relation between the antecedent and the consequence.

The most appealing solution is Richard Wright's NESS test – a test for factual causation that has grown out of John Stuart Mill's covering law analysis.[59] The NESS test for factual causation stipulates that an antecedent is a factual cause if it is a member of a set of the minimum number of necessary antecedents which, when they spatio-temporally converge, are sufficient to create the consequence.[60] This test is not without its critics,[61] but its superiority over the but for test has been recognised by the most prominent legal theorists on causation, including those writing in the context of international law.[62] For these reasons, when applicable,[63] it will serve as the test for factual causation in the new theory for causation developed in the second half of this chapter.

3.3 *The Problems of Legal Causation*

By substituting the but for test for the NESS test, a rescue attempt for the factual-legal cause theory could be made, but any such attempt would be a futile undertaking. This futility is on account of the significant problems that the principles of legal causation engender. First, turning to the meaning of

---

[55] Honoré, 'Necessary and Sufficient Conditions', 364.
[56] Wright and Puppe, 'Causation', 475.
[57] See Hart and Honoré, *Causation in the Law*, 491.
[58] Honoré, 'Necessary and Sufficient Conditions', 363–364; Wright and Puppe, 'Causation', 475–476.
[59] Wright and Puppe, 'Causation', 482.
[60] Hart and Honoré, *Causation in the Law*, 112.
[61] For an overview, see Wright, 'Causation, Responsibility, Risk', 1023–1039; Stapleton, 'Causation in the Law', 765–767.
[62] Plakokefalos, 'Causation in the Law of State Responsibility', 477–478.
[63] The NESS test is only applicable with respect to causal questions arising out of relations between events in the real world; see Honoré, 'Causation in the Law', § 3.1. For this reason, it has no application in respect of causal questions for 'physical conduct consequences' (see section 4.3.3.2 below), 'legal circumstance consequences' (see section 4.3.6 below), 'legal conduct consequences' (see section 4.3.6 below), and 'artificial consequences' (see section 4.3.7 below).

legal causation in international investment law, this jurisprudence is so under-developed as to be useless. This conclusion cannot be emphasised enough because it is feared that arbitral tribunals will take up the idea that legal causation examines a cause's causal potency – a concept so vague that it is bound to be used to cloak arbitrary[64] and unreasoned decision making.[65] An example can be found in *El Paso v. Argentina*. After a lengthy account of the facts relating to the causal question,[66] the arbitral tribunal simply concluded:[67]

> In the light of the preceding analysis and after due consideration of the Parties' arguments and the evidence in the file, the Tribunal concludes that the [host state's] measures were, if not the only, certainly the prevailing reason for [the investor's loss].

The jurisprudence from domestic law is no more promising. Its problems begin with the vagueness of foreseeability,[68] the pseudo-application of which over its many years of existence reinforces the point on causal potency's (unfortunate) likely future use. But foreseeability's vagueness is the lowest hanging fruit. Its more substantive problem is that foreseeability is a circumstance that is more relevant to faultworthiness than to causation. Generally, the primary criterion, although causally not the only criterion, for the satisfaction of a rule's fault legal element is that the performing person has knowledge of the wrongful nature of his or her conduct – knowledge that arises if the person foresees the harm flowing from his or her conduct. One person can injure another person, but it usually becomes a legal problem only if that first person was reckless, or intended or should have known (negligence) that such harm would occur. By making foreseeability part of the equation for legal causation, the cause legal element becomes polluted with fault concepts.

This is not a fatal blow, although the next problem could qualify as such. Referring to the two rules[69] that were used to exemplify the harm within the risk principle – the first mandating that sheep must be placed in pens during

---

[64] Picking up on a theme of William Andrews' famous dissent in *Palsgraf v. Long Island Railroad*: 'What we do mean by the word "proximate" is, that because of convenience, of public policy, of a rough sense of justice, the law arbitrarily declines to trace a series of events beyond a certain point. This is not logic. It is practical politics'; see *Helen Palsgraf v. The Long Island Railroad Company* (1928) 248 N.Y. 339 per Andrews J.

[65] Hart and Honoré, *Causation in the Law*, 3.

[66] See *El Paso v. Argentina* §§ 488–507.

[67] Ibid. § 507.

[68] As Leon Green noted: 'To attempt to draw the line between the foreseeable and the unforeseeable in the world of everyday affairs raises even more difficulties than the determination of where space leaves off and outerspace begins'; see Green, 'Foreseeability in Negligence Law', 1413.

[69] See section 2.2.1 above.

their naval transportation and the second prohibiting access to firearms for youths – it will be noted that both are very specific rules. The reason for this is that the harm within the risk principle cannot operate with respect to more open-textured rules, which by their nature should apply to a variety of cases. The relevance of this limited application of harm within the risk is that the rules of international investment law are open-textured.[70]

The killer blow for the use of legal causation principles from domestic law is that they were specifically developed for rules that have no place in international investment law. In Anglo-American jurisdictions, this rule is the tort of negligence. The principles of legal causation work alongside the duty legal element with one purpose in mind: to control the liability that respondents are exposed to by the malleability of the tort of negligence.[71] But international investment law already has rules that serve as gatekeepers: the rules limiting claimants to 'investors' that hold 'investments' in the host state.

Finally, it is respectfully submitted that Stern's rules for identifying legally relevant factual causes are unhelpful, and not only because their scope is limited to factual causes attributable to claimants. As regards the commentary on exclusive interventions, it confirms that omissions can be causal. The idea of cumulative interventions is the most convincing, but it is guilty of mixing circumstances relevant to the questions of fault and apportionment with causation. Finally, it is unclear how complementary interventions can become legally relevant.

4 A NEW THEORY OF CAUSATION FOR INTERNATIONAL INVESTMENT LAW

The above critique paves the way for this chapter's main objective: the pronouncement of a new theory[72] on causation for international investment law. Like all theories, the content of some of its components draws from the fruits

---

[70] For example, in *Lemire v. Ukraine*, the arbitral tribunal commented that the applicable investment treaty's provision containing the rules on arbitrary and discriminatory measures, fair and equitable treatment, and protection and security was couched in 'Delphic economy of language'; see *Joseph Charles Lemire v. Ukraine*, ICSID Case No. ARB/06/18, Decision on Jurisdiction and Liability (14 January 2010) § 246.

[71] Stapleton, 'Legal Cause', 945.

[72] Technically, the process involves constructing a definition of the word 'cause', but its complexity means that this task is more in the nature of laying down a methodology; see Bar, *Common European Law of Torts*, 437.

of other scholarly work, but many components are genuinely novel, beginning with its ideas on what amounts to a potential cause in law.

4.1 Potential Causes

Potential cause refers to the object that acts as the antecedent in any test for factual causation. In common discourse[73] and in law, there are usually no restrictions on what this object can be. The theory advanced here, however, advocates that only voluntary human conduct can serve as the antecedent.[74] In this context,[75] conduct is voluntary if its performance is instructed by the brain of the performing person, thereby excluding conduct such as sleepwalking and sneezing as forms of voluntary human conduct. Accordingly, signing a contract under duress is voluntary conduct, although, as explained section 4.4.1.2, the person who signs would not be causally responsible for this conduct.

The fundamental reason for restricting antecedents to voluntary human conduct is that law can only regulate human conduct,[76] as the following rule demonstrates:

The weather must be sunny on Sundays (the 'Sunny Sunday rule').

Ignoring the desirability of such a rule, it is absurd because its subject is a non-human force. It follows that any rule that imposes liability has to have a human as its subject, but that does not mean that the rule can be amended to provide as follows:

X person must cause the weather to be sunny on Sundays. Non-compliance will result in a fine of 50,000 ducats.

Again, this rule is absurd because the unfortunate X person has potential liability for an outcome over which he or she has no control. What underlies these absurdities is a more fundamental point: liability rules seek to change the world in which they apply. That change can be effected only if the rule that seeks change can be understood in that world. Understanding legal rules is a faculty reserved for humans, which explains why a human is the only

---

[73] Beebee and others, 'Introduction', 2.
[74] Kelsen, *Principles of International Law*, 10.
[75] Unfortunately, the expression 'voluntary' is afflicted by ambiguity. In some contexts it refers to a person's intention to cause some consequence, while in others it refers to a person's mind when he or she is not subject to any duress. For an example of the failure to clearly delineate between these different meanings, see Phelps and Lehman (eds.), *West's Encyclopedia*, 248–249.
[76] Fuller, *Morality of Law*, 74.

potential subject of a rule. Merely understanding, however, is not enough. There must be an incentive for the subject to comply, and that incentive is the avoidance of the rule's legal consequence. To effect such avoidance, the subject must have control over the object of the rule's predicate however, which explains why any potential cause must be voluntary.

4.1.1 The Exclusion of Natural Circumstances and Natural Forces

The major ramification of restricting potential causes to voluntary human conduct is the exclusion of natural circumstances and natural forces as causes in law.[77] This means that a person's death is not caused by a loss of blood,[78] but by the conduct causing that loss of blood. Similarly, a bike rider who hits a falling tree cannot claim that this fall caused his or her injury unless a human planted that tree,[79] because that act of planting is human conduct. Yet, even if the person who planted the offending tree could be identified and brought before an adjudicative body, he or she will not necessarily be liable for the injury. If the rule allegedly breached has a fault legal element, the respondent will be able to argue that it cannot be satisfied because he or she could not have foreseen this injury, which exemplifies the point that the natural circumstances and natural forces are usually relevant to the fault legal element.

There are no exceptions to this exclusion, but it can be circumvented in one of two ways. First, the causal responsibility for one person's (the claimant's) conduct can be transferred to another person (the respondent) – an idea elaborated on in section 4.4 below. For example,[80] if the claimant (the employee) is ordered to work outside and is struck by lightning, he or she could argue that causal responsibility for the conduct of working outside should be pinned to the respondent (employer) by way of 'legal imperative'.[81] Second, a person could cause the consequence by omission.[82] For example, if a dog drinks nitroglycerine and subsequently explodes, thereby injuring the claimant, the claimant might assert that the cause was another person's failure to stop the dog drinking.[83]

---

[77] Edgerton, 'Legal Cause II', 347. Although in international law natural forces are generally recognised as causal; see Crawford, *State Responsibility*, 497.

[78] Wright and Puppe, 'Causation', 480.

[79] See, for example, *Berry v. Borough of Sugar Notch*. There, the claimant was hit by a falling tree that had been planted by the respondent, who was held to have caused this injury; see *Berry v. Borough of Sugar Notch* (1899) 191 Pa. 348 per Fell J.

[80] Example taken from Nolan, 'Are Railroads Liable When Lightning Strikes?', 1551.

[81] See section 4.4.1.1 below.

[82] Whether omissions constitute legal causes is a question addressed in section 4.1.2 below.

[83] Example taken from Green, *Rationale of Proximate Cause*, 195.

4.1.2 The Status of Omissions

This assumes that omissions are potential causes – an idea that has generated plenty of controversy in philosophical circles. Proceeding from the King Lear's logic that 'nothing can be made out of nothing',[84] or, more eloquently, 'causation is a relation between events',[85] it could be objected that an omission cannot constitute a cause.[86] This objection should not be entertained for the purposes of causation in law.[87] As a preliminary point, the classification of omissions as causes in law is demanded by society, which the law ultimately serves,[88] on account of the pervasive and powerful intuition[89] that omissions are causal. For a more logically satisfying explanation, Mill's theory on omissions as causes can be invoked:[90]

> From nothing, a mere negation, no consequences can proceed. All effects are connected, by the law of causation, with some set of *positive* conditions; negative ones, it is true, being almost always required in addition. In other words, every fact or phenomenon which has a beginning, invariably arises when some certain combination of positive facts exist, provided certain other positive facts do not exist.

This theory is somewhat contradictory. Mill does not name omissions as causes,[91] yet it is apparent that he thought that they were causally relevant. They gain this relevancy because of their derivative relationship to actions; effectively, they create the environment for the performance of the action. These omissions are what this monograph calls cause-prevention omissions.

4.1.2.1 *Cause-Prevention Omissions*

A cause-prevention omission is a failure to make a person perform, or prevent a person from performing, certain conduct. Instances of failing to make a person perform are rare. An example would be where a person fails to inform another person, such as a worker at a fire brigade, about a fire that threatens to

---

[84] Shakespeare, *King Lear*, Act I, Scene IV. In German jurisprudence, the same idea is encapsulated in the expression: 'Ein Nichtgeschehen kann nicht wirken, ein Nichts kann keine Folgen haben'; see Lehmann, *Recht der Schuldverhältnisse*, 75.

[85] Beebee, 'Causing and Nothingness', 292.

[86] In the early twentieth century, German law did not recognise omissions as causes; see Jansen, 'Developing Legal Doctrine', 122–123.

[87] But see Moore, *Causation and Responsibility*, 54–55.

[88] Wasserstrom, *Judicial Decision*, 10.

[89] Dowe, 'Causal Processes', § 6.1.

[90] Mill, *System of Logic*, 199.

[91] Mackie, *Cement of the Universe*, 63.

burn down a building, with the result that this latter person does not engage in fire fighting. What are more common are cases of preventing a person from performing, with an example coming from *CME v. Czechia*. There, the conduct in question was the counterparty's termination of a contract that was the investor's principal cash flow source. The counterparty was not a Czech organ, but a private company. However, the investor managed to convince the arbitral tribunal that Czechia's failure to stop this termination was the cause of the investor's loss.[92] The arbitral tribunal did not explicitly spell out why it transferred causal responsibility to Czechia, but an analysis of the arbitral award, and the reasoning of arbitral tribunals in other investment arbitrations where cause-prevention omissions were found, reveals four salient factors: preventability, capacity, awareness, and special relationship.

Preventability refers to the idea that there was a particular action that could have thwarted the performance of the conduct in question. The arbitral tribunal in *CME v. Czechia* gave voice to this requirement by noting that Czechia could have refrained from supporting the partnership agreement's termination and informed the investor's partner that such termination would not be condoned by it.[93] Considering the nature of these actions, it can be assumed that Czechia had the capacity to perform them – an assumption that applies generally if the non-performing person is a state. But this assumption should not always apply, as the case of *Pantechniki v. Albania* illustrates. There, the investor's investment was damaged during large-scale rioting across the host state.[94] The claimant argued that this breached the rule on full protection and security.[95] In rejecting this argument, the arbitral tribunal held that the:

> Albanian authorities were *powerless* in the face of social unrest of this magnitude.[96]

If the non-performing person needs to have the capacity to prevent the conduct in question, then it stands to reason that an awareness of that conduct is also required. This requirement was satisfied in *CME v. Czechia* because the counterparty openly declared its intention to harm the investor by terminating the contract.[97]

---

92 Ibid. § 554.
93 *CME Czech Republic B.V. v. The Czech Republic*, Ad Hoc Arbitration (UNCITRAL Arbitration Rules), Partial Award ('*CME v. Czechia*, Partial Award') (13 September 2001) § 600.
94 *Pantechniki v. Albania* § 13.
95 Ibid. § 71.
96 Ibid. § 82 (emphasis added).
97 *CME v. Czechia*, Partial Award § 600.

Turning to the final factor, special relationship, it is proposed that the relationship between the performing person and the non-performing person must be such that the latter has an obligation to thwart the conduct in question. One avenue by which this relationship arises is if the non-performing person acknowledges it. An example is the rule on full protection and security. According to its terms, the host state acknowledges that it is obliged to stop third persons from harming investors' investments. The other avenue is by imposition of the law. As Czechia did not acknowledge that it accepted causal responsibility for the counterparty's conduct, this must have been the avenue through which the special relationship in *CME v. Czechia* arose, but it is admittedly difficult to detect what facts could justify this imposition. One fact that the arbitral tribunal repeatedly mentioned was the coercion[98] that Czechia exerted on the investor to change the contract with the counterparty some years prior to its termination. This change placed the investor in a legally vulnerable situation – a situation that the counterparty later took advantage of. Extrapolating from these facts, it is submitted that a special relationship arises if the non-performing person's earlier conduct increases the vulnerability of the person who suffers the harm to such harm.

4.1.2.2 *Consequence-Avoidance Omissions*
Another variety of omission, which Mill's theory on omissions does not contemplate, is the consequence-avoidance omission.[99] This is a failure to perform some conduct which, if performed, would have avoided the occurrence of the relevant consequence. It can be figuratively thought of as the missing antecedent in a causal constellation that, if present, would have produced a consequence other than the consequence that actually occurred. An example would be failing to close a fire door through which a fire later spreads, which incidentally explains the absence of consequence-avoidance omissions in Mill's theory. Their existence can be traced back to the exclusion of natural circumstances and natural forces from acting as potential causes – an exclusion that Mill never made. It will be noted that in this example the consequence-avoidance omission is failing to stop a natural force, whereas the failure to stop that natural force's ignition would be a cause-prevention omission.

---

[98] The most explicit endorsement of this view can be inferred from the following statement: '[Czechia], after having coerced the 1996/1997 change in the legal basis for [the investor's] investment ... was obligated to re-establish and secure the legal protection for CME's investment'; see *CME v. Czechia*, Partial Award § 573.

[99] It seems that Puppe had a similar concept in mind with her 'hindrances of rescuing event'; see Puppe, 'Concept of Causation', 82.

Investment arbitrations involving consequence-avoidance omissions will be rare, but they will arise if the investor fails to counteract the effect of the host state's (wrongful) conduct. For example, if the host state enacts a carbon tax and the investor suffers a substantial devaluation of its shareholding as a result, the host state might be able to argue that the investor could have nullified this tax's effect by reducing its carbon footprint. For that argument to succeed, the host state must establish 'avoidability': that the conduct which was not performed would have avoided the actual consequence through the realisation of a more beneficial consequence.

A second requirement is that the non-performing person has the actual or constructive capacity to perform the conduct in question. Actual capacity is the non-performing person's factual ability to perform, while constructive capacity refers to the non-performing person's normative ability to perform. Referring to the carbon tax example, the investor might complain that the cost of switching to non-carbon-based energy sources would make the company in which the shareholding exists insolvent. While this would exclude its actual capacity, the investor might yet have constructive capacity. If, for example, the carbon tax's introduction was flagged well before it came into effect, then it could be argued that the company could have saved funds to prepare for this event,[100] rather than distributing those funds through dividend payments. From this example, two salient aspects of constructive capacity should be appreciated. First, the preparation time for performing the conduct that avoids the consequence begins when the non-performing person actually or constructively knows of the actual consequence's potential occurrence. Second, the content of this preparation depends on the non-performing person's actual capacities. If, for example, the company had in place a dividend freeze and could not have saved to prepare for the carbon tax's implementation, then it would not have had constructive capacity.

Before concluding, it is worth mentioning why two potential requirements for consequence-avoidance omissions – an awareness of the conduct that would avoid the consequence, and the reasonableness of that conduct – are pretenders. As regards awareness, it should be assumed that the investors and host states, considering their resources, are aware of any conduct that can potentially avoid a negative consequence. For reasonableness, this is a non-causal concept because it evaluates a person's behaviour.[101] The theory

---

[100] This is a tactic many large corporates have employed to prepare for the implementation of new carbon taxes; see Hertsgaard, 'If It's Good Enough for Big Oil'.

[101] MacCormick, *Rhetoric and The Rule of Law*, 179.

of causation advanced here seeks to clear out the pollution that non-causal concepts have brought to the factual-legal cause theory.

4.1.2.3 *Significance of Distinction between Cause-Prevention Omissions and Consequence-Avoidance Omissions*

Aside from the conceptual distinction between cause-prevention omissions and consequence-avoidance omissions, and the different circumstances that must exist for one or the other to operate, there is an important practical distinction. If the former is proven, causal responsibility for the action that should have been prevented is transferred from the performer of that action to the non-performing person. Consequence-avoidance omissions have no such effect. They become part of the causal constellation that creates the actual consequence. Finally, the concepts of cause-prevention omissions and consequence-avoidance omissions should not be confused with the rules on attribution. These rules have a facilitative purpose.[102] Recognising the impracticalities of a principal performing all the requisite acts for its legal purposes, they permit an agent to perform those tasks, although they legally tie them back to the principal,[103] disregarding factors such as whether the principal could have prevented such conduct. Moreover, the concepts of cause-prevention omissions and consequence-avoidance omissions are ultimately concerned with 'causal responsibility', a concept explained in section 4.4 below, whereas attribution transfers liability from an agent to a principal.[104]

4.2 A Taxonomy of Legal Consequences

The question of what a potential cause in law should look like having now been settled, the next definitional question can be tackled: what is the proper meaning of consequence?

---

[102] This is uncontroversial in international law; see Crawford, *State Responsibility*, 113. In Anglo-American law, however, many policies have been proposed to support the existence of vicarious liability. For an overview of these policies, see Neyers, 'Theory of Vicarious Liability', 291–301.

[103] Condorelli and Kress, 'Rules of Attribution', 221. See also Frederick Pollock's conception of vicarious liability in Pollock, *Essays in Jurisprudence and Ethics*, 130–131. It expresses the idea that a principal has to accept both the benefits and burdens of other persons doing his or her bidding; see Keating, 'Idea of Fairness', 1360. For a critique of this conception, see Neyers, 'Theory of Vicarious Liability', 298–300.

[104] Crawford, *State Responsibility*, 113–114.

4.2.1 Seven Consequences

It is proposed that law knows of seven types of consequences, starting with organic consequences.[105] They are either the necrotic death of[106] or a change in the usual functioning of the cells of an organism – admittedly, a type of consequence that is very unlikely to be seen in an investment arbitration. A second type is physical circumstance consequences, which are changes in the location or form of physical objects. Examples include a bodily injury or damage to land or goods. The third is physical conduct consequences. They include not only physical movements but also information-creating conduct such as warning consumers about the dangers of tobacco products.[107]

The fourth type – mental consequences – refers to either desires or beliefs. Emotions, such as happiness or melancholia, are better understood as organic physical consequences as they are neurophysiological in nature.[108] A desire is a state of mind where a person wants to cause an advantageous consequence,[109] as assessed according to that person's reward system. For investors and host states, the primary rewards should be profit and the social welfare of their populations,[110] respectively. A belief is a state of mind where a person thinks that a fact exists or evaluates a certain fact as superior to another fact.[111] Facts refer to various concepts, including causal relationships, features of the natural world, or artificial concepts, like the value of an investment.

The fifth and sixth types are legal circumstance consequences and legal conduct consequences. The former are changes to the nature, status, or extent of a legal concept, which is any concept that is created by law, with examples being intellectual property, marriage, companies, and ownership. The latter are actions or omissions with legal consequences. Examples include a private person entering into a contract or a state enacting a new law. The final type is artificial consequences. These are changes in the nature or extent of a societal,

---

[105] The term 'organic consequence' is borrowed from Tony Honoré; see Honoré, 'Causation in the Law', § 3.1.
[106] As opposed to apoptotic death, which is the natural and normal death of cells, first recognised by Kerr and others, 'Apoptosis', 239.
[107] Such conduct was the basis of the disputes in *Philip Morris v. Australia* and *Philip Morris v. Uruguay*.
[108] Matsumoto (ed.), *Cambridge Dictionary of Psychology*, 179 (definition of 'emotion').
[109] This conception of desire is inspired by the 'action-based theory' of desire; see Schroeder, 'Desire', § 1.1.
[110] Essentially a form of parental care, which is one form of primary rewards in humans; see Schultz, 'Neuronal Reward and Decision Signals', 857.
[111] This is a stipulative definition influenced by the two forms of beliefs that can serve as antecedents in a causal constellation leading to a physical conduct consequence; see section 4.3.3 below.

as opposed to a legal, concept having no physical form. In international invest-ment law, the prime example is the devaluation of a shareholding.

4.2.2 Continuous Causality

The main operative feature of the theory being advanced here is what is called continuous causation. Causation in law does not have any dead-ends. If there were to be a starting junction, it would be mental consequences. Mental consequences lead to physical conduct or legal conduct, which in turn lead to, one, physical circumstances or organic consequences or, two, legal circumstances, respectively. As a simple example, while out hunting for food, a person sees a fish (forming a belief), throws a spear at it (physical conduct), thereby causing its death (organic consequence). How that organic consequence becomes causal is that it acts as information for the beliefs that cause subsequent conduct, such as eating the fish. For this conception to be accepted, two challenges must be met and they set the agenda for the rest of this part.

4.3 *Causality*

The first challenge is constructing a test for causality that facilitates con-tinuous causation. The key tool in this endeavour is the 'causal constellation'. For each consequence, there is a causal constellation made up of its direct causes. How a potential cause becomes a direct cause depends on the type of consequence in question. For consequences in the physical world, such as organic consequences and physical circumstances, and mental consequences, the NESS test is deployed. For other types of consequence, their direct causes are predetermined, as described in the sections below. If the applicable cause legal element comes from a rule containing a fault legal element, the test for factual causation must be supplemented by a test for fault causation.[112] If the potential cause fails the test for fault causation, it cannot be labelled a direct cause.

The theory being expounded here cannot be properly illuminated by description only. What is required is its exemplification, with reference to each type of consequence. This is admittedly a very laborious task, but it cannot be avoided because it demonstrates how the idea of continuous caus-ation operates in practice.

---

[112] See section 3.1 above.

4.3.1 Causal Constellations for Organic Consequences

The causal constellations for organic consequence differ according to whether the organic consequence is a genetic condition or an environmentally induced condition. Applying the rule that only human conduct can constitute a cause,[113] the only forms of human conduct that can create a causal constellation for a genetic condition are consequence-avoidance omissions.[114] These omissions are failing to, one, stop the genetic condition's development and, two, submit the organism to the treatment. For example,[115] if the consequence were a person having to live with a genetic condition, these omissions would usually[116] take the form of, one, a doctor failing to terminate the pregnancy and, two, the person's mother failing to submit to that procedure.

For environmentally induced conditions, the causal constellation minimally consists of, excluding any potential consequence-avoidance omissions, a positional antecedent and a change antecedent. The positional antecedent is the positioning of the organism at the time and place of its collision with the change antecedent. The change agent is lack of nutrition or malnutrition, trauma, or the introduction of a virus into the organism.[117] An example is any asbestos case. There, the malnourishing effects of asbestos dust are introduced into the organism, which will be that of the claimant. The conduct constituting this introduction is the change antecedent, while the claimant's conduct of coming into contact with the asbestos is the positional antecedent. These antecedents collide when they spatio-temporally converge. For example, if the consequence is an HIV infection, the change antecedent might be the doctor's injection of HIV-infected blood into the patient's arm, with the patient's presence at this time being the positional antecedent. However, the person performing the two antecedents need not necessarily meet: an HIV-infected drug user might discard a syringe on a beach (the change antecedent), only for a beach-goer to later step on it (the positional antecedent).[118]

After identifying these antecedents, their factual causality and, if applicable, fault causality can be tested by applying the NESS test. This application will

---

[113] See section 4.1 above.

[114] See section 4.1.2.2 above for an explanation of consequence-avoidance omissions.

[115] In Anglo-American law, these are usually referred to as 'wrongful birth' or 'wrongful conception' cases; see Stretton, 'Birth Torts', 319.

[116] At the time of writing, gene therapy was still in its infancy, meaning that the management of the symptoms of genetic conditions is the default option; see Phelps and Hassed, *Genetic Conditions*, 1.

[117] These being the circumstances leading to necrosis; see Dye (ed.), *Dictionary of Stem Cells*, 224 (definition of 'necrosis').

[118] Admittedly, the chances of being infected in such circumstances are very low; see Canadian Paediatric Society, 'Needle Stick Injuries', 207.

usually involve recourse to the causal laws developed by medical science. Given that knowledge of such causal laws is incomplete, this will occasionally lead to evidentiary difficulties in which the applicable standard of proof is vital.[119]

4.3.2 Causal Constellations for Physical Circumstance Consequences

As with environmentally induced organic consequences, the causal constellations for physical circumstance consequences minimally consist of a positional antecedent and a change antecedent. The positional antecedent is the positioning of the relevant physical object such that it collides with some other physical force (the change force).[120] For example, if the consequence is a broken leg to a pedestrian who was hit by a car while crossing the road, the positional antecedent is the pedestrian's presence on the road at the time of the change agent, being the car-driving.

4.3.3 Physical Conduct Consequences

Assuming that mental causation[121] exists for physical conduct consequences,[122] then their causal constellations must be made up of mental states, all of which must temporally converge. Drawing on the theory of folk psychology,[123] these mental states are, one, a desire for some advantageous outcome, two, the belief that the conduct will cause the outcome ('causality belief'), three, the belief that the conduct is within the performing person's capacity ('capacity belief') and, four, the belief that the conduct is the most effective method to achieve that outcome ('most effective method belief').[124] As desire

---

[119] In Anglo-American law jurisdictions, the standard is 'on the balance of probabilities', which is a relatively low standard compared to continental European jurisdictions; see Bar, *Common European Law of Torts*, 470.

[120] Applying David Fair's idea that the source of all causes are energy flows; see generally Fair, 'Causation and the Flow of Energy', 219. Although accepting this thesis, this paper limits the relevance of energy flows to physical circumstance consequences. Puppe also supports the idea that energy flows carry causes, but expresses doubts as to whether they are relevant for all causes; see Puppe, 'Concept of Causation', 81.

[121] Sometimes referred to as 'psychological causation'; see Bar, *Common European Law of Torts*, 443.

[122] Although in the latter half of the twentieth century there have been numerous attacks on mental causation; see Robb and Heil, 'Mental Causation', § 1.1.

[123] Also referred to as 'common sense psychology', although some argue that 'common sense psychology' has a narrower ambit than 'folk psychology'; see Radcliffe, 'From Folk Psychology to Commonsense', 223.

[124] See Horgan and Woodward, 'Folk Psychology is Here to Stay', 144.

has been already been explained in section 4.2.1 above, this section will focus on the three beliefs.

Regardless of whether his or her belief corresponds to the objective truth,[125] the performing person must believe that his or her conduct will potentially achieve some advantageous outcome and that he or she can perform such conduct.[126] For example, a smoker wants to avoid premature death (the advantageous outcome). As this person believes that he or she can stop smoking (the capacity belief) and that smoking causes premature death (the causality belief), then he or she quits smoking (the physical conduct consequence).

The third belief is that the performing person believes that the conduct is the most effective method to achieve the advantageous outcome.[127] Forming this belief necessarily involves an evaluative comparison between the relevant physical conduct consequence and other forms of conduct. For example, if the student desires a high grade, he or she might identify either studying hard or cheating. After assessing the benefits and detriments of both, he or she (thankfully) concludes that studying hard is the most effective method to achieve a high grade.

4.3.3.1 Defence of Folk Psychology

For some, folk psychology's influence might be objectionable because it seemingly does not match the rigour of scientific[128] psychology or neuroscience.[129] The main tenet of the criticism is that scientific psychology might yet show that desires and beliefs do not exist at all.[130] For the purposes of causation in the law, however, folk psychology should be embraced.[131]

First, the fact that folk psychology is informed by common experience does not necessarily mean that it is invalid as a theory,[132] and it may yet be validated by science.[133] Second, jurists should be inclined to ground decisions on

[125] Matsumoto (ed.), *Cambridge Dictionary of Psychology*, 80 (definition of 'beliefs').
[126] Horgan and Woodward, 'Folk Psychology is Here to Stay', 144.
[127] Ibid.
[128] See, for example, the following definition: ' "Folk Psychology" denotes the *prescientific*, common-sense conceptual framework that all normally socialized humans deploy in order to comprehend ... the behaviour of humans' (emphasis added); see Churchland, 'Folk Psychology', 3.
[129] This is known as the 'status issue'; see Baker, 'Folk Psychology', 318.
[130] Stich, *From Folk Psychology to Cognitive Science*, 228.
[131] This accords with the law's general acceptance of folk psychology; see Birmingham, 'Folk Psychology and Legal Understanding', 1716.
[132] As one commentator has noted, if beliefs and desires do not exist, it would be: 'the greatest intellectual catastrophe in the history of our species'; see Fodor, *Psychosemantics*, xii.
[133] Horgan and Woodward, 'Folk Psychology is Here to Stay', 145.

causality in theories which find broad acceptance among the general populace,[134] who are the intended recipients of justice.[135] Third, and most importantly, there is no alternative to the concepts of desires and beliefs in causally explaining human conduct as there is no other vocabulary available for this purpose.[136]

4.3.3.2 *Testing Causality for Physical Conduct Consequences*

It will have been noted that in deploying folk psychology to explain physical conduct consequences, the question of factual causality does not arise.[137] Folk psychology spells out a causal law for physical conduct consequences. If the relevant circumstances fit within the dictates of that causal law, then there is factual causality. What will be the main hurdle in this context is proving what beliefs the performing person had.[138]

Further, the question of fault causation does not arise with respect to beliefs because it could never be accurately tested. As an illustration of this, consider the following rule:

> A person must not defy official party ideology because of a belief that Big Brother is wicked.[139]

Although apocryphal, the idea of causally linking conduct to mental states is evident in anti-discrimination laws,[140] incidentally proving why mental states have to be viewed as potential causes in law. The question is: how would this thought that Big Brother is wicked be reformulated? Potentially, the non-faultworthy thought could be that Big Brother is slightly less than wicked, but this starts to enter the realm of the fanciful and non-scientific.

---

[134] This view is generally accepted in Anglo-American criminal law; see Morse, 'Determinism and the Death of Folk Psychology', 20.

[135] Wasserstrom, *Judicial Decision*, 10.

[136] Fodor, 'Persistence of the Attitudes', 228–229.

[137] Presumably explaining Tony Honoré's contention that Mill's covering law analysis has no application for consequences other than physical circumstance consequences; see Honoré, 'Causation in the Law', § 3.1.

[138] For example, in English tort law there is a presumption of inducement in cases of negligent misrepresentation; see *Edwards v. Ashik* [2014] EWHC 2454 (Ch).

[139] Drawing inspiration from George Orwell's *Nineteen Eighty-Four* –although, in the novel, thought crimes did not have any conduct legal element as merely thinking improper thoughts was a crime; see Orwell, *Nineteen Eighty-Four*, 21.

[140] For example, consider the following rule: 'No covered entity shall discriminate against a qualified individual *on the basis of* disability in regard to job application procedures' (emphasis added); see Americans with Disabilities Act of 1990 (United States of America) s. 12112(a).

4.3.4 Causal Constellations for Mental Consequences

Causal constellations for mental consequences minimally consist of some information-creating conduct (the change antecedent) and the receipt of that information by the person holding the belief (the positional antecedent). Accordingly, if the mental consequence is a belief that smoking causes premature death, then the causal constellation could be the placement of warning signs on tobacco products (the change antecedent) and the consumer's reading of those warning signs (the positional antecedent). Although information-creating might conjure up thoughts of human conduct involving the use of language, it need not. Any human conduct has the potential to create information. For example, if the consequence is a belief that an olive in a martini is pitted, the information-creating could be cutting a hole at one end of the relevant olive, thereby indicating that it is pitted.[141]

When it comes to assessing the factual causality of the information-creating antecedent, the NESS test returns. The only caveat regarding its application is that if the mental consequence is a belief, then the degree of belief should ideally be defined. For example, if the degree of belief is mere suspicion, then one act of information-creating might be sufficient, whereas more information-creating might be required for certainty.[142] As this is patently a very difficult determination to make,[143] adjudicative bodies are inclined to presume that certain information-creating, from ostensibly qualified persons, causes a person to develop a belief, without any reference to the degree of belief.[144]

4.3.5 Causal Constellations for Legal Circumstance Consequences

The causal constellations of legal circumstance consequences minimally consist of a change antecedent and a positional antecedent. The change antecedent is some legal conduct that changes the nature or extent of a legal concept, while the positional antecedent is the positioning of that same legal

---

[141] Phillips, 'Product Misrepresentation', 562. The example comes from an actual case, *Hochberg v. O'Donnell's*. There, the claimant, believing that an olive was pitted, bit into an olive placed in his martini, with the consequence that a tooth was injured. The claimant was ultimately successful. See *Hochberg v. O'Donnell's Restaurant, Inc.* (D. C. App. 1971) 272 A. 2d 846.

[142] See Schwitzgebel, 'Belief', § 2.4.

[143] As noted by Lord Cranworth when this question came before the English courts in the 1850s: 'It is impossible so to analyse the operation of the human mind as to be able to say how far any particular representation may have led to the formation of any particular resolution'; see *Reynell v. Sprye* (1852) 1 De G. M. & G. 708 per Cranworth LJ.

[144] See, for example, *Gould v. Vaggelas*, where it was held: 'A representation need not be the sole inducement in sustaining the loss. If it plays some part, even if only a minor part, in

concept in the time and space of the change antecedent's period of effectiveness. For example, in cases of direct expropriation where the investor's legal ownership of its investment is lost, the change antecedent might be the host state's enactment of a law depriving the investor of ownership, while the positional antecedent is the investor's ownership of the investment at the time and place of this law's effectiveness.[145]

The likely objection to this conception of causal constellations for legal circumstance consequences is that merely owning an investment, or more precisely the legal conduct of taking ownership, cannot constitute a cause. The presumed basis for this objection is that this positional antecedent is a 'condition' and not a 'cause'.[146] This objection should be rejected. Aside from invoking common sense to distinguish between conditions and causes,[147] there is no scientific basis for this distinction.[148] Moreover, this positional antecedent performs the same role as the positional antecedent in causal constellations for physical circumstance consequences.[149] However, it would be unthinkable to dismiss an example of a physical circumstance consequence's positional antecedent, such as the injured person's running in front of a speeding car, as non-causal. Thus, by analogy, the positional antecedents in causal constellations for legal circumstances should also be viewed as causes. Another matter worth emphasising is that the change antecedent must be legal conduct, as opposed to purely physical conduct. Although legal conduct must be expressed through physical conduct, it distinguishes itself because the law gives it some legal effect. For example, the action of signing a contract is the physical conduct of putting pen to paper, but it also serves the legal purpose of entering into that contract.

For legal circumstance consequences, testing for factual causality and fault causality does not involve the NESS test. It is actually misleading to describe this process as causality because all that is being asked is whether the applicable law recognises some change to the nature, status, or extent of the relevant legal concept after the change antecedent takes effect. If the answer is yes for factual causality, which is admittedly a misnomer in this context, and no for fault causality, then the antecedents are causes.

---

contributing to the course of action taken a causal connection will exist'; see *Gould v. Vaggelas* (1985) 157 C.L.R. 236 per Wilson J.

[145] For a similar case, see *Venezuela Holdings v. Venezuela*.

[146] Hart and Honoré, *Causation in the Law*, 111.

[147] Ibid.

[148] Mill, *System of Logic*, 399–400. Admittedly, jurists would retort, however, that causation in the law is not a task for science; see Bar, *Common European Law of Torts*, 459–460.

[149] See section 4.3.2 above.

4.3.6 Causal Constellations for Legal Conduct Consequences

As with physical conduct consequences, the causal constellation for legal conduct consequences is made up of four antecedents. The three antecedents[150]
of desire, causality belief, and most effective method belief remain the same,
but the capacity belief changes form. The law applicable to the legal conduct
consequence determines whether the performing person has capacity to perform the legal conduct. For example, if a person seeks to enter into a contract,
the law applicable to his or her contractual capacity is relevant,[151] not his or her
belief that he or she is capable of performing this legal conduct. As for causality, this is simply a matter of proving the existence of the relevant beliefs and
their temporal coincidence.

4.3.7 Causal Constellations for Artificial Consequences

A causal constellation for an artificial consequence will vary according to the
specific consequence. Given its prevalence in international investment law,
this section is interested in putting forward the causal constellation for a shareholding devaluation. In constructing that causal constellation, the first task is
to determine the meaning of value. That meaning could be the highest price
that a hypothetical buyer is willing to pay, and, if reliable evidence is available on that,[152] arbitral tribunals in international investment law have shown
a preference for using it to define value.[153] But this is a mental consequence –
the buyer's belief regarding the shareholding's fair market value. Artificial
consequences are objective concepts,[154] such as the shareholding's intrinsic

---

[150] See section 4.3.3 above for descriptions of these antecedents.

[151] Under English law, this is the law of the jurisdiction to which the contract is most closely
connected or the person's domicile; see Collins and others (eds.), *Dicey, Morris and Collins
on the Conflict of Laws*, Rule 228. Under German law, pursuant to § 7(1) of the Introductory
Act to the Civil Code, this law is the law of the person's nationality; see Junker, *Internationales
Privatrecht*, 231. However, both English law (at the time of writing) and German law are subject to the exception that Article 13 of the Rome I Regulation creates to these rules.

[152] For example, this evidence could be a share's spot price on an exchange; see *CMS Gas
Transmission Company v. The Republic of Argentina*, ICSID Case No. ARB/01/8, Award (12
May 2005) § 403.

[153] Ripinsky and Williams, *Damages*, 189.

[154] Ultimately, fair market value according to the hypothetical buyer is subjective speculation, as
encapsulated in the following remark from intrinsic value's founder, John Burr Williams: 'Both
wise men and foolish will trade in the market, but no one group by itself will set the price. Nor
will it matter what the majority, however overwhelming, may think; for the last owner, and he
alone, will set the price'; see Burr Williams, *Theory of Investment Value*, 12.

value. Intrinsic value can be formulated in any number of ways[155] but at its core is rather simple:[156]

> The value of any stock ... is determined by the cash inflows and outflows – discounted at an appropriate interest rate – that can be expected to occur during the remaining life of the asset.

This formula reveals intrinsic value's four variables: cash inflow, cash outflow, weighted average cost of capital ('discounted at an appropriate interest rate'), and asset's remaining life. The challenge now is to craft a causal constellation from this formula.

Because numerous antecedents lay behind them, WACC and asset's remaining life are unlikely to move as frequently as cash inflows and cash outflows. Cash inflow and cash outflow are examples of legal conduct as they are conduct effecting a change in respect of a legal concept; in other words, it is the symbolic act of a buyer transferring ownership of money to the company in which the shareholding exists. As with other causal constellations, these change antecedents need to be complemented by a positional antecedent, which is the antecedent of the investor owning the shareholding at the time when and place where the relevant change antecedent becomes active.

With shareholding devaluations, the problem of causality should not arise. In all cases, the process of its determination will consist of comparing value before and after the breach. If the value has decreased and the conduct in breach can be classified as one of the antecedents for the shareholding devaluation, or one of the antecedents in the causal constellations behind 'WACC' or 'asset's remaining life' and that conduct is the characteristic conduct for the relevant causal constellation (an idea detailed in section 4.4.2 below), then it will be a cause. But in the vast majority of disputes, this conduct will be cash inflow or cash outflow. If the conduct constituting any of these antecedents is proven, then it is a factual cause. For example, if consumers, encouraged by the host state, discontinue their purchases of a company's products, then this legal conduct of omitting to buy should be viewed as the factual cause of the devaluation of that company's shares.[157]

---

[155] Price, *Conscious Investor*, 12.

[156] Buffett, *1992 Letter*, ¶ 62. This is a simplified version of the discounted cash flow formula; see Damodaran, *Investment Valuation*, 11–13.

[157] For a similar case, see *Azurix v. Argentina*. There, the host state encouraged consumers not to pay for their consumption of water provided by the investor. This conduct breached the rule on fair and equitable treatment. See *Azurix Corp. v. The Argentine Republic*, ICSID Case No. ARB/01/12, Award (14 July 2006) ('*Azurix v. Argentina*') § 376.

4.4 Causal Responsibility

Many would object that the consumers' conduct is not the 'real cause'. That title rather belongs to the conduct making up the host state's encouragement – a position that reflects what arbitral tribunals have decided in similar cases. It might appear that the theory expounded here is diverging from the practice,[158] although the opposite is true. This theory of causation does hold that the consumers' conduct is causal because it forms part of the consequence's causal constellation, but that does not mean that the consumers have causal responsibility for that cause, which introduces the concept that this part of the chapter deals with. The rules on causal responsibility determine on whom the blame for the consequence is pinned. If that person is the subject of the rule from which the cause legal element originates, then the element is satisfied.

4.4.1 Causal Responsibility for Physical Conduct and Legal Conduct

Drawing on the Aristotelian axiom[159] that a person controls his or her own conduct, the default rule is that the person who performs any physical or legal conduct, including information-creating, is causally responsible for it. This rule admits of a number of exceptions, however, such as when a non-performing person is found to have performed a cause-prevention omission in respect of the performing person's cause, as discussed in section 4.1.2.1.

4.4.1.1 Legal Imperatives

Another exception is when the performing person is acting pursuant to a legal imperative. Channelling John Austin,[160] legal imperatives are commands that the performing person is subject to. These legal imperatives may be created by any source, excluding the performing person. Accordingly, if a performing person performs pursuant to a contract that he or she is a party to, this performance is not obligated by a legal imperative.[161] This exception is particularly important for international investment law because host states create legal imperatives with the enactment of their laws. If those laws stipulate that an investor must perform some act contrary to its interests, this exception makes the host state causally responsible for the consequences relating thereto. For

---

[158] For an example of that practice, see the discussion of *Azurix v. Argentina* above.
[159] Meyer, *Aristotle on Moral Responsibility*, 1.
[160] Austin, *Province of Jurisprudence*, 5.
[161] Practically, the originators of legal imperatives are states, as John Austin envisioned, although he referred to them as 'lawgivers'; see ibid., 13.

example,[162] if the conduct of placing warning labels on tobacco products is obligated by the host state's law, it is the enactment of this law that is the cause of the consequences relating to this conduct. In this way, a legal imperative more than transfers causal responsibility; it subsumes the performing person's conduct to become the cause in the relevant causal constellation.

4.4.1.2 Factual Imperatives

Factual imperatives[163] are the conceptual cousins of legal imperatives. They consist in unlawful conduct of a person that causes the performing person to reasonably believe that his or her conduct will avoid some harm (the 'hypothetical harm'). The hypothetical harm must be greater than the actual harm that the performing person's conduct causes. A belief's reasonableness is determined by approximating the objective chance that the unlawful conduct will cause the hypothetical harm. If that objective chance is more likely than not, then the belief is reasonable. Further, the affliction of the hypothetical harm must not have been consented to by the performing person, and his or her conduct must be proportionate. Proportionality is established if the performing person's conduct avoids the hypothetical harm in the manner least harmful to the other person who creates the factual imperative. If the performing person's conduct exceeds this limit, then he or she has causal responsibility for the surplus.

The concept of factual imperative transfers causal responsibility in a variety of cases, including chases[164] and rescues.[165] For international investment law, its relevance is mostly felt in respect of consequential losses.[166] Consider, for example,[167] a dispute where the host state revokes the investor's

---

[162] Drawing on the facts of *Philip Morris Brands Sàrl, Philip Morris Products S.A. and Abal Hermanos S.A. v. Oriental Republic of Uruguay*, ICSID Case No. ARB/10/7 and *Philip Morris Asia Limited v. The Commonwealth of Australia*, PCA Case No. 2012-12.

[163] The concept is similar to that provided for in ILC Articles on State Responsibility, Art. 18. Factual imperative has a wider scope, however, because Article 18 focuses on circumstances constituting coercion; see ILC Articles on State Responsibility (with commentaries), Art. 18 (cmt 2).

[164] For example, if a person escapes police custody and a police officer, the performing person, is hit by a car while giving chase, then the first person's act of escaping is the factual imperative for the police officer's act of chasing. With this conclusion, the respondent becomes causally responsible for the claimant's broken legs. This example is based on a case from the German Federal Supreme Court (12 March 1996), BGHZ 132, 164. For an English translation, see Markesinis and Unberath, *German Law of Torts*, 638.

[165] For example, if a person is thrown out of a train because of the train's excess speed and the performing person jumps out of the train to rescue the first person, the performing person's conduct is causally attributable to the train company. This example is based on the facts of *Arthur Wagner v. International Railway Company* (1921) 282 N.Y. 176.

[166] Although incidental loss is another descriptor; see Ripinsky and Williams, *Damages*, 301.

[167] Drawing on the facts of *Middle East Cement Shipping and Handling Co. S.A. v. Arab Republic of Egypt*, ICSID Case No. ARB/99/6, Award (12 April 2002) §§ 81–85.

business permit. To avoid the losses associated with paying the salaries of idle employees, the investor begins to move its assets from the host state, thereby ceasing its business activities there. The investor incurs significant costs in this process. Applying the general rule, the investor's conduct will be the cause of these losses, but, if the host state's conduct constitutes a factual imperative, this unpalatable outcome can be avoided. Assuming that the revocation was unlawful, the two questions that this example raises relate to the elements of 'harm' and 'proportionality'. For harm, it would have to be established that the hypothetical harm of employees' salary costs would exceed the actual harm of the moving costs. For proportionality, it would be a matter of determining whether the moving of the investor's assets was conducted in the most cost-efficient manner.[168]

4.4.1.3 Inducements

The third mechanism for transferring causal responsibility for physical or legal conduct is the concept of inducement. The distinction between inducements and factual imperatives is that the former lack a harm element. Moreover, inducements usually acquire their status because they implicitly promise a gain for the performing person. By contrast, factual imperatives usually imply some harm to the performing person.

Although rarely recognised,[169] causal responsibility can transfer from a performing person to a person who induces that performance. As with legal imperatives, if an inducement becomes the legal cause of a loss, then it becomes relevant for other legal purposes, most particularly when assessing the foreseeability of a consequence. Inferring from Anglo-American law[170] and German law,[171] this transfer is premised on, one, the inducement being unlawful or contrary to good morals,[172] two, the inducing person believing that

---

[168] Arbitral tribunals generally accept that the investor's conduct was proportionate. For example, *Siemens v. Argentina*, where the investor's post-expropriation costs were unquestioned; see *Siemens A.G. v. The Argentine Republic*, ICSID Case No. ARB/02/8, Award (17 January 2007) § 329 (for a list of these costs) and § 387 (for the arbitral tribunal's confirmation that the host state effectively caused these costs).

[169] Seavey, 'Reliance upon Gratuitous Promises', 914. English courts are always at pains to limit circumstances where liability arises through an inducement; see, for example, *White and another v. Jones and others* [1995] 2 AC 207 per Goff of Chieveley LJ.

[170] For American law, see particularly Restatement (Third) of Torts: Liability for Economic Harm (Tentative Draft No. 1) § 5. For an overview of English law, see Walton and others (eds.), *Charlesworth & Percy on Negligence*, 80–92.

[171] For an overview, see Markesinis and Unberath, *German Law of Torts*, 890–891.

[172] This borrows from the expression '*contra bonos mores*' ('gegen die guten Sitten'), formerly the guiding principle of German competition law; see Act on Unfair Competition 1909 (Germany) § 1. In the new legislation on unfair competition, 'fairness' is the new guiding principle, a term more in keeping with European Union law; see Vrey, *Towards a European Unfair Competition Law*, 156.

the performing person will likely perform,[173] and three, a fiduciary relationship or special relationship between those two persons. Aside from the circumstance where the inducing person recognises this relationship, this special relationship might also arise where the inducing person can, relative to the performing person, one, verify the accuracy or, two, control the performance of the conduct that is the subject of the inducement.

As regards their scope, inducements only transfer causal responsibility in respect of conduct that is consistent with, and proportionate to, the inducing person's representation during its period of validity. Accordingly, if the inducing person retracts that representation, then there is no transfer of causal responsibility after the retraction.[174] An example[175] of disproportionate conduct would be where, after the host state represents that the investor can legally pursue a foreign investment, the investor purchases prestige office space when more modest office space would have been sufficient to complete the investment activities. The case of *Azurix v. Argentina* illustrates how inducements transfer causal responsibility. There, the host state encouraged the investor's customers to stop paying their debts to the investor.[176] The host state's conduct was held to breach the rule on fair and equitable treatment.[177] Evidently, encouraging contractual parties to breach their obligations is unlawful.[178] Further, it is considered that there is a fiduciary relationship between a host state and its citizens as an aspect of a state's primary obligation to protect its citizens.[179]

4.4.2 Causal Responsibility for Other Causes

It will be rarely be necessary to determine causal responsibility for causes other than physical conduct or legal conduct because rules typically stipulate that a

---

[173] See, for example, Feldthusen, *Economic Negligence*, 54; Perry, 'Protected Interests and Undertakings', 282.

[174] For an example of this principle, see *MTD v. Chile*. There, after the host state informed the investor that it could pursue its investment, it was held that all the investor's costs thereafter were not caused by the host state; see *MTD v. Chile*, Award § 240(ii).

[175] This example is based on the facts in *MTD v. Chile*. For an analysis of how this theory of causation applies to label the investor's conduct in that case causal, see section 2.1.1 of chapter 4.

[176] *Azurix v. Argentina* § 125.

[177] Ibid. § 376.

[178] In Anglo-American law, it is known as the tort of interference with contractual relations. The leading case in English law is *OBG Limited and others v. Allan and others* [2007] UKHL 21. For American law, see Restatement (Second) of Torts, chap. 37. In German law, this conduct would be unlawful per Civil Code § 826 or Act on Unfair Competition 2010 § 4(4); see Gerhard Wagner in Säcker and others (eds.), *Münchener Kommentar zum Bürgerlichen Gesetzbuch*, Book VI, § 826 (¶ 62); Hartwig Sprau in Palandt, *Bürgerliches Gesetzbuch*, § 826 (¶ 59).

[179] As Emmerich de Vattel noted: 'Whoever uses a citizen ill, indirectly offends the state, which is *bound to protect this citizen*' (emphasis added); see Parlett, 'Diplomatic Protection', 87.

person's conduct must be a cause of the relevant consequence. Sometimes, however, causal responsibility for other causes will come into question. For beliefs, causal responsibility attaches to the person who publishes the information from which the belief develops. For example,[180] if a person believes that only 3,700 km separate the Canary Islands from Japan travelling in a westerly direction, then causal responsibility for that belief is cast upon the person who created the belief in the believer. However, this causal responsibility does not translate into causal responsibility for conduct performed on the basis of that belief. Again reverting to the Aristotelian axiom of personal autonomy,[181] a person has a duty to inform him or herself about the facts relevant to his or her conduct.[182]

Determining causal responsibility for physical circumstances, legal circumstances, and shareholding devaluations is more difficult because they occur through two or more performances of conduct. The question is: which of the performing persons has causal responsibility for the circumstance or shareholding devaluation if viewed as a cause? The question becomes significant if the relevant type of circumstance assumes the role of information-creating. For example,[183] after rioters destroy an investor's factory, the investor fears that its employees are in danger and relocates them to a neighbouring state. Here, the circumstance is the factory's destruction, which serves as the cause of the investor's belief regarding the danger for its employees. The causal constellation for the factory's destruction consists of, one, the rioting and, two, the positioning of the factory at the time and place of the rioting.[184] The question is: of the persons performing these two causes, who is causally responsible for the factory's destruction, if it is viewed as a cause? Patently, the rioters must assume causal responsibility and the reason for this is their faultworthiness. Accordingly, the general principle provides that whoever performs the faultworthy conduct in a circumstance's or shareholding devaluation's causal constellation assumes causal responsibility for that consequence if it operates as a cause. If two or more persons perform faultworthy conduct, then they share causal responsibility according to their degrees of fault.[185]

In those cases where the conduct making up a circumstance's or shareholding devaluation's causal constellation is not subject to any determination regarding faultworthiness, causal responsibility is assumed by the person

---

[180] This example draws inspiration from Christopher Columbus's beliefs about taking the westerly route from Europe to Asia; see Fernández-Armesto, *Columbus*, 30.

[181] Meyer, *Aristotle on Moral Responsibility*, 1.

[182] Sorabji, *Necessity, Cause, and Blame*, 227.

[183] *Pantechniki v. Albania* serves as the inspiration for this example; see *Pantechniki v. Albania* § 13.

[184] See section 4.3.2 above for a discussion of the causal constellations for physical circumstance consequences.

[185] This is the standard approach for cases involving contributory fault; see section 2.3 of chapter 4.

who performs the most characteristic conduct. For physical circumstances and legal circumstances, the characteristic performances are their change antecedents.[186] For shareholding devaluations, it is the conduct constituting the variable that negatively changes the shareholding's value; for example, if a shareholding devalues 50 per cent over one year and its cash outflows remain steady but its cash inflows fall, then the conduct constituting the reduction in cash inflows is the characteristic performance. It should be noted, however, that shareholding devaluations can only become causal if they act as information-creators.

4.4.3 Illustration of the Theory on Causal Responsibility for Other Causes

Before concluding, it is worth exemplifying how the present theory on causal responsibility applies. Again, suppose that rioters destroy the investor's factory and the investor relocates its employees. Applying the general rule, the investor is causally responsible for the conduct giving rise to these relocation costs, but it seeks to transfer that causal responsibility to the host state.

4.4.3.1 *Transferring Causal Responsibility for Payment of Relocation Costs to Rioters*

To achieve that objective, the investor must first establish that the rioting operates as a factual imperative[187] in respect of its own conduct of paying the relocation costs. This first step involves proving that the rioting, one, was unlawful, which is evidently the case, and, two, reasonably caused the investor to believe that relocating its employees would avoid some hypothetical harm, presumably physical harm to them. Remembering that information-creating is one of the potential causes of beliefs,[188] some information-creating, which the rioters are causally responsible for, needs to be identified. This information-creating could be either the rioting itself, if the investor perceived it, or the circumstance of the factory's destruction. For either source of information-creating, the rioters are causally responsible. As regards the reasonableness point, this is a two-stage inquiry. First, the hypothetical harm to the employees must be graver than the relocation costs. Second, the chance of this hypothetical harm occurring must be more likely than not. This is designed to be a generous standard that makes provision for the difficulty of accurately determining causal relations involving other persons' conduct.

---

[186] See sections 4.3.2 and 4.3.5 above for explanations of these change antecedents.
[187] For a summary of factual imperatives, see section 4.4.1.2 above.
[188] See section 4.3.4 above.

The final points to prove are that the hypothetical harm must not have been consented to by the investor and the investor's relocation of its employees was proportionate. For illustrative purposes, suppose that the investor's employees travelled first class in the relocation process, an example of a disproportionate response. The rioting still acts as a factual imperative, but only in respect of consequences that would have resulted from proportionate conduct. Using this example, the consequence would be the costs of economy-class tickets. For the surplus between the actual relocation costs and the costs of economy-class tickets, the general rule that the performing person has causal responsibility applies.

4.4.3.2 Transferring Causal Responsibility of Rioting to Host State

Taking stock, the investor's conduct has caused the relocation costs, but causal responsibility for this cause is shared between the investor and the rioters. Now the task is to transfer causal responsibility for the rioting to the host state. That can be achieved by establishing that the host state's failure to stop the rioting constitutes a cause-prevention omission in respect of it. Cause-prevention omissions have four attributes.[189] First, the rioting must be preventable; second, the host state must be aware of it; and three, the host state must have the capacity to prevent it. If the host state maintains a police force, the satisfaction of these three might be presumed. The fourth attribute is a special relationship between the host state and rioters. The proof of this is uncontroversial because, via the rule on protection and security, the host state acknowledges this relationship.

In summary, it can be asked: who legally caused these costs? Generally, the investor, but the investor's causative conduct was performed on account of the factual imperative of rioting, thereby meaning that the rioters are causally responsible for this conduct. This causal responsibility is only partial, however, because the investor's conduct of purchasing first-class tickets was disproportionate. Accordingly, both the investor and the rioters are causally responsible for the conduct causing the actual consequence, namely the costs of relocating the employees. In respect of the rioters' proportion of causal responsibility, that proportion can be transferred to the host state. This final transfer comes about because the host state failed to prevent the rioting, with such failure constituting a cause-prevention omission.

---

[189] See section 4.1.2.1 above.

5 CONCLUSION

Cause is a central concept in the law, but it is a word that has engendered confusion like no other.[190] For 150 years, jurists have conceived a cause as a difference-maker.[191] After identifying a range of factual causes, the difference-maker is selected via the application of rules that supposedly reflect common sense. This theory of causation proposed here turns this dominant theory on its head. It sees causation in the law as defined by continuity, where causes lead to consequences, which in turn become causes. For an antecedent to be counted as a cause of a consequence, it must be a member of that consequence's causal constellation. This begins to create a picture of what an investor's contribution for the purposes of contributory fault should look like: a member of the relevant consequence's causal constellation. As will be shown, however, this is only one type of investor contribution, a type relevant for the defence of mismanagement.

---

[190] Hume, *Treatise of Human Nature*, 156.
[191] See Hart and Honoré, *Causation in the Law*, 35.

4

Mismanagement

1 THE CONCEPT OF MISMANAGEMENT

Stability is touted as a virtue of any body of jurisprudence,[1] which might explain why newly proposed legal concepts often fail to find traction.[2] For this reason, it is with some trepidation that the following two chapters introduce three legal concepts into the corpus of international investment law: mismanagement, investment reprisal, and post-establishment illegality. Whatever their destiny as regards their future incorporation into this jurisprudence, they are used in this work to identify three separate defences.

The first two are subspecies of contributory fault, while the latter is an entirely separate species. What distinguishes mismanagement from investment reprisal is that the former requires that the investor directly contribute to the relevant consequence, while the latter involves an indirect contribution; using the terminology developed in chapter 3, the investor's contribution for mismanagement is part of the causal constellation for the investor's loss, whereas the investor's contribution for investment reprisal sits behind this constellation. The importance of this distinction cannot be overstated. Aside from the obvious point that the conduct constituting these contributions will be different, what it entails is a different fault standard for each of mismanagement and investment reprisal. In short, while the investor's foresight of the host state's impending breach makes for *mis*management, fault for investment reprisal is established because the investor's conduct amounts to an affront to the host state's sovereignty.

A picture of mismanagement should be beginning to take shape: investing in the host state when it was foreseeable that the host state could perform some

---

[1] Famously encapsulated in a headline in the fictitious kingdom of King Rex: 'A law that changes every day is worse than no law at all'; see Fuller, *Morality of Law*, 37.

[2] For a similar sentiment, see Williams, *Joint Torts and Contributory Negligence*, 3.

conduct that would harm the investment. An example would be purchasing a shareholding in a company conducting stem cell research in the host state sometime after the main opposition party announces its policy to criminalise stem cell research. After this party wins the next election and implements this policy, the value of the investor's shareholding is reduced to a pittance.

1.1 *The Doctrinal Foundations of Mismanagement*

Its novelty ostensibly means that this could be a difficult task, but the existence of mismanagement can legitimately be grounded in Article 39 of the ILC Draft Articles on State Responsibility:[3]

> In the determination of reparation, account shall be taken of the contribution to the injury by wilful or negligent action or omission of the injured State or any person or entity in relation to whom reparation is sought.

Within this rule, there are two legal elements: the investor's contribution to its injury and the wilfulness or negligence of that contribution. Mismanagement takes these legal elements and crafts a more specific rule from them.

All this ignores a more fundamental question, however: does sound policy support the recognition of mismanagement? The basic reason against its recognition is its potential to stifle investment activities. If investors know that that host states can escape liability on proof that their breaches were foreseeable, many might forego their investing.[4] Given the omnipresence of political risk in much foreign investment, this point holds significant weight. It is buttressed by a second reason that investors' contributions for the purposes of mismanagement fundamentally differ from those tort-like scenarios that Article 39 would ordinarily apply to. Take the case of *SS Wimbledon*.[5] There, Germany argued that the injured person partially contributed to its losses, which consisted in various expenses connected to the prolongation of the voyage, because it moored in Kiel for several days instead of continuing its voyage after Germany (wrongfully) refused passage through the Kiel Canal.[6] Although this argument was unsuccessful because the majority judges found that it was reasonable for the vessel to wait in Kiel[7] in case negotiations opened the way for SS *Wimbledon*, it illustrates that the typical claimant contribution

---

[3]   ILC Articles on State Responsibility, Art. 39.

[4]   A similar argument was made by the investor in *Philip Morris v. Australia*; see *Philip Morris v. Australia*, Award on Jurisdiction and Admissibility § 434.

[5]   *Case of the S.S. 'Wimbledon' (United Kingdom and others v. Germany)*, 1923 P.C.I.J. (Ser. A) No. 1 (17 August 1923). ('*SS Wimbledon*').

[6]   ILC Articles on State Responsibility (with commentaries), Art. 39 (cmt 4 (fn. 625)).

[7]   SS *Wimbledon* § 53.

adds nothing of value to the respondent state. By contrast, an investor's contribution, which is usually the making of an investment, will by definition economically benefit the host state. The injustice of the host state accepting this benefit, while having the option of suspending its investment treaty obligations by giving prior warning of a potential future breach, is obvious because it violates the grand bargain[8] at the core of international investment law.

Equally, there are weighty reasons for recognising mismanagement as a defence. For a host state, such recognition would offer more certainty for future policy decisions. Presumably in formulating policies that are likely to adversely impact existing investments, a host state will seek out information on what costs it is likely to face. That assessment becomes more difficult, however, if investments established subsequent to this policy's becoming public knowledge, but before its implementation, are blessed with investment treaty protections. Another reason provides that if mismanagement immunises a host state from liability, then investors will look for other (more blameworthy) candidates to claim from, such as their professional advisors or managers. But the most powerful reason is more intuitive: there is a risk of moral hazard if mismanagement is not recognised. Effectively any announcement of a policy which is likely to adversely affect investments, could act as an advertisement for investors to invest in the host state with limited to no risk.[9]

1.2 The Legal Function of Mismanagement

Fortunately, the choice between mismanagement's recognition or non-recognition is not as binary as it appears. The best option is to recognise mismanagement as a partial defence through which liability can be apportioned between the investor and the host state. Not only does this accord with the vision of contributory fault projected by Article 39;[10] it also enables a process whereby the factors for and against such recognition can be incorporated into the apportionment equation to fairly distribute liability – an equation

---

[8] This is the foreign investment (and thereby economic development) for treaty protections bargain; see Salacuse and Sullivan, 'Do BITs Really Work?', 77.

[9] As arbitral tribunals are at pains to point out, 'it is not the function of international law of expropriation ... to eliminate the normal commercial risks of a foreign investor'; see *Waste Management, Inc. v. United Mexican States*, ICSID Case No. ARB(AF)/oo/3, Award (30 April 2004) ('*Waste Management v. Mexico (II)*') § 177. Another oft-repeated line is: 'insurance treaties are not insurance policies against bad business judgments'; see ibid. § 144 (citing *Emilio Agustín Maffezini v. The Kingdom of Spain*, ICSID Case No. ARB/97/7, Award (9 November 2000) § 64).

[10] Moutier-Lopet, 'Contribution to the Injury', 644. Equally, in domestic law contributory fault is universally recognised as a partial defence where liability is apportioned; see Artigot i Golobardes and Gomez Pomar, 'Contributory and Comparative Negligence', 375.

that is detailed in section 2.3.1 below. Moreover, labelling mismanagement as a partial defence, as opposed to a complete defence, avoids the obvious injustice of pinning full liability on the investor when it is only partially at fault.[11]

2 MISMANAGEMENT – LEGAL CONTENT AND ATTRIBUTION

2.1 *Investor Causal Contributions*

The starting point for deciphering mismanagement's legal content is drawing an image of what the relevant investor's causal contribution should look like. Applying the theory on causation proposed in chapter 3, this is any cause in the relevant loss's causal constellation for which the investor assumes causal responsibility. Admittedly, this statement of the theory does not bring this image into focus. To this end, the cases of *MTD v. Chile* and *Philip Morris v. Australia* serve as instructive guides.

2.1.1 The Investor Causal Contribution in *MTD v. Chile*

The seminal case on contributory fault in international investment law,[12] *MTD v. Chile*, concerned an investment project to build a new township south of Santiago.[13] The investor purchased a shareholding in a company that owned land in this area. That land was zoned for agricultural use,[14] although the investor paid a purchase price that reflected its residential-use value. It did so because it assumed, primarily on the basis of representations made by the seller and the support that the projected received from the Chilean authorities, that rezoning was a mere formality.[15] Its proposed investment was approved by Chile's foreign investment committee[16] and foreign investment permits authorising the purchase were signed with the same body,[17] but the rezoning application was rejected in line with official governmental policy.[18] For the investor, this meant that it had substantially overpaid for the shareholding. The inconsistency in Chile's actions amounted to a breach of the

---

[11] ILC Articles on State Responsibility (with commentaries), Art. 39 (cmt (2)); Prosser, 'Comparative Negligence', 469.
[12] See Kantor, 'Impact of Contributory Investor Conduct', 551.
[13] *MTD v. Chile*, Award § 41.
[14] Ibid. § 49.
[15] Ibid. § 42.
[16] Ibid. § 53.
[17] Ibid. § 54.
[18] Ibid. § 81.

fair and equitable treatment rule in the applicable investment treaty.[19] Most relevantly, the arbitral tribunal also found that the investor's lack of due diligence[20] contributed to its loss – a contribution weighted at 50 per cent.[21]

The challenge now is to identify this contribution. That process begins by forming the relevant consequence's causal constellation. There are two candidates for the relevant consequence, either a shareholding devaluation or a loss of the purchase price for the shareholding, but the former should be discounted on the ground that the project company was not generating revenue.[22] Remembering that the latter is a legal circumstance consequence because it is a circumstance in respect of a legal concept (ownership of money),[23] the causal constellation includes the investor's act of transferring the purchase price and the seller's acceptance.[24] This transfer is not the investor's contribution, however. Using the principle of inducement,[25] causal responsibility for this conduct should shift to Chile as its representations caused the transfer. The three requirements for this principle to operate are fulfilled because, one, the representations constituted an unlawful act, two, Chile must have believed that its representations would cause the investor to act, and, three, Chile had a special relationship vis-à-vis the investor because it alone controlled the subject of its representations (the rezoning approval). The investor's contribution was a consequence-avoidance omission:[26] the failure to include a condition precedent in the share purchase contract specifying that that document would have no effect if the land was not rezoned. This conduct was also implicitly identified as the investor's contribution by the arbitral tribunal. The only obstacle in establishing it as a cause is proving that the investors could have performed it, which in this case means convincing the seller to accept this condition precedent. This acceptance should be readily assumed, because the seller accepted a similar condition precedent with respect to the approval of the investment project by Chile's foreign investment committee.[27]

2.1.2 The Investor Causal Contribution in *Philip Morris v. Australia*

As it never proceeded beyond the jurisdictional phase, *Philip Morris v. Australia* is not usually counted as a case involving mismanagement. However, Australia

---

[19] Ibid. § 166.
[20] Ibid. § 168.
[21] Ibid. § 246.
[22] See *Venezuela Holdings v. Venezuela* § 382.
[23] See section 4.2.1 of chapter 3.
[24] See section 4.3.5 of chapter 3.
[25] See section 4.4.1.3 of chapter 3.
[26] See section 4.1.2.2 of chapter 3.
[27] *MTD v. Chile*, Award § 49.

indicated in its Response to the Notice of Arbitration that it would effectively plead mismanagement in the merits phase.[28]

The facts are that the investor owned a company that carried on the business of manufacturing and distributing tobacco products in Australia.[29] Australia enacted 'plain packaging legislation' that saw most of the branding on tobacco products replaced with health warning labels and graphic pictograms.[30] In the lead-up to the enactment of this legislation, the investor acquired the Australian operating company from another holding company in its corporate group,[31] ostensibly for reasons of corporate planning.[32] The arbitral tribunal, however, held that this acquisition was made primarily with a view to securing the investor's status as an 'investor' under the applicable investment treaty[33] after the investor had foreseen the likelihood of a dispute arising.[34] This was held to constitute an abuse of rights and the arbitral tribunal ruled that it lacked jurisdiction for this reason. Had the arbitral tribunal ruled otherwise, Australia might have pleaded mismanagement in the merits phase, although, as argued in section 2.1.3 below, any such plea would have had to have been rejected.

In making this plea, Australia could have pointed to the investor's acquisition of the Australian operating company as its contribution. For this contribution, the relevant consequence is a shareholding devaluation because the Australian operating company was a going concern. Any causal constellation for a shareholding devaluation consists of numerous causes,[35] with the investor and Australia being causally responsible for one cause each. For the investor, this is the positional antecedent of owning the company at the relevant time and place. As the acquisition makes the investor causally responsible for this legal circumstance, this explains why it operates as the investor's contribution.[36] Australia's contribution is the antecedent of a decrease in cash inflow. Although it is Australian consumers who actually fail to make purchases of tobacco products, Australia would assume causal responsibility for the cash

---

[28] *Philip Morris Asia Limited v. The Commonwealth of Australia*, PCA Case No. 2012-12, Australia's Response to the Notice of Arbitration (21 December 2011) § 7(b).

[29] *Philip Morris Asia Limited v. The Commonwealth of Australia*, PCA Case No. 2012-12, Notice of Arbitration (21 November 2011) § 4.2.

[30] For the history of this legislation, see *Philip Morris v. Australia*, Award on Jurisdiction and Admissibility §§ 99–140 and §§ 165–177.

[31] Ibid. § 176.

[32] Ibid. § 142.

[33] Ibid. § 584

[34] Ibid. § 585.

[35] See section 4.3.7 of chapter 3.

[36] See section 4.4.2 of chapter 3.

inflow decrease through its inducement of this consumer behaviour by way of the health warning labels and graphic pictograms.[37]

2.1.3 Capital Injections or Related Omissions as Investor Causal Contributions

These analyses depict the investor's conduct in *MTD v. Chile* and *Philip Morris v. Australia* as causal contributions for the purposes of mismanagement. Between them, however, there is a significant qualitative difference. In *MTD v. Chile*, the investor's contribution was an omission relating to a capital injection into Chile. That capital injection resembled an 'investment' as per the jurisdictional requirement. By contrast, the investor's contribution in *Philip Morris v. Australia* was an intra-group change of ownership. This conduct cannot constitute an investor causal contribution, because it merely relabels an existing causal contribution, namely the investor's original capital injection into Australia. Moreover, as *Philip Morris v. Australia* aptly demonstrates, changing the investment's ownership is a jurisdictional issue for which specific rules have been developed.[38]

The outstanding question concerns the status of extra-group acquisitions of established investments for fair value: should they be recognised as causal contributions? Again, a general reason militating against recognition as a causal contribution is that changing ownership is a jurisdictional issue. Additionally, such recognition seemingly grants the host state a gratuitous windfall as, for no other reason than the fortuitous circumstance of the investor's acquisition at the relevant time, the option to plead mismanagement arises. But there are weightier reasons that mandate that recognition as a causal contribution should be accorded. Primarily, acquisitions for fair value are properly described as investments into the host state, and they are recognised as such for the purpose of establishing the arbitral tribunal's jurisdiction.[39] Moreover,

---

[37] For this purpose, it should be understood that the first requirement for transferring causal responsibility by inducement – that the conduct constituting the inducement be unlawful – would necessarily be satisfied. This is because if mismanagement is being considered as a defence, then Australia must have breached one of its treaty obligations, thereby fulfilling the unlawfulness requirement. See section 4.4.1.3 of chapter 3 for the theory behind this.

[38] For an overview of the cases dealing with this issue, other than *Philip Morris v. Australia*, see McLachlan and others, *International Investment Arbitration*, §§ 5.159–5.170.

[39] This principle was first recognised in *Fedax v. Venezuela*. There, the investor subsequently acquired its investment from another person – an acquisition that the arbitral tribunal classified as making an investment for the purposes of its jurisdiction; see *Fedax N.V. v. The Republic of Venezuela*, ICSID Case No. ARB/96/3, Decision of the Tribunal on Objections to Jurisdiction (11 July 1997) § 43. Subsequent jurisprudence has sought to limit the effect of this ruling, but those efforts have been directed towards excluding certain financial instruments from the definition of investment. The point here is that an acquisition of established investments is recognised as making an investment because this act involves a commitment of capital, which

mismanagement is a more equitable route through which to resolve issues relating to post-establishment acquisitions made with the foresight of a future dispute with the host state. The rule on the timing of the investor's ownership has a particularly sharp edge: non-fulfilment means that the arbitral tribunal lacks jurisdiction, which effectively terminates the investor's claim. By contrast, mismanagement, as a partial defence, has a scalar function that is amenable to being flexed according to the prevailing circumstances.

2.2 *The Fault Legal Element*

Putting the analyses above together, investor causal contributions will usually take the form of a capital injection, a post-establishment acquisition, or some omission relating to either of these. After identifying such conduct, the next step involves the establishment of its faultworthiness. To this end, Article 39 of the ILC Articles on State Responsibility stipulates that wilfulness or negligence is the relevant standard. Wilfulness presumably encompasses the two most well-known subjective fault standards in the English language, intention and recklessness.[40] As the idea of intentional mismanagement is near-inconceivable, because it would be economically irrational, the sections below examine the concept of reckless mismanagement.

2.2.1 Reckless Mismanagement

Recklessness might be a creature of criminal law, but, particularly on account of how optimism bias pervades investment activities, it could be exported into international investment law. Borrowing from its core meaning in criminal law, a definition would read: an investor who foresees the occurrence of the relevant consequence at the time it performs its causal contribution.[41] Within this definition, the key concept is foresight. Rather than being a singular concept,

---

is the most basic aspect of making an investment. See Schlemmer, 'Investment, Investor, Shareholders', 61–62.

[40] Rapp, 'Wreckage of Recklessness', fn. 3.

[41] There is arguably another attribute to this definition: that the relevant conduct also be unreasonable. Originally, English criminal law only required that the defendant subjectively foresee the chance of harm, but this was later amended; see *R v. G and Another* [2004] 1 AC 1034 per Lord Bingham. Similarly, reasonableness is not featured in any of the definitions of recklessness produced by the American Law Institute in its first two Restatements of Torts; see Restatement (First) of Torts (1934) § 500 (Reckless Disregard of Safety Defined) and Restatement (Second) of Torts (1979) § 500 (Reckless Disregard of Safety Defined). However, in the Restatement (Third) of Torts, the reasonableness requirement was included; see Restatement (Third) of Torts: Liability for Physical and Emotional Harm § 2 (Recklessness). As explained in section 2.2.3.1 below, the proposed fault legal element for mismanagement should be shorn of any

it has three aspects, all of which should be proven to establish the investor's recklessness.

The first aspect is foresight of the consequence's nature. For example, a respondent who directs insulting comments towards the claimant, a member in a large audience, might foresee reputational harm, but not a brain haemorrhage.[42] In the context of investment disputes, this aspect is unlikely to be controversial because there is usually only one consequence in play: an investment loss. What might be controversial is the second aspect: foresight of the consequence's extent.[43] If the consequence is an investment loss, this aspect requires that the investor foresee its approximate value.[44] The final aspect is foresight of the consequence's causes. Accordingly, an investor who foresees an investment loss through the host state's enactment of a new tax, when that same consequence actually results from new regulations affecting its manufacturing processes, will not have the requisite foresight.

Foresight with these three aspects might be called specific foresight. It is conceptually distinct from the requisite degree of foresight. This latter concept refers to a person's degree of belief regarding the three aspects of specific foresight. Degree of foresight could be measured by reference to some continuum of belief, ranging from absolute certainty to complete disbelief. But using such a continuum is unnecessary for reckless mismanagement. If an investor recognises that certain future conduct of the host state merely *might* – as opposed to *will* – cause an investment loss of an approximate value, regardless of the fact that it does not believe that those events will come to pass, the requisite degree of belief is present.[45] This is a strict standard, but sound reasons support it. Foremost, if an investor has knowledge of the relevant facts, it can be expected to properly assess them. Further, the alternative

---

reasonableness element because this ultimately invites an examination of an investment's utility – an examination which should not be undertaken.

[42] Inspired by an unusual German case where the respondent made what were described as some mildly insulting remarks to the claimant, with the claimant shortly thereafter suffering a brain haemorrhage; see German Federal Supreme Court (3 February 1976), *Neue Juristische Wochenschrift* (1976) 1143. Example taken from Christian Grüneberg in Palandt, *Bürgerliches Gesetzbuch*, preliminary remarks on § 249 (¶ 36).

[43] This principle is inspired by the 'eggshell skull' rule. For an overview of the various conceptions of this rule in European jurisdictions, see Bar, *Non-Contractual Liability*, 754–772.

[44] This principle was implicitly recognised in *Blusun v. Italy*. There, the investor was in a precarious financial situation, similar to the victim with an eggshell skull. Italy's conduct struck the mortal financial blow to the investment, but this was held not to be the 'operative cause' – an example of confusingly introducing normative elements into the question of causation, as noted in section 3 of chapter 3. It is submitted that this was not the 'operative cause' because Italy could not have foreseen that its conduct would cause this degree of harm; see *Blusun v. Italy* § 394.

[45] Otherwise known as 'awareness of risk'; see Brady, 'Recklessness, Negligence, Indifference, and Awareness', 383.

standard of actual belief that the events will occur transforms reckless mismanagement into another concept: intentional mismanagement.[46]

2.2.2 A Complete Defence of Reckless Mismanagement?

The present theory dictates that one avenue for the host state to establish
the fault legal element for mismanagement is to prove that the investor subjectively foresaw its investment loss by reason of the host state's breach. That
accords with one of the foundations of mismanagement: that it should operate
to dissuade investments fraught with perceptible political risk.[47] But there is
the potential to take the concept of reckless mismanagement one step further
by crafting a separate defence for it. Much in the same way that domestic
criminal law distinguishes between reckless homicide and negligent homicide, mismanagement could be divided between reckless mismanagement
and negligent mismanagement. Not only could these two forms of mismanagement be differentiated by their fault legal elements, they could also have
different legal functions. Given the greater culpability attaching to recklessness, reckless mismanagement could function as a complete defence – a characterisation that can be further supported on the ground that investors who
consciously ignore political risk are undeserving of any recovery.

But rather than justifying the idea of a complete defence of reckless mismanagement, what this reasoning actually illustrates is the danger of unquali-
fied transpositions of domestic law theory into international law.[48] In domestic
criminal law, culpability assumes a place of prime importance because of the
correlation between its level in the defendant and any punishment that he or
she should receive.[49] This relevance does not extend into international investment law. More than the reason that international investment law is primarily
concerned with economic development,[50] not punishment, the irrelevance
of the degree of culpability is explained by the practice of holding the agent
of any poor investment decision responsible on account of any foresight of
the relevant risk. An investment manager cannot hope to exculpate him or
herself from a poor investment decision by explaining that he or she had no

---

[46] Actual knowledge of future harm is another expression for intention; see Sebok, 'Purpose,
Belief, and Recklessness', 1166; Williams, 'Unresolved Problem of Recklessness', 75; Brady,
'Recklessness, Negligence, Indifference, and Awareness', 383. In English criminal law this is
known as the 'identity view' of intention; see Kaveny, 'Inferring Intention from Foresight', 81.

[47] See section 1.1 above.

[48] See Bederman, 'Contributory Fault and State Responsibility', 338 and 363.

[49] See Hart, *Punishment and Responsibility*, 114.

[50] Parra, *History of ICSID*, 11–12.

knowledge of an objectively foreseeable risk – a factor that further underscores the need for two alternative fault standards for this legal element: reckless-ness and negligence. There are also procedural reasons that support this con-struction. With these two alternatives, it makes the host state's task of proving the investor's foresight more manageable – a benefit that host states should enjoy considering the difficulties involved in proving non-perceptible matters such as foresight. An example of this can be seen in *MTD v. Chile*. There, Chile alleged[51] that, before the investor purchased its investment, a meeting between the state's representatives and the investor took place, during which the investor was warned of the legal difficulties involved in rezoning the land earmarked for development. The investor denied this meeting ever took place[52] and, in the absence of any meaningful corroborating evidence,[53] the arbitral tribunal sided with the investor.[54] Accordingly, Chile could not prove actual knowledge. Chile did succeed, however, in convincing the arbitral tri-bunal that the investor should have foreseen the rejection of the rezoning application,[55] most particularly because that decision was in line with Chile's official, and publicly available, land development policy, which information could have been obtained through a legal advisor.[56]

More than any other reasons, there is one particularly cogent reason for discarding the notion of a complete defence of reckless mismanagement. According to this conception of recklessness, the investor's cognisance of the mere chance of its investment loss operates to deny it any recovery, regardless of the merits of the investment decision in light of the relevant political risk. For example, an investor invests in a company conducting embryonic stem cell research. All the host state's political parties accept the current regulation on this practice, which is very minimal. One conservative political party that gen-erally attracts 2–3 per cent of the popular vote advocates its criminalisation – a policy position well known to the investor when it invested. If political forces operate to place this minor political party in a governing coalition and that coalition adopts the criminalisation policy, the host state could successfully plead reckless mismanagement in any subsequent investment dispute with the investor. Considering that the chances of these circumstances materialising

---

[51] As noted by the arbitral tribunal, the respondent 'place[d] great significance' on the November 1996 meeting; see *MTD v. Chile*, Award § 150.
[52] Ibid. § 124.
[53] The only contemporaneous evidence was a marking of 'Malaysia' in a minister's calendar on 6 November 1996; see ibid.
[54] Ibid. § 158.
[55] Ibid. § 178.
[56] Ibid. § 173.

are very minimal, this visits a great inequity on the investor. Moreover, it demonstrates how reckless mismanagement would discourage investments with any hint of political risk, which is a significant negative considering that many investments face this risk. This problem might be solved by stipulating that a certain risk threshold needs to be met, but this option creates new problems. Most particularly, it is unclear what that threshold should be. Yet even if it could be rationally determined, its operation would offend the notion of proportionality. While one investment decision that falls marginally over this threshold qualifies as reckless mismanagement, with the outcome that the host state escapes all liability, another on the other side of the threshold avoids this outcome with the result that the host state's liability stays completely intact.

2.2.3 Negligent Mismanagement

All this means that mismanagement should be viewed as one defence with two alternative fault standards, the second of which is negligence. Again, the main task is to ascribe the proper meaning to this concept. The factor complicating this task is, at least in international law, the distinct lack of commentary on it.[57] Reference might be made to domestic law notions, but any guidance they might offer is similarly limited because of the inapplicability of the dominant theory on its meaning. In American tort law, this is known as the Hand Formula.[58] This simple equation labels the conduct in question negligent if the gravity of the relevant harm multiplied by the chance of that harm's occurrence upon performance of this conduct has a value greater than the costs of taking precautions to avoid this harm.[59] It will be noted that it does not account for any gains that might follow upon the particular conduct and, considering that it was developed to assess the negligence of conduct such as failing to properly secure a barge to a wharf,[60] it should not be expected to. Yet, the qualitative assessment of any investment activity will always factor in its potential gains.

---

[57] See, for example, Anaïs Mouiter-Lopet's commentary on Article 39 of the ILC Articles on State Responsibility, which contains no discussion of the meaning attributable to negligence; Moutier-Lopet, 'Contribution to the Injury', 639–645.

[58] Restatement (Third) of Torts: Liability for Physical and Emotional Harm § 3 (Negligence) (cmt d). But for a view that challenges this dominance, see Zipursky, 'Reasonableness In and Out of Negligence Law', 2131.

[59] Gilles, 'On Determining Negligence', 817–819.

[60] As was the case in *US v. Carroll Towing*, where Judge Learned Hand outlined the Hand Formula; see *United States and others v. Carroll Towing Co., Inc., and others* 159 F.2d 169.

2.2.3.1 *Investment Utility*

There is, however, another tool that takes account of potential gains in evaluating the qualitative aspect of certain conduct: the von Neumann-Morgenstern expected utility theory.[61] In short, this theory sets forth a formula by which the expected utility of certain conduct can be measured.[62] If the application of that equation produces a positive number for the outcome in question, then it is labelled normatively rational. Given that it is habitually used to evaluate investment decisions,[63] the temptation might be to extrapolate it for the purpose of determining the negligence of an investment decision (an investor's causal contribution). In this way, any investment decision with 'investment utility' would not satisfy the fault legal element because it would be classed as a reasonable economic decision. The idea of using expected utility theory in international investment law butts up against a myriad of problems, however.

The first of these is that the current equation for expected utility theory is ill-suited for assessing singular investment decisions faced with political risk, as opposed to lottery-like uncertainties.[64] Suppose that the supply of cannabis is legal in the host state to those aged 18 or over, but there is a proposal to lift this age restriction to 27. Around the same time that this proposal is made public, the investor buys a shareholding in a company supplying cannabis. In assessing that conduct's investment utility, the key element would be the age restriction proposal. Expected utility theory directs that this 'state' should be assigned a utility value, which in turn should be multiplied by the probability of its occurrence. But there is another relevant variable: the probability that this age restriction proposal will negatively impact on investment utility, which will be assumed to be profit. For example, if the cannabis company's customers are generally baby boomers, the proposal will have limited negative impact, while the opposite holds true if its customers are millennials.

Assuming that this problem could be overcome by reformulating its equation, expected utility theory is not viable for another reason. Admittedly this contention is mostly informed by intuition, but arithmetically determining whether an investor has been negligent is unlikely to find any favour among arbitral tribunals. Besides resembling automated adjudication, this method is prone to delivering disproportionate outcomes. This is because investment

---

[61] This is a popular reference, but it ignores the contribution to this theory by many scholars over the years, beginning with Blaise Pascal; see Lengwiler, 'Origins of Expected Utility Theory', 536.

[62] For an overview, see Briggs, 'Normative Theories of Rational Choice', § 1.

[63] The chief proponent of which is Jack Hirschleifer; see particularly Hirschleifer, 'Investment Decision under Uncertainty', 509.

[64] Understanding games of pure chance were the backdrop to the development of expected utility theory and its use has been limited to situations involving pure uncertainty; see Machina, 'Expected Utility Hypothesis', 4211.

decisions with marginal investment utility are not negligent, with the result that the host state's liability remains wholly intact, while other investment decisions with slightly negative investment utility are classified as negligent.

Yet, all of these problems pale into insignificance compared to the final problem. This problem grows out of a smaller problem, which is determining what gives an investment decision its utility. In the cannabis example, it was assumed that investment utility equalled profit, as is usually the case. However, a profitable investment does not necessarily have utility for the host state. From its perspective, investment utility should be referenced according to positive economic outcomes, such as employment and knowledge transfer. Yet, even if it can be convincingly reasoned that one form of investment utility should be preferred over the other, a bigger problem is encountered. Whether investor profit or host state economic outcomes inform investment utility, the arbitral tribunal will be straying beyond its scope of legitimacy. This is because when an arbitral tribunal determines that an investment decision has positive investment utility, it effectively designates it as prospectively profitable or likely to produce positive economic outcomes, and for that reason not negligent. What this line of reasoning communicates to the host state is that the relevant investment was meritorious and should have been welcomed, which is a question that should be reserved for host states.[65]

2.2.3.2 *Objective Foreseeability*

The failure of expected utility theory to provide meaning to negligence mandates the use of another option, with the most preferable being objective foreseeability. According to this conception of negligence, if any of the known political risks pertaining to an investment materialise as the relevant breach, the corresponding investment decision will be deemed faultworthy. As was the case with defining recklessness by reference to subjective foresight, this conception gives effect to the policy underlying mismanagement whereby investments made in the face of perceptible political risk should not be accorded full protection. The objection that this conception gives the fault legal element of mismanagement an excessive scope of application is likely to be raised, but it should be dismissed on two grounds. First, as one of the factors for apportioning liability is the investor's degree of foreseeability in respect of its investment loss,[66] cases

---

[65] Considering that one cause of the legitimacy crisis is arbitral tribunals' ability to take decisions affecting public interests, they should avoid any unnecessary rulings to this effect; see Harten, 'Perceived Bias', 449.

[66] See sections 2.3.1.2 and 2.3.1.3 below.

involving very minimal foresight will have a limited effect on the investor's final recovery. Second, as explained in section 2.2.1 above, foresight refers to specific foresight, meaning, for the purposes of negligence, that the investor must have been objectively aware of the relevant consequence's nature, its extent, and its cause. All of this leads to the most pressing question: how does the investor become objectively aware?

First, the relevant information on the three elements of specific foresight must have been available at the time of the investor's causal contribution. Available information includes not only information in the public domain, but also information that could have been obtained through appropriate professional advice, as indicated by the arbitral tribunal in *MTD v. Chile*. In concluding that the investors had objective foresight of their investment loss, the arbitral tribunal agreed[67] with Chile that, had the investor sought professional advice on the rezoning of the land, those efforts would have revealed that governmental policy prohibited urban development on it.[68]

If available information includes professional advice, it should also extend to information that could have been obtained through meeting with the host state's representatives,[69] assuming it can be proven that those representatives would have divulged it. But this available information will rarely act as the basis for imputing objective foresight to the investor on account of the second requirement: that the available information be accessible. Information obtainable through professional advice should generally be accessible, unless the unusual case arises where the costs outweigh the benefit of ascertaining the information. As for available information from governmental sources, it will only be accessible if the investor had the necessary clout to arrange the meetings.

2.3 Apportionment

What is apparent is that the core of mismanagement is simple: the investor performs a direct causal contribution with respect to its investment loss with subjective or objective foresight of this consequence. Attention now shifts from mismanagement's legal content to its legal function, which, as it is a partial defence,[70] involves the apportionment of liability between the disputants. This

---

[67] *MTD v. Chile*, Award § 242.
[68] Ibid. § 173.
[69] This was another form of information allegedly available to the investor in *MTD v. Chile*; see ibid. § 150.
[70] See section 1.1 above for an analysis of why mismanagement should operate as a partial defence.

is a notoriously difficult task.[71] In *MTD v. Chile*, the annulment committee commented that:[72]

> As is often the case with situations of comparative fault, the role of the two parties contributing to the loss was very different and only with difficulty commensurable, and the Tribunal had a corresponding margin of estimation. Furthermore, in an investment treaty claim where contribution is relevant, the respondent's breach will normally be regulatory in character, whereas the claimant's conduct will be different, a failure to safeguard its own interests rather than a breach of any duty owed to the host state. In such circumstances, it is not unusual for the loss to be shared equally.

Given the authority standing behind this view that liability should be shared equally, the reflex thought is to wave the white flag in the quest for reason-based apportionment.[73] But this is an opportunity to develop a new theory. There are two possible approaches.[74] The first approach would be to align the investor's fault with its liability by ascertaining the investor's degree of fault and subtracting it from the host state's notional liability of 100 per cent. However, finding a suitable method to value the investor's degree of fault presents an impassable obstacle. The obvious option is foreseeability because it is a scalar concept, but accurately approximating 'high foreseeability', for example, in percentage form poses a dilemma. Expected utility theory can produce more specific numbers, but the reasons barring its invocation in investment arbitration in respect of determining the fault legal element have equal force here.[75]

Yet, even if the degree of foresight could be accurately valued, this approach would not be viable because of its potential to produce inequitable outcomes. Suppose that the investor's degree of foresight is rated at 70 per cent, thereby reducing the host state's liability to 30 per cent. This apportionment hardly seems doctrinally correct, however, given that the host state has breached a strict liability rule.[76] The arbitral tribunal reasons that a strict liability rule is

[71] Pearson, 'Apportionment of Losses', 347.
[72] *MTD Equity Sdn. Bhd. and MTD Chile S.A. v. Republic of Chile*, ICSID Case No. ARB/01/7, Decision on Annulment (21 March 2007) § 101 ('*MTD v. Chile*, Decision on Annulment').
[73] This seems to be the view that holds sway in international investment law; see Merizalde, 'Proportionality, Contributory Negligence and Other Equity Considerations', 317.
[74] This assumes that the principle guiding the apportionment is fault, but potentially cause could be used for this purpose; see Williams, *Joint Torts and Contributory Negligence*, 157. Further, Bederman has noted that under international law cause has been used to this end, although he does not cite any decisions to support his contention; see Bederman, 'Contributory Fault and State Responsibility', 359–360. The dominant view, however, is that fault guides apportionment; see Pearson, 'Apportionment of Losses', 345.
[75] See section 2.2.3.1 above.
[76] The general rule in international law is that, unless specifically included in the liability rule, a fault legal element should not be read into the liability rule; see ILC Articles on State

robbed of its defining characteristic if the host state's liability sinks too low. To remedy this, the arbitral tribunal proposes to raise the host state's liability to 50 per cent. This proposal, however, effectively compares the investor's fault with the host state's, which is a comparison the jurisprudence does not permit because two different forms of fault are being compared. Moreover, this approach has arrived back at the original position, namely a 50-50 split of liability.[77]

2.3.1 Restitutionary Apportionment

In constructing another approach, the main lesson to be drawn from the failure of this reduction approach is that principles other than fault should guide the way. Taking heed of this, the equation should not begin from the point that the host state is 100 per cent liable, but has starting liability of 0 per cent on a finding of mismanagement. This seemingly means that mismanagement acts as a complete defence – a starting position that is supported by the weight of the reasons in favour of recognising mismanagement as a defence. At this juncture, the reasons for not according such recognition become relevant, most particularly that mismanagement gives an undeserved gain to the host state. This is because mismanagement can operate to let the host state take advantage of the economic benefits that the investor brings without being accountable for its own wrongful conduct.

2.3.1.1 *Direct Contributions*
Drawing from this principle, the host state should be fully liable for all the direct contributions that the investor makes to its economy. Direct contributions include capital that is transferred from the investor directly to the host state, the most common example being tax payments. Referring back to the facts of *MTD v. Chile*, if the investor's purchase of the shareholding included the payment of a transaction tax, the host state should be liable for that amount. Importantly for any capital injection that purchases an established investment, the subsequent investor should be credited with any direct contributions of the initial investor. The reasoning behind this is that the purchase price will presumably take account of these costs.

Responsibility (with commentaries), Art. 2 (cmt 10). See also Sabahi, *Compensation and Restitution*, 42. The annulment committee in *MTD v. Chile* made a similar point when it noted that the host state's breach will usually be regulatory, whereas the investor's conduct will be faultworthy; see *MTD v. Chile*, Decision on Annulment § 101.

77   As noted by the annulment committee in *MTD v. Chile*, 'it is not unusual for the loss to be shared equally'; see *MTD v. Chile*, Decision on Annulment § 101.

2.3.1.2 Indirect Contributions

The direct contributions are not the only source of the host state's enrichment. Through the investor's payments for goods and services relating to its investment provided by local participants in the host state's economy, the host state's economic development is promoted. Again, the host state should remain fully liable for the tax payments that these indirect contributions give rise to, including income tax payments and the transaction tax payments on the proven or likely transactions that have been made from the net income. The question now is how the remaining net income to the host state's economy from these indirect contributions should be treated. The difficulty is that their benefit to the host state is difficult to ascertain and measure, meaning that the principle of unjust enrichment cannot be invoked with the same conviction, as compared to direct contributions, to hold the host state liable. Moreover, if the host state is forced to reimburse these unaccounted-for amounts, the host state begins to resemble an insurer for foreseeable political risks, thus raising moral hazard concerns.

With the relevant principles pointing in different directions, partial liability for net income from indirect contributions is the answer. In undertaking the requisite apportionment, proper account needs to be taken of these principles, which is an objective that can be achieved by burdening the investor with liability according to the degree of political risk. Calculating degree of political risk involves two steps, the first of which considers the transparency of the information from which the host state's breach becomes foreseeable. That first step poses a binary question: is the clarity of this information such that the conduct constituting the breach can be readily identified? If that question is answered affirmatively, the arbitral tribunal should proceed to the second step, while a negative answer entails that there was no political risk. In the absence of any political risk, liability shifts to the host state – an outcome that penalises the lack of transparency in the host state's communications. Accordingly, if a host state relies on a vaguely worded rule to perform the conduct constituting its breach, mismanagement will not operate in its favour.

The second step examines the likelihood that the host state would perform the conduct in question. How that examination is conducted depends on the type of information, with a division being made between statements on future conduct and rules of the host state's domestic law. Statements on future conduct refer to information indicating that the host state intends to perform the conduct – a statement that might typically be conveyed through a policy statement. Valuing the likelihood of performance against statements on future conduct is not an exact science, but it can be guided by two factors. First, there is the political capacity to perform.[78] In considering this factor, arbitral tribunals should seek to recognise the prevailing political circumstances that will affect the host state's chances of performance. For example, if performing the conduct involves a change to the host state's constitution and the political party controlling the host state's legislature does not have the requisite numbers to pass the amendment, the political capacity should attract a low rating. The second factor is the political will to perform, a factor principally informed by the nature of the document that contains the information. If information is covered with officialese, it can be expected that it is more likely to be performed, compared to political noise in the news media.[79] Once each factor has been ascertained, the difficult task of valuation can begin. This involves rating the first and second factors on scales of 0 to 1 and 0 to 10, respectively, and then multiplying those values.

If the information is a rule of the host state's internal order, the valuation proceeds differently. The focus is on how frequently the host state applies this rule or similar rules. Referring to the facts in *MTD v. Chile*, consideration of this factor would involve looking at the historical practices of the governmental body that took the decision to reject the rezoning application, to see the extent to which its decisions applied local planning rules. In this way, the rating for this factor hinges on the strength of the rule of law in the host state.

2.3.1.3 *Other Contributions*

As with direct contributions, a subsequent investor in respect of an established investment can be credited with the initial investor's indirect contributions. This is a convenient lead-in to the final question: the treatment of the remaining contributions that make up the investor's capital injection. These other contributions are only likely to be found in purchases of established investments or pre-existing assets in the host state. As direct contributions and indirect contributions cover the costs of establishing and operating the investment, these other contributions will usually represent the profit margin for the initial investor or owner in the sale price of the investment. When this is understood, the question arises as to whether they are contributions at all. If

---

[78] The investor in *Philip Morris v. Australia* made an argument that invoked this factor. It argued that as the political party advocating the plain packaging legislation was only a minority government, it lacked the political capacity to enact this legislation, thereby eliminating or reducing the political risk the investor faced. See *Philip Morris v. Australia*, Award on Jurisdiction and Admissibility §§ 559–560.

[79] Again referring to *Philip Morris v. Australia*, the arbitral tribunal held that the political risk that materialised in Australia's alleged breach of the applicable investment treaty arose when the Australian prime minister and health minister jointly released an official media statement announcing the government's intention to perform the relevant conduct; see ibid. § 566.

they are likely to find their way into the local economy, they should be counted as potential contributions and the investor should assume liability according to the relevant degree of political risk. Deductively, this means that the investor assumes full liability for other contributions that are unlikely to filter into the local economy, which would presumably be the case if they are paid to persons who do not have their main centre of business in the host state. The reasoning behind that outcome is that the principle of unjust enrichment, which has served to justify the various assumptions of liability by the host state in cases of mismanagement, has no application here. In its absence, reversion is made to the default position that the host state assumes no liability.

But this reasoning should not extend to cases where the investor's loss also includes future profits of an investment that it established. Taking the cannabis example set down above,[80] imagine that the investment is a 100 per cent shareholding in the company producing and supplying cannabis in the host state. Six months after the investor's capital injection of EUR 1,000,000, the necessary infrastructure for this business has been built. After 12 months of trading, supplying cannabis is recriminalised in the host state – a risk that was foreseeable. Immediately before this recriminalisation, the investor's shareholding was worth EUR 2,500,000. As the profit portion of EUR 1,500,000 is more in the form of a contribution to the investor, the principle of unjust enrichment cannot shift any liability to the host state. Another reason, however, can be invoked to justify this shift: rewarding the investor for creating a profitable investment, thereby incentivising investing. Accordingly, the starting position is that the host state is fully liable for the investor's lost profits for an investment that the investor has established itself, subject to a partial transfer of that liability to the investor according to the relevant degree of political risk. This means that the investor will always recover some of its lost profits in cases involving findings of mismanagement, but there are other defences that the host state might rely on to avoid paying compensation for this loss, such as the police powers defence.

2.3.2 Exemplification of Restitutionary Apportionment

With the theory being expounded here, a new approach has emerged: restitutionary apportionment. It cannot deliver precise figures, but that is not its objective. Rather, it accurately approximates the disputants' share of liability in accordance with defeasible principles. It is more doctrinally sound than the current arbitrary approach and leaves some room for adjudicative

---

[80] See section 2.2.3.1 above.

discretion, but those factors will not necessarily lead to its adoption. To further that objective, the paragraphs below demonstrate how it applies.

2.3.2.1 *Criminalisation of Embryonic Stem Cell Research Case*

In the first case, the investor holds a shareholding in a local company ('Embryco') that carries on the business of embryonic stem cell research. The host state has a two-party political system where the two major political parties usually attract around 90 per cent of the popular vote. The third political force, the 'Christianity First' political party, typically garners about 5 per cent of the popular vote, with the remaining 5 per cent being distributed among the fringe political parties. Immediately before the investor invests the starting costs of EUR 10,000,000 in Embryco, the left-leaning major political party, which controls the government, completely deregulates embryonic stem cell research – a world first. Christianity First vehemently opposes this deregulation and releases a policy statement announcing that its primary objective is to criminalise embryonic stem cell research and the supply of any fruits of that research in the host state. After four years, it manages to achieve this objective when, after an election, it forms a coalition government with the right-leaning major political party – a first for the host state's political system. By this time, Embryco has managed to develop an effective treatment for Alzheimer's disease, a very lucrative drug in the host state considering its greying population.

The arbitral tribunal rules that the host state has breached the applicable investment treaty, but also finds that the investor has engaged in mismanagement. In apportioning the liability, the arbitral tribunal should first ascertain any direct contributions, of which there are none because the capital injections into Embryco did not trigger any tax obligations, nor has Embryco been subject to any corporate income tax obligations.

As regards the indirect contributions, the evidence shows that the capital injections went towards employee salaries paid to local workers (EUR 8,000,000), equipment from local suppliers (EUR 800,000), and rental costs for laboratories (EUR 200,000). The host state has a flat tax of 25 per cent on personal income, meaning that its employee salaries and rental costs have generated tax payments amounting to EUR 2,050,000. The transactions for the equipment were subject to a value-added tax of 5 per cent, thereby bringing the host state's enrichment through the investor's indirect contributions to EUR 2,090,000. The next variable is likely tax payments to the host state levied on the net income (EUR 6,910,000) from these indirect contributions. Adducing the relevant evidence to exactly calculate this amount is one of the limits of restitutionary apportionment, but this problem can be overcome. Applying the 50/30/20 rule, it might be assumed that 80 per cent of this net income (EUR 5,528,000) went towards transactions in the host state, noting that the indirect contributions were paid to participants in the host state's economy. With a value-added tax of 5 per cent, the likely tax payments come to EUR 276,400.

For the remaining amount of EUR 6,633,600, the investor assumes liability according to the degree of political risk that the investment faced. Given that Christianity First's policy was clearly stated via its website and was extensively covered in the local news media, it exhibits the requisite degree of publicity and clarity. Its likelihood of performance, however, is low. Given that it was a minor political party that had never formed part of a government, its political capacity should be rated at 0.1, although the strength of the Christianity First's conviction on this matter means that the political will should be rated at 10. After multiplying these values, the degree of political risk comes to 10 per cent, thus entailing that the investor assumes liability amounting to EUR 663,360. The final part of the equation looks at other contributions, of which there are none in this case. Of its EUR 10,000,00 capital injection, EUR 9,000,000 was spent, with the remaining EUR 1,000,000 being repatriated once it became clear that Embryco's business was not viable. What is relevant in this context is Embryco's lost profit of EUR 40,000,000, representing the estimated profit to be generated from the sales in the host state of its treatment for Alzheimer's disease. As explained in section 2.3.1.3 above, liability for this loss is shared between the host state and the investor with the latter accepting a percentage of the liability corresponding to the relevant degree of political risk, which applied to this case means that it accepts liability in the amount of EUR 4,000,000 for this loss.

Putting this together, the investor suffered an investment loss of EUR 49,000,000, for which the investor and the host state assume liability amounting to EUR 4,663,360 (9.5 per cent) and EUR 44,336,640 (90.5 per cent), respectively. Mismanagement has not applied in this case to grant the host state the advantage that would usually accrue to it, but this outcome is well justified. It has operated to preserve the fruits of the investor's labour in the face of marginal political risk, thereby ensuring that mismanagement does not operate to dissuade profitable investments. Not all applications of mismanagement so obviously favour the investor, however.

2.3.2.2 Creation of Nature Reserve over Oil Field

In this second case, the investor purchases from another foreign investor, for EUR 50,000,000, a major shareholding in Adrioil, a local oil company. While working an exploration permit, Adrioil finds a large offshore oil field. After this discovery is announced via its website, local hotel and restaurants owners begin exerting pressure on politicians in the regional government to stop the development of this oil field, often voicing their thoughts in local newspapers. On account of this pressure, the regional government announces that it will conduct a review into the environmental significance of the coastal waters adjacent to its jurisdiction. That review concludes that these waters contain globally unique biodiversity and recommends the creation of a nature reserve over this area. It is at around this time that the investor purchases its investment. One month after that review is released, the regional government announces that it accepts the review's findings and within six months the proposed nature reserve is created. This spells disaster for the investor because national law provides that an exploration permit cannot be upgraded to a production permit if the permit area falls within a nature reserve.

After the investor proves that the applicable investment treaty has been breached, the host state successfully pleads mismanagement. In the apportionment of liability, this case presents some new difficulties because it involves an established investment. The figure of EUR 50,000,000 has solely been used to purchase this established investment. However, the former owner's direct contributions and indirect contributions are credited to the investor. As regards direct contributions, these include all the various licence fees that the former owner paid, amounting to a total of EUR 500,000. Another EUR 19,500,000 was spent on rental costs for office space (EUR 500,000), employees' salaries (EUR 9,000,000), and equipment (EUR 10,000,000). The amounts paid for office space and employees' salaries triggered tax obligations in the host state amounting to EUR 4,000,000, but the equipment was purchased from foreign supplier, meaning that it is not included as an indirect contribution. Applying the 50/30/20 rule and assuming that the host state has a value-added tax of 10 per cent, the likely tax payments on the net income from the eligible indirect contributions come to EUR 440,000.

This leaves an amount of EUR 5,060,000, which is subject to division according to the degree of political risk. As regards the first question of whether the host state's breach was identifiable from the information available at the time of the investor's purchase, the evidence (reports in the news media and government report) establishes that this was the case. The valuation of political capacity should be very high ('1') as the regional government had the legal authority to create the nature reserve. The political will might be valued at 7, taking into account that the information on the creation of the nature reserve, at the relevant time, came from a governmental report. Accordingly, the investor assumes 70 per cent liability for these costs.

An amount of EUR 30,000,000 remains unaccounted for in this equation, representing the profit portion of the investor's purchase. As this amount went to another foreign investor, it cannot be counted as a contribution to the host state. Because of this, liability in this case is apportioned between the investor and the host state as follows: EUR 43,542,000 (87 per cent) and

EUR 6,458,000 (13 per cent), respectively. For the investor, this means that it takes on liability for the costs of the equipment (EUR 10,000,000), 70 per cent of its investment funds that probably found their way into the host state's economy (EUR 3,542,000), and the profit portion of the investment's purchase (EUR 30,000,000). Thus, in this case, a heavy burden falls on the investor, reflective of the fact that its investment contributed little to the host state's economy. Most of its contribution went to the former owner, against whom the investor might seek recourse for breach of the contract through which the shareholding was purchased. But in the absence of any circumstances giving rise to a breach, such as misrepresentation regarding the creation of the nature reserve, the loss rightly lies with the investor.

2.4 Attribution

With this outcome, the investor might feel cheated by the former owner, but it is ultimately the former owner's direct and indirect contributions that allow the investor to receive any recovery at all from the host state. This process of crediting contributions is vulnerable to attack, however. Effectively, the payments for these credited contributions are transferred from the former owner to the investor by attribution. Reflecting the fact that attribution of conduct to investors is one of the most undeveloped areas of international investment law, no rule can be invoked to support this crediting. Moreover, the rules on attribution in general international law, which have been adopted into international investment law,[81] have been developed to apply to states, thereby making them formally[82] inapplicable to attribution of conduct to investors.

This is not the occasion to build the jurisprudence on the attribution of conduct to investors in international investment law. Rather, it is proposed that a general principle can be sourced to doctrinally ground this rule, which may be called a 'continuation of investment business doctrine'. This doctrine is product of self-creation, although it draws much inspiration from the rules of domestic law on corporate succession to assets and liabilities. It provides that if an investor purchases an established investment and continues its business, then the conduct of the former owner is attributed to the investor.

---

[81] Arbitral tribunals in investment arbitrations have accepted Articles 4–11 of the ILC Articles on State Responsibility as the definitive statement of rules on attribution; see *Jan de Nul NV and Dredging International NV v. Egypt*, ICSID Case No. ARB/04/11, Award (12 October 2005) § 69, citing Crawford and Olleson, 'Application of the Rules of State Responsibility', 423.

[82] Although the principles underlying them can guide the creation of rules for the attribution of conduct to investors; see further section 2.4.2.1 of chapter 5 for an example of how these rules can be used for this purpose.

The foundation of this attribution is that the investor must accept both the benefits and the burdens of the former owner's conduct in creating the enterprise that is the investment,[83] meaning that the investor should be credited with the former owner's direct and indirect contributions.

This is not the only peculiar question of attribution that mismanagement raises. The case involving the criminalisation of stem cell research offers an example. There, the information that made this criminalisation foreseeable was the policy announcement of a minor party. At that time, this party was not in power, thus begging the question of whether this conduct could be attributed to the host state. A similar question arose in *Vivendi v. Argentina (II)*.[84] In its submission, the investor argued that when members of opposition parties in the host state's legislature expressed their opinions on political matters, they were exercising their legislative functions, thus making the host state liable for them under the rule that any conduct of the three branches of government are attributable to it.[85] Unfortunately, the arbitral tribunal did not rule on the issue owing to the investor's failure to prove a breach of the fair and equitable treatment rule based on that conduct,[86] but relevant commentary has filled the void by concluding that this argument lacks merit. The three reasons supporting that view are that members of the host state's legislature, one, are 'mere constituent elements of that organ', two, individually lack legislature power, and, three, represent the public, not the state.[87]

This is a cogent argument to exclude the attribution of conduct of individual members of parliament to the host state pursuant to Article 4 of the ILC Articles on State Responsibility, but there is another rule that can serve as the basis for attribution: Article 11. That provision stipulates that conduct is attributed to a state if the state acknowledges and adopts it as its own.[88] Admittedly, the commentary on Article 11 does not contemplate the specific question of the attribution of minor parties' policy announcements to the host state,[89] but it can be presumed that if such policy were subsequently enacted

---

[83] See Keating, 'Idea of Fairness', 1360. For a critique of this idea, see Neyers, 'Theory of Vicarious Liability', 298–300.

[84] *Compañía de Aguas del Aconquija S.A. and Vivendi Universal S.A. v. Argentine Republic*, ICSID Case No. ARB/97/3, Award (20 August 2007).

[85] Ibid. §§ 5.4.1–5.4.3.

[86] It did, however, comment that the acts of the Ombudsman were attributable to Argentina; see ibid. § 7.4.44. Note that the investor was able to prove a breach of the fair and equitable treatment standard based on other conduct; see ibid. § 7.4.43.

[87] Olleson, 'Attribution in Investment Treaty Arbitration', 474.

[88] See ILC Articles on State Responsibility, Art. 11.

[89] See, for example, Frouville, 'Attribution of Conduct to the State', 273–275.

into law, then such enactment would fall within the definitional ambit of 'acknowledge and adopt'.

3 MISMANAGEMENT – JURISDICTION AND ADMISSIBILITY

Proving that mismanagement's legal elements are satisfied and the relevant conduct can be attributed to the disputants does not mean that it has been successfully pleaded. The habitually neglected questions of the arbitral tribunal's jurisdiction to entertain this plea and its admissibility remain. As regards the question of jurisdiction, this neglect can be forgiven, however, as it is difficult to envision any jurisdictional questions that a plea of mismanagement could raise.[90]

By contrast, there is potentially a question of admissibility. To illustrate this, consider a situation where the respondent, who is an academic, posts a sign on her door that any person who knocks on her door outside her consultation hours will be punched in the face. A student seeking help with an assessment task decides to visit this professor outside her consultation hours. Before knocking on the professor's door, he notices the warning, but reasons that it is worth taking the risk. Unfortunately for him, the professor opens the door and promptly punches him in the face, thereby breaking the student's eye socket. In the subsequent trial, the professor pleads the defence of voluntary assumption of risk,[91] a plea that the judge summarily rejects because this defence cannot be pleaded as an answer to intentional assaults.[92]

What is more interesting is the reason for this exclusion.[93] Commentary is sparse on this topic, but it is submitted that the best explanation is that the professor's wrongful conduct is vastly graver than the student's conduct. Extrapolating this principle, if a host state's breach is particularly egregious, a plea of mismanagement could be ruled inadmissible. The question is: what

[90] See section 2.2 of chapter 1 for an overview of the rules on arbitral tribunals' jurisdiction over defences.

[91] Consent could not be pleaded because one of its core elements – that the person giving the consent (the victim) believes that the other person's otherwise wrongful conduct will deliver some benefit to him or her – is absent, whereas with voluntary assumption of risk the victim (wrongly) believes that a risk will not materialise and thus proceeds to act. See further section 4.1 below.

[92] Kenneth Simons offers a similar example involving an intentional tort committed on Harry Houdini, although he concludes that either consent or voluntary assumption of risk could be pleaded; see Simons, 'Exploring the Relationship', 272–274. It is considered that the only applicable defence was consent, however, because Houdini believed that his reputation as a performer would be enhanced by agreeing to the intentional tort.

[93] See also the Restatement (Third) of Torts: Intentional Torts to the Persons (Tentative Draft No. 1). There, voluntary assumption of risk is not listed as a defence.

constitutes a particularly egregious breach in international investment law? Opinions will differ on what this breach should look like, but given that international investment law's liability rules are designed to encourage good governance,[94] this factor should guide the answer. One possible instance would be where the host state's conduct is tainted by corruption. An example might be where the host state's breach eliminates the investor's investment for the purpose of gifting that investment's market share to a company owned by a member of the president's family.

4 MISMANAGEMENT AND OTHER RELATED LEGAL CONCEPTS

The theory expounded here creates a potential admissibility rule for pleas of mismanagement, a rule that is founded on a principle relating to voluntary assumption of risk. It assumes that voluntary assumption of risk is a legal concept equivalent to mismanagement, an assumption seemingly liable to correction. This assumption, however, is well founded.[95] As with mismanagement, voluntary assumption of risk fundamentally involves claimants who foresee that their conduct might directly cause their harm.[96] But while voluntary assumption of risk can be equated with mismanagement, the latter should be rigorously distinguished from other related legal concepts – distinctions that the current jurisprudence habitually confuses.

4.1 Mismanagement and Consent

The first of these legal concepts is consent, a defence recognised in international law by virtue of Article 20 of the ILC Articles on State Responsibility. In both international law[97] and domestic law[98] consent is confused with voluntary assumption of risk, and by extension with mismanagement. This confusion arises out of the tendency to interpret the claimant's performance of the conduct that directly causes the relevant consequence as the giving of implied consent,[99] particularly if that claimant has actual knowledge of the respondent's potential forthcoming breach. Applying this reasoning, the

---

[94] For an overview of the history of how good governance became the core of these liability rules, see Sattorova, *Impact of Investment Treaty Law*, 2–5.

[95] See Sabahi, *Compensation and Restitution*, 175.

[96] Phelps and Lehman (eds.), *West's Encyclopedia*, 166 (definition of '*volenti non fit injuria*').

[97] See, for example, Mansour, 'Circumstances Precluding Wrongfulness', 439.

[98] In the Anglo-American world, the most prominent author on this topic is Kenneth Simons; see particularly Simons, 'Exploring the Relationship', 272 and Simons, 'Puzzling Doctrine', 1693.

[99] See, for example, Wade, 'Place of Assumption of Risk', 7–8.

student who knocked on the professor's door would be said to have implicitly consented to being punched in the face. Similarly, when the investor
in the nature reserve example purchased its investment, that purchase could
serve to express the investor's consent to the subsequent creation of the nature
reserve.[100] But if these claimants were asked whether they consented to the
respondent's conduct, both would surely answer no, and for good reason.
The act of giving consent communicates to the respondent that the claimant
permits the respondent's otherwise wrongful[101] conduct – a quality that is
always absent in the claimant's conduct for mismanagement. In some cases, it
may seem difficult to draw a line between these types of conduct, but that line
will always be readily visible. This is because conduct indicating consent will
relate to conduct of the respondent that the claimant believes will benefit him
or her, such as submitting to an invasive surgical procedure with the result
that claimant is no longer burdened with the upbringing of a child that she
cannot raise. With cases of mismanagement, the claimant does not have this
belief. On account of his or her optimism bias, he or she concludes that the
risk will not materialise.

4.2 *Mismanagement and Devaluation of Loss*

What this emphasises is that mismanagement fundamentally involves a poor
business decision, but not all poor business decisions leading to a loss can
found a plea of mismanagement.[102] An example[103] of such a business decision
comes from the case of *Azurix v. Argentina*. In *Azurix*, the investors financed
the purchase of a USD 438,555,554[104] concession for water distribution and
sewerage treatment services in return for shareholdings in the company
holding the concession, ABA. After a series of actions by the provincial government that deprived ABA of the economic benefit of the concession, the
provincial government terminated the concession.[105] The investors claimed
at least[106] USD 608,414,000 in compensatory damages for various breaches.[107]

---

[100] See section 2.3.2.2 above.
[101] Hurd, 'Moral Magic of Consent', 123.
[102] See Merizalde, 'Proportionality, Contributory Negligence and Other Equity Considerations',
309; Ripinsky and Williams, *Damages*, 317; Dugan and others, *Investor-State Arbitration*, 603.
[103] It was also described as such by the arbitral tribunal; see *Azurix v. Argentina* § 426.
[104] Ibid. § 41. Although the currency of the payment was Argentine pesos, one Argentine peso
equalled one US dollar at the time of payment.
[105] For a summary, see ibid. § 43.
[106] The investors gave the arbitral tribunal different options for the valuation of their investment;
see ibid. § 411.
[107] Ibid. § 414.

They were successful,[108] but their award was limited to USD 165,240,753, including the loss of the concession.[109] The arbitral tribunal calculated the fair market value of the concession to be USD 60,000,000.[110]

Overpaying for an asset might be mismanagement in the ordinary sense, but not in the legal sense.[111] The arbitral tribunal's decision did not apply any notions of mismanagement, but merely calculated the value of the investor's loss. Because that valuation reflected the concession's fair market value, rather than the purchase price, it created an effective loss for the investor of its own creation. That loss is not the type of investment loss that mismanagement is concerned with, however. Additionally, the factor giving the investor's conduct its faultworthy character for mismanagement is the investor's foresight of the host state's breach, not purchasing an asset for a price well above its fair market value.

4.3 Mismanagement and Unviable Business Plan

This is not the only type of poor business decision to have been confused with mismanagement. Commentators have noted that in two cases, *Olguín v. Paraguay*[112] and *Waste Management v. Mexico (II)*,[113] the respective arbitral tribunals made effective findings, albeit in obiter,[114] of mismanagement. The better view, however, is that the investors in these cases chose to pursue unviable business plans. In *Olguín v. Paraguay*, the investor's investments

---

[108] Ibid. § 377 (for breach of the rule on fair and equitable treatment), § 393 (for breach of the rule on arbitrary or discriminatory measures), and § 408 (for breach of rule on protection and security).

[109] Ibid. § 442.

[110] Ibid. § 427.

[111] Some commentators, however, have viewed *Azurix v. Argentina* as a case involving contributory fault and, by extension, mismanagement. See Merizalde, 'Proportionality, Contributory Negligence and Other Equity Considerations', 309; Ripinsky and Williams, *Damages*, 317; Dugan, and others, *Investor-State Arbitration*, 603.

[112] See Merizalde, 'Proportionality, Contributory Negligence and Other Equity Considerations', 309. Additionally, although not labelling the case as one involving contributory fault or similar, Markus Burgstaller and Jonathan Ketcheson indicate that the claimant failed because it had knowledge of the likelihood of the breaches, which would constitute an effective finding of reckless mismanagement; see Burgstaller and Ketcheson, 'Should Expropriation Risk Be Taken into Account?', 196.

[113] See Merizalde, 'Proportionality, Contributory Negligence and Other Equity Considerations', 322.

[114] In both of these cases, the investors failed to establish that the host states had breached the investment treaties; see *Eudoro Armando Olguín v. Republic of Paraguay*, ICSID Case No. ARB/98/5, Award (26 July 2001 (unofficial English translation)) ('*Olguín v. Paraguay*') §§ 70–71; *Waste Management v. Mexico (II)* § 178.

were cash deposits with a Paraguayan bank. The interest rate on these deposits was 33 per cent and the bank made the interest payments until a financial crisis hit Paraguay, one result of which was the bank's insolvency and the subsequent loss of the investor's deposits. The investor claimed that Paraguay's inadequate financial supervision caused this outcome, although the arbitral tribunal found that, while Paraguay's conduct was negligent,[115] it did not amount to a breach of the investment treaty. Most pertinently, the arbitral tribunal also noted that the investor 'contributed significantly' to his predicament – an idea that it failed to flesh out unfortunately. A clue as to its meaning can be gleaned, however, from earlier in the award. There, the arbitral tribunal emphasised that the bank was unlikely to be able to continuously pay the very high interest rates that it offered – a risk that materialised with the coming of the financial crisis. This was simply an investment unlikely to bear fruit, much like the investment in *Waste Management v. Mexico (II)*. In that case, the arbitral tribunal explicitly called out the investor on this:

> [The] business plan … was, in the circumstances, founded on too narrow a client base and dependent for its success on unsustainable assumptions about customer uptake and contractual performance.[116]

The arbitral tribunal in *Waste Management v. Mexico (II)* found that although the host state had breached its contract with the investor,[117] this contractual breach did not amount to a treaty breach.[118] This finding conveniently avoided the question of duplicative causation that would have arisen: does the host state's breach or the investor's investing in an unviable business cause the investment loss? Applying the NESS test discussed in chapter 3, both could be classified as causes. But the idea of making a host state liable to compensate an investor for an otherwise bad investment is so unpalatable that an arbitral tribunal would probably rule that causation was lacking.

5 CONCLUSION

These analyses show that mismanagement is a concept distinct from others, but one that remains largely unrecognised. This needs to change. It has solid doctrinal foundations in Article 39 of the ILC Articles on State Responsibility and

---

[115] *Olguín v. Paraguay* § 71.
[116] *Waste Management v. Mexico (II)* § 177. In *Olguín v. Paraguay*, the arbitral tribunal also noted that the claimant had to accept the outcome of his 'speculative, or at best, a not very prudent investment'; see *Olguín v. Paraguay* § 65(b).
[117] *Waste Management v. Mexico (II)* § 165.
[118] Ibid. § 178.

some arbitral awards. The more difficult question relates to its legal function. The very high standard of diligence expected of investment managers creates an argument for mismanagement to operate as a complete defence. That argument provides that if any investor is so imprudent as to invest with fore-sight of a possible investment loss, then that investor is undeserving of any protection under an investment treaty. But that is too simplistic. Considering the prevalence of political risks, that option would serve only to disincentivise investing. Moreover, it would apply unfairly in cases of minor political risk. The solution is to make mismanagement a partial defence. Its legal content is unproblematic, but, like any partial defence, deciding how liability should be apportioned presents a considerable challenge. On account of the great difficulty involved in measuring the disputants' fault, the default method in international investment law is to split liability 50-50 between the disputants. Determined to move beyond this simplicity, another theory for apportionment was put forward: restitutionary apportionment. Rather than being rooted in arbitrariness, restitutionary apportionment is a principled approach to appor-tionment. Objections might be made to its complexity, but these should be disregarded on account of the truism that complexity is often a necessary inci-dental of developing the law.

5

Investment Reprisal and Post-Establishment Illegality

1 THE CONCEPTS OF INVESTMENT REPRISAL AND POST-ESTABLISHMENT ILLEGALITY

Investment reprisal has previously been encountered in the opening to chapter 4. This concept could go by any number of names, such as 'civil provocation', 'incitement of host state', or 'investment countermeasures', but the first two alternatives are too rooted in domestic criminal law. As regards 'investment countermeasures', it is feared that this expression would be too readily confused with the concept of state-to-state countermeasures, as codified in the ILC Articles on State Responsibility.[1] In current jurisprudence, the expression 'reprisal' has overtones of conduct that is illegal, but that too makes an appropriate descriptor because the conduct which is the reprisal must amount to a breach of the applicable treaty before this defence can be pleaded. More importantly, the notion of reprisal, as conceived by Rayneval in the late eighteenth century,[2] accurately conveys the content of this concept: some blameworthy conduct performed by the investor that provokes the host state's breach. As such, it is immediately distinguishable from mismanagement as the latter requires that the investor directly cause its investment loss. Strictly, the investor contribution does not cause the investor's loss because it does not form part of the causal constellation for such consequence, but it nonetheless has a causal relationship to it. Although they are of a different nature, this shared causative element makes them both contributory fault defences. It is the absence of this element that marks out the other defence with which this chapter is concerned: post-establishment illegality. Most closely related to investment reprisal, thereby explaining their simultaneous examination, a

---

[1] See *Corn Products International, Inc. v. United Mexican States*, ICSID Case No. ARB (AF)/04/1, Decision on Responsibility (15 January 2008) § 145.

[2] Spiegel, 'Origin and Development of Denial of Justice', 74–76.

plea of post-establishment illegality is founded on investor (mis)conduct in breach of a liability rule. Aside from their multiple doctrinal similarities, what both investment reprisal and post-establishment illegality have in common is their lack of explicit recognition in the current jurisprudence. On account of that, the starting point is to establish their doctrinal foundations.

1.1 The Doctrinal Foundations of Investment Reprisal and Post-Establishment Illegality

For the most part, the task of establishing investment reprisal's and post-establishment illegality's doctrinal foundations is unproblematic. As a form of contributory fault, investment reprisal can source its existence to Article 39 of the ILC Articles on State Responsibility. Additionally, there are a growing number of arbitral awards in which it has been implicitly found,[3] which is also the case for post-establishment illegality. While post-establishment illegality is not recognised in the ILC Articles on State Responsibility,[4] some academic literature vouches for its existence. Most particularly, eminent authority[5] holds that the defence of illegality in general international law is a manifestation of the general principle[6] that a person should not be permitted to profit from his or her own illegality. By extension, post-establishment illegality could also ground its existence in the same principle.

1.1.1 Treaty-Based Post-Establishment Illegality

In the future, however, it is likely that post-establishment illegality will not peg its doctrinal foundations to this principle because investment treaties will codify this defence, with the Morocco-Nigeria bilateral investment treaty offering an example:[7]

ARTICLE 18

POST-ESTABLISHMENT OBLIGATIONS

1) Investments shall, in keeping with good practice requirements relating to the size and nature of the investment, maintain an environmental

---

[3] See, for example, *Occidental v. Ecuador*, Award § 665; *Yukos v. Russia* § 1633; *Copper Mesa Mining Corporation v. Republic of Ecuador*, PCA Case No. 2012-2, Award (15 March 2016) ('*Copper Mesa v. Ecuador*') § 6.133.
[4] It is not one of the 'circumstances precluding wrongfulness' in the ILC Articles on State Responsibility. See Crawford, *State Responsibility*, 278 for a discussion of its exclusion.
[5] See Fitzmaurice, *General Principles*, 117.
[6] See Dworkin, *Taking Rights Seriously*, 22.
[7] Morocco-Nigeria BIT, Art. 18. For a similar article, see Belarus-India BIT, Art. 11.

management system. Companies in areas of resource exploitation and high-risk industrial enterprises shall maintain a current certification to ISO 14001 or an equivalent environmental management standard.

2) Investors and investments shall uphold human rights in the host state.
3) Investors and investments shall act in accordance with core labour standards as required by the ILO Declaration on Fundamental Principles and Rights of Work, 1998.
4) Investors and investments shall not manage or operate the investments in a manner that circumvents international environmental, labour and human rights obligations to which the host state and/or home state are Parties.

The advantage of treaty provisions such as these is that they clarify legal content and provide a more secure doctrinal foundation for a plea of post-establishment illegality than grounding a plea in the general principles of law. But once it is recognised that such provisions impose an obligation on a third person, the affected investor, a neon light appears above them reading 'validity questionable'. The problem is Article 34 of the Vienna Convention on the Law of Treaties:

A treaty does not create either obligations or rights for a third state without its consent.

The obvious objection is that an investor is not a third state as per this rule, but there is jurisprudence indicating that third state includes non-state entities, although this jurisprudence is sparse.[8] Yet even if this rule only applies to states, this problem does not disappear. The view restricting the application to states is ultimately informed by Article 1 of the Vienna Convention on the Law of Treaties and it stipulates that the Convention only applies to treaty relations between states. Because of that provision, recourse can be made to the fall back position, the rules of customary international law, following Article 3(b). In customary international law, it is trite law that treaties cannot impose obligations on third persons.[9] Admittedly, there is a substantial body of jurisprudence that assumes the opposite,[10] but, with respect, there is limited doctrine marshalled behind it to substantiate that opposing view.[11] Accordingly, treaty provisions that seek to create a defence of post-establishment illegality are presumably invalid, unless the impractical step of seeking out the explicit consent of all the affected investors is pursued as per Article 35 of the Vienna

---

[8]   Proelss, 'Article 34', 661.
[9]   Tomuschat, 'International Organizations as Third Parties under the Law of Treaties', 120.
[10] Dumberry and Dumas-Aubin, 'How to Impose Human Rights?', fn. 18.
[11] See, for example, Chinkin, *Third Parties in International Law*, 121.

Convention on the Law of Treaties. To avoid that outcome, it can be argued that either an investor is not a third person or an exception to this rule should be crafted. In considering the workability of these options, reference is made to the Vienna Convention on the Law of Treaties as it is assumed that its provisions accurately reflect the rules of customary international law.

The second option is not a viable one. Considering that host states have the option of enacting their own laws to regulate investors, there is an argument that treaty-based obligations are unnecessary. Nonetheless, there are good reasons why host states might prefer treaty-based obligations, particularly those that designate other bodies of international law as standards according to which investor misconduct will be measured. When states agree to incorporate these standards in their law, they can be comfortable in the knowledge that their investors will be the subjects of obligations that meet international standards. Further, it might be more convenient for states to impose those obligations via a treaty, rather than going through what might be an arduous process of transposing them into domestic law. But notwithstanding the force of those reasons, they cannot overcome the fact that there is no jurisprudence supporting the idea that Article 35 admits any exceptions.

1.1.1.1 Valid Offers for Investor Accession

The first option has better prospects. It would involve the construction of an argument that, rather than being a third person, an investor can become, or is actually, a party to the relevant investment treaty. The most viable method to that end is accession pursuant to Article 15 of the Vienna Convention on the Law of Treaties. The problem afflicting this method concerns how states that are party to an investment treaty should indicate their willingness for investors to accede. Article 15 lays down three possible avenues, the first and second being respectively explicit and implicit offers of accession to the treaty, and the third being either an explicit or implicit offer after the treaty's conclusion. It is difficult to envision how states that are party to an investment treaty could implicitly offer accession. Typically, such offers are found in multilateral treaties, with the corollary of that being that they rarely arise out of bilateral treaties.[12] This jurisprudence, however, assumes that it is a state seeking accession. Thus, the question remains: by merely extending rights to and imposing obligations on investors in investment treaties, do states implicitly offer accession to investors? In the current climate where any measure addressing the asymmetry of investment treaties would be viewed favourably,[13] an arbitral tribunal would probably answer this question in the

---

[12] Hoffmeister, 'Article 15', 218.
[13] Hepburn, 'In Accordance with *Which* Host State Laws?', 559.

affirmative. This answer might make for good political optics, but more is needed to bind the investor than this form of implicit offer.

1.1.1.2 *Investor's Act of Accession*

What informs this conclusion is the required form of the investor's act of accession. Fundamentally, this act has to be evidence of the investor's consent to be bound.[14] Article 16 of the Vienna Convention envisions that it should be a formal act, such as the deposit of an instrument of accession with the treaty's depositary, but this general procedure is subject to any specific dictates of the relevant treaty. Using this exception to the general procedure, states to investment treaties should designate the one act that should most obviously serve as the investor's act of accession: the making of its investment. This is a practical solution, but it runs into a doctrinal problem. To understand this problem, it must be accepted that if an investor accedes to an investment treaty, it only accedes to the obligations placed on it because, by virtue of the states' unilateral promises to it, it already has the benefit of that treaty's rights, a conclusion that is reinforced by Article 36 because it provides that a person holding rights under a treaty is presumed to assent to them.[15] If an investor can accede to an investment treaty's obligations by merely making an investment, then the regime of formalities created by Article 35 to ensure that the acceding party knows of their obligations is completely compromised.

It follows that something more is needed than mere investing for an investor's act of accession. That something has to be more practical than requiring that each investor, for example, sign a declaration that they consent to the relevant obligations, but also strong enough to satisfy an arbitral tribunal that the investor has been informed that its investing serves to bind it to the applicable investment treaty. With these factors in mind, it is proposed that, at a minimum, the treaty should contain a provision informing investors that the making of their investments will lead to their accession and, taking inspiration from the jurisprudence on denial of benefits clauses,[16] notices in the government gazette.

It is now apparent that there is a better alternative to implicitly offering accession to investors. If states are required to give notice in the treaty, then such notice effectively operates as an explicit offer for investors' accession. In this way, states' options for making offers of accession become limited to this form of offer. Finally, it should be noted that if the investor's act of

---

[14] Vienna Convention on the Law of Treaties, Art. 16.
[15] See Dolzer and Schreuer, *Principles of International Investment Law*, 79.
[16] See, for example, *Plama Consortium Limited v. Republic of Bulgaria*, ICSID Case No. ARB/03/24, Decision on Jurisdiction (8 February 2005) § 157.

investing serves as its act of accession, then that limits the scope of its consent to obligations relating to that particular investment.

1.1.2 The Recognition of Investment Reprisal

As was the case with mismanagement, another question that this section needs to address is the recognition of investment reprisal as a defence. This is not a problem that afflicts post-establishment illegality. The reason for this is that investment reprisal is a form of self-help,[17] whereas post-establishment illegality is not. In cases of investment reprisal, the host state takes the liberty of exacting revenge (which is also the conduct constituting its breach) on the investor for the latter's wrongdoing, rather than asking for redress before an adjudicative body, as is the case with a plea of post-establishment illegality. Good reason supports the view that limited credence should be given to forms of self-help in the law.[18] Foremost, self-help, by its nature, erodes the rule of law. Moreover, its recognition represents a jurisprudential regression as there has been a concerted effort to pare down the application of reprisal over the past century.[19]

These are powerful arguments not to recognise investment reprisal. With such non-recognition, the fact that the investor performed wrongful conduct that provoked the host state would become irrelevant – an outcome that could be objected to on account of the maxim that 'for every wrong, the law provides a remedy'. But this objection does not possess the necessary weight to unseat the reasons for not recognising investment reprisal. This is because the maxim rests on the strength of the rule of law in the system where the rule providing for that remedy is found. However, the rule of law must be underpinned by a functioning adjudicative apparatus – a feature that has not been developed in respect of investor misconduct under international investment law.[20] Except in cases where the investor has given its consent for an arbitral tribunal to adjudicate on its conduct,[21] which is always the case with pleas of post-establishment illegality,[22] the host state cannot bring an action under international investment law to hold the investor accountable. Seeking recourse before its own

---

[17] Crawford, *State Responsibility*, 684–685.

[18] Ibid., 686.

[19] Ruffert, 'Reprisals', § 17.

[20] This reflects Emmerich de Vattel's conception of reprisal in international law as it could be resorted to 'in order to obtain justice when it cannot otherwise be had'; Vattel, *Law of Nations*, 228. Additionally, counterclaims are subject to the principle of proportionality under international law; see ILC Articles on State Responsibility, Art. 51.

[21] For an example of this (rarely given) consent, see *Burlington v. Ecuador*, Decision on Ecuador's Counterclaims § 60.

[22] See section 3.1.1 below.

courts might be a potential option, but this is a weak rebuttal for two reasons. First, responding to the investor's conduct may be a matter best reserved for the host state's legislature because new laws should be implemented. Second, the development of the host state's law might be such that recourse to the courts is futile, such as when they have no jurisprudence to draw on to determine the legality or otherwise of the investor's conduct.

1.2 *The Legal Functions of Investment Reprisal and Post-Establishment Illegality*

What this entails is that investment reprisal should be recognised as a defence. This conclusion, however, assumes that investment reprisal and post-establishment illegality are defences – an assumption that cannot marshal much support behind it from the current jurisprudence. That jurisprudence holds that, as a form of contributory fault, investment reprisal is a remedy rule. However, as detailed in sections 1.6.1 and 1.6.2 of chapter 2, that view cannot be correct, with the corollary being that the contributory fault defences are properly designated as defences. There is no reason to revisit that debate. What is more contentious is the legal function of post-establishment illegality – a circumstance that has variously been held to be relevant to admissibility or jurisdiction.

1.2.1 Post-Establishment Illegality as an Admissibility Issue

Its purported relation to admissibility can be readily dismissed. Usually, this proposition is justified on the basis that entertaining a claim tainted with illegality is an abuse of process.[23] This logic is difficult to accept. What constitutes[24] an abuse of process is using an adjudicative process for a purpose other than that for which it was established.[25] Adjudicative bodies, however, are fundamentally established to determine the rights and wrongs of conduct.[26] Accordingly, by entertaining claims that are allegedly tainted by illegality, and passing judgment on this alleged illegality, adjudicative bodies fulfil their primary purpose. Secondly, an investor's illegal conduct has no bearing on its claim *itself*. As previously explained, the topic of admissibility

---

[23] See, for example, *Churchill Mining Plc and Planet Mining Pty Ltd v. Republic of Indonesia*, ICSID Case Nos. ARB/12/14 and ARB/12/40, Award (6 December 2016) ('*Churchill Mining v. Indonesia*') § 492.

[24] This definition is largely inspired by the description of the Anglo-American law cause of action 'abuse of process' as found in the Restatement (Second) of Torts (1977) § 682.

[25] Some examples might include claims brought in pursuit of political ends, to generate media attention to advertise a commercial product, or to exert pressure on the respondent to pay an amount relating to another dispute.

[26] Finnis, 'Adjudication and Legal Change', 399.

examines the maturity of a claim for adjudication,[27] not its rightfulness or wrongfulness by evaluating the quality of the conduct making up the matrix of the dispute from which the claim arises. Finally, finding a claim inadmissible on account of the investor's illegality can lead to a disproportionate outcome. Effectively, the punishment this finding inflicts on the investor is an amount equal to its investment, as recovery for that loss becomes procedurally barred.[28] The value of that loss, however, bears no relation to the gravity of the investor's wrongdoing.

1.2.2 Post-Establishment Illegality as a Jurisdictional Issue

Post-establishment illegality is generally irrelevant to jurisdiction, although the situation is far more nuanced. This is because post-establishment illegality's counterpart – establishment illegality – is a circumstance that, if proven, will mean that the legality requirement for jurisdiction cannot be fulfilled. Aside from the question of how establishment and post-establishment illegalities should be distinguished (which is answered below), there is another complication that burdens this conception. In many investment treaties, the legality requirement is not specifically provided for, which, in those investment arbitrations where such investment treaties apply, raises the question of whether this requirement must still be fulfilled? The answer is important because if it is negative, then it raises an additional question on the relevance of establishment illegality in those cases.

There is a wealth of jurisprudence on this question, but unfortunately it is inconsistent.[29] With the bulk of the academic literature[30] and dicta from *Plama v. Bulgaria*[31] and *Bear Creek v. Peru*[32] in its corner, the negative answer

---

[27] See section 3 of chapter 1.

[28] This principle is taken from Weinrib, 'Illegality as a Tort Defence', 45. Although Weinrib was discussing illegality in Anglo-American tort law, the principle has equal applicability here.

[29] *Bear Creek Mining Corporation v. Republic of Peru*, ICSID Case No. ARB/14/21, Award (30 November 2017) (*'Bear Creek v. Peru'*) § 318.

[30] For a list of these academic authorities, see Dumberry, 'State of Confusion', 236 and fn. 42.

[31] In *Plama v. Bulgaria*, the investor had misled the host state about its capacity to complete its investment project, but the applicable investment treaty contained no 'compliance with the host state's law' provision. The arbitral tribunal found that it had jurisdiction, thereby implicitly indicating that this provision must be included in the applicable investment treaty for it to operate as a jurisdictional requirement, although it subsequently ruled that it could not 'lend its support to Claimant's request and cannot, therefore, grant the substantive protections of the [applicable investment treaty]', meaning the claim was inadmissible; see *Plama Consortium Limited v. Republic of Bulgaria*, ICSID Case No. ARB/03/24, Award (27 August 2008) § 146. See also *Anatolie Stati, Gabriel Stati, Ascom Group S.A., and Terra Raf Trans Trading Ltd. v. Republic of Kazakhstan*, SCC Case No. V (116/2010), Award (19 December 2013) § 812 for a similar outcome.

[32] *Bear Creek v. Peru* § 320

enjoys the most theoretical support. The better view, however, and one that the arbitral tribunals in *Minnotte v. Poland*,[33] *Phoenix Action v. Czechia*,[34] and *Cortec v. Kenya*[35] adopted, is that the 'legality of investment' requirement is universally applicable for the following reasons. First, if the opposite view prevails, then it opens the door for investors who are subject to the legality requirement under the investment treaties applicable to their disputes to raise an argument invoking the most-favoured-nation clause to exclude it. The specifics of that argument are that the affected investor would be at a disadvantage as compared to those investors who arbitrated under investment treaties where the legality requirement was absent, assuming the host state was a signatory to such an investment treaty. The merits of this argument are controversial,[36] but if it were successful, many legality requirements would be rendered ineffective.

The other reason is more compelling. It holds that establishment illegality voids the arbitration agreement that underpins any investment arbitration. Two premises support this contention, the first of which provides that the investor's investing in the host state is the action, along with any formal requirements, that partially expresses its consent to arbitration. Admittedly, this interpretation has to overcome the weight of much entrenched jurisprudence. That jurisprudence holds that the investor's initiation of arbitration acts as its acceptance – an interpretation that has been trumpeted by prominent scholars of international investment law and embraced by arbitral tribunals.[37] For this interpretation to work, it must be assumed that the host state gratuitously gives up its right of state immunity[38] and the home advantage that it would enjoy in any litigation before its own courts, both of which are necessary incidents of submitting to arbitration. Rationality dictates that this assumption should not be accepted. Deductively, this means that such

---

[33] *David Minnotte and Robert Lewis v. Republic of Poland*, ICSID Case No. ARB(AF)/10/1, Award (16 May 2014) §§ 131–132.

[34] This decision actually goes further by holding that the legality requirement applies in any ICSID arbitration; see *Phoenix Action, Ltd. v. The Czech Republic*, ICSID Case No. ARB/06/5, Award (15 April 2009) § 114. But the most comprehensive commentary on the ICSID Convention states that any requirement for establishment legality can only arise via the applicable investment treaty; see Schreuer and others, *ICSID Convention*, Art. 25, §§ 199–201.

[35] *Cortec Mining Kenya Limited, Cortec (Pty) Limited and Stirling Capital Limited v. Republic of Kenya*, ICSID Case No. ARB/15/29, Award (22 October 2018) § 319.

[36] For an overview, see McLachlan and others, *International Investment Arbitration*, §§ 7.317–7.342.

[37] Schreuer, 'Consent to Arbitration', 837.

[38] This is recognised as a legal right of states under customary international law; see Crawford, *Brownlie's Principles*, 487.

forbearance must be made with some benefit in mind. One candidate is the same promise made by the other signatory state to the host state's investors, but, as no benefit accrues to the host state *itself* from this promise, it can be dismissed. The only other candidate is the investor's investment. But this is not a victory by default. Rather, it applies the most basic of rules on treaty interpretation: that any interpretation must seek to promote the purpose underlying the relevant treaty provision.[39] Putting all this together, it follows that the investor's investment is an integral part of any arbitration agreement upon which an investment arbitration is based.

The second limb provides that establishment illegality permanently poisons an investment. As detailed below, it takes on this quality because it is, one, necessary for the investment's existence and, two, undermines the host state's economic development.[40] To prove necessity, the following question must be answered in the negative: if the investor had performed the relevant conduct legally, would the investment have come into being? 'Undermining economic development' potentially takes a number of forms, such as some negative macroeconomic outcome. The realities of proof, however, mean that the host state should usually designate a microeconomic outcome as the negative consequence caused by the illegal conduct. Without limiting what such an outcome might look like, it should usually take one of two forms. First, it could be a reduced economic contribution from the investment on account of the illegal conduct; for example, if the investor pays transaction bribes to secure its legal permits, this should be seen as a reduced economic benefit because the same money could have been paid into the host state's public funds. A second kind of negative microeconomic outcome is the exclusion or disincentivisation of more economically beneficial investments.[41] Using the same example, if the transaction bribes made the governmental officers look past another investment that had made a higher bid for the legal permits, then that more beneficial bid will have been excluded. Whether these circumstances amount to a mistake or misrepresentation, they act to vitiate the host state's consent to arbitration because the investor's consideration achieves the opposite of what motivated the host state to make this offer, thus voiding the arbitration agreement.

This proposed universal applicability of the legality requirement could be excluded if the applicable investment treaty contained a rule specifically to

---

[39] Vienna Convention on the Law of Treaties, Art. 31(1).
[40] For a similar sentiment, see Wells, 'Backlash to Investment Arbitration', 347.
[41] See also Llamzon, *Corruption*, 35–36.

that effect. Arguably, such a provision can be found in the Canada-Peru Free Trade Agreement:[42]

> Nothing in Article 803 shall be construed to prevent a Party from adopting or maintaining a measure that prescribes special formalities in connection with the establishment of covered investments, such as a requirement that investments be legally constituted under the laws or regulations of the Party, provided that such formalities do not materially impair the protections afforded by a Party to investors of the other Party and covered investments pursuant to this Chapter.

This provision was at issue in *Bear Creek v. Peru*. Following the arbitral tribunal's interpretation, it bestowed on each of Canada or Peru the right to elect to create a legality requirement. In the absence of any election to that effect by Peru, the legality requirement was not applicable.[43]

With respect, that interpretation fails to take proper account of how Article 803 shapes this provision. Article 803 contains this treaty's national treatment rules. As rules relating to an investment's establishment are often more demanding on foreign investors compared to local investors, any enactment of these rules would prima facie breach Article 803. Article 816 clarifies that this is not the case with its opening words: 'Nothing in Article 803 shall be construed to prevent a Party from adopting or maintaining a measure that prescribes special formalities in connection with the establishment of covered investments'. Effectively, it carves out from Article 803 an exception for rules relating to investment establishment.[44] By contemplating the application of such rules, Article 803 does not exclude a legality requirement, but supports its inclusion.

1.2.2.1 *Meaning of Investment Establishment*

This analysis establishes the importance of distinguishing establishment illegality from post-establishment illegality, but it does not illuminate that distinction. The arbitral tribunal in *Hamester v. Ghana* is one of the few arbitral tribunals that has attempted this task:[45]

> The Tribunal considers that a distinction has to be drawn between (1) legality as at the initiation of the investment ('made') and (2) legality during the performance of the investment.

---

[42] Canada-Peru FTA, Art. 816.

[43] *Bear Creek v. Peru* § 319.

[44] This provision gives rise to a defence to a breach of the national treatment rule; see section 1.4 of chapter 2 for an explanation of why rules that limit the definitional scope of a legal element in the correlative liability rules are properly called defences.

[45] *Gustav F W Hamester GmbH & Co KG v. Republic of Ghana*, ICSID Case No. ARB/07/24, Award (18 June 2010) § 127.

With respect, equating establishment with 'initiation' and post-establishment with 'during performance' does not offer any real insight. What is required is a definition with greater detail:

> Establishment illegality means that the investor has committed serious illegal acts to procure the necessary legal permits or business assets to undertake its investment activity.

As with any proposed definition of general application in international investment law, the stipulations of the applicable investment treaty have priority.[46] For a legality requirement arising by default or an 'in accordance with the host state's law' provision, however, this definition can be applied.

Any illegal conduct not falling within this definition is an instance of post-establishment illegality. But post-establishment illegality does not encompass every form of, what is usually viewed as, investor misconduct. Most notably, this definition excludes conduct relating to the investor's ownership of the investment, which should be considered as a separate requirement for the arbitral tribunal's jurisdiction (the ownership requirement). Accordingly, if the investor's mere ownership of the investment is illegal under the host state's law, then that is a circumstance relevant to the ownership requirement.[47]

By contrast, 'investment establishment' directs arbitral tribunals' focus to the conduct relating to the acquisition of the legal permits and business assets for the investment's income-generating activities. For example, if the investment is a shareholding in a television company, then this legal permit would be its broadcast licence. For those investments which progress through an exploratory phase, investment activities also cover the work that defines that exploratory phase. But this expanded reading gives rise to a difficult question. Imagine, for example, that the investment is a shareholding in a company in the natural resources sector. To secure its exploration permit, the investor makes multiple fraudulent misrepresentations about its financial standing and the insurance policies that it must hold. After discovering a large deposit, it seeks to upgrade to a production permit. As its financial position has dramatically improved, it no longer needs to resort to fraudulent misrepresentations. Accordingly, while the investment activities for the exploratory phase are stained with illegality, the investment activities for the income-generating phase are not, with the consequential question being: does this stain remain with the investment? Following the general principle that subsequent lawful conduct does not exculpate the performer of wrongful conduct from the

---

[46] *Libya v. Chad* [1994] ICJ Reports 6, Judgment (3 February 1994) § 41; Crawford, 'Treaty and Contract', 355.
[47] Kalicki and others, 'Appropriate Remedies', 722; Schill, 'Illegal Investments', 295.

consequences thereof,[48] this subsequent lawful conduct with respect to the production permit should not be seen as cleaning the stain.

The conceptual closeness of the legality requirement and the investment approval requirement makes the distinction harder to draw, as evidenced by arbitral tribunals' tendency to conflate them.[49] This distinction, however, is not illusory. While the legality requirement focuses on the legality of the investor's activities leading up to the establishment of its investment, the investment approval requirement examines whether the host state has admitted the specific investment under any applicable investment approval laws. The satisfaction of one does not necessarily entail the satisfaction of the other. For example, while the investor may be able to establish that its capacities are such that it can build and operate a power plant with the result that it should be granted the relevant permit, the host state may refuse to admit the investment because the investor is ultimately controlled by a hostile state.[50] Another alleged point of distinction is that the investor must strictly comply with the host state's investment approval laws,[51] whereas, as argued below, certain establishment illegalities do not necessarily operate to deprive the arbitral tribunal of jurisdiction. The chance to opine on this question came to the arbitral tribunal in *Philip Morris v. Australia*, although it decided that the rules that allegedly acted as investment approval laws were not properly classified as 'mandatory', seemingly indicating that they were not legal rules at all.[52]

1.2.2.2 *Meaning of Establishment Illegality*
Proving establishment illegality requires more than merely proving that the investment's establishment was tainted with illegality. Synthetising from the numerous arbitral awards in which this question is addressed, it is apparent that the illegal conduct must be serious. This seriousness qualifier aims to create proportionality between the outcome and the illegality.[53] A prominent example comes from *World Duty Free v. Kenya*, where it was implicitly held that a USD 2 million bribe to the host state's president to procure a permit to open retail outlets at an airport breached the seriousness threshold.[54] Similarly,

---

48 See further section 1.1 of chapter 2. In essence, conduct that does not form part of the factual matrix in which the wrongful conduct was performed has no relevance to the wrongfulness of that conduct.
49 For a list of these arbitral awards, see Brown, 'Regulation of Foreign Direct Investment', 315.
50 For example, in Australia investments may not be admitted if they are deemed to be 'contrary to the national interest'; see Foreign Acquisitions and Takeovers Act 1975 (Australia) s. 67(1)(b).
51 Brown, 'Regulation of Foreign Direct Investment', 316.
52 *Philip Morris v. Australia*, Award on Jurisdiction and Admissibility § 516.
53 Hepburn, 'In Accordance with *Which* Host State Laws?', 546.
54 *World Duty Free Company Limited v. The Republic of Kenya*, ICSID Case No. ARB/00/7, Award (4 October 2006) § 180.

in *Churchill Mining v. Indonesia*, an associate of the investor was found to have implemented an elaborate scheme to forge mining exploration and production permits for the investor's benefit.[55] By contrast, in *Tokelés v. Ukraine*, the investor allegedly failed to correctly designate the legal form of his operating company when it was registered and also failed to properly formalise certain corporate documents.[56] Without deciding whether these allegations were proven, the arbitral tribunal ruled that such 'minor errors' were not sufficiently serious.[57]

From *World Duty Free v. Kenya* and *Churchill Mining v. Indonesia*, it can be inferred, respectively, that both corruption and fraud are potentially serious illegalities. This observation is not particularly insightful, however, because both concepts are scalar; in other words, forging exploration permits is on a very different plane compared to, for example, embellishing the curriculum vitae of the investor's chief executive officer. What are needed are more objective markers for seriousness. For this purpose, inspiration can be drawn from the factors that explain why the legality requirement is universally applicable. The first of these is that the illegality must have been necessary for the investment's existence. Applying the test outlined for this element to the curriculum vitae embellishment example, if the host state would have granted the investor the relevant permit even if the curriculum vitae was accurate, then the illegal conduct is not serious. For cases where the illegal conduct affects the exploratory phase, this requirement will be satisfied if the illegal conduct was indirectly necessary for the legal permits needed for the income-generating phase.

The second requirement provides that the investor's illegal conduct must act as a negative force on the host state's economic development.[58] Adding to what has been written above on the meaning of undermining economic development, it is worth looking at what this does not cover. As an example, suppose that the investor tables the highest bid for the relevant legal permit, but bribes a governmental officer to ignore the fact that it has not taken out all the requisite insurance policies for performing the investment activities. This is not serious establishment illegality for the simple reason that it does not inflict any economic harm on the host state. This conduct would be classified as post-establishment illegality as it does not vitiate the host state's

---

[55] *Churchill Mining v. Indonesia* § 528.

[56] *Tokios Tokelés v. Ukraine*, ICSID Case No. ARB/02/18, Decision on Jurisdiction (29 April 2004) § 83.

[57] Ibid. § 86.

[58] The inspiration for this requirement comes from *Kim v. Uzbekistan*. There, the arbitral tribunal held that a denial of jurisdiction on the basis of illegality could only be justified if a 'significant interest' of the host state was compromised, see *Vladislav Kim and others v. Republic of Uzbekistan*, ICSID Case No. ARB/13/6, Decision on Jurisdiction (8 March 2017) § 413.

consent.[59] This classification means that this conduct is not relevant to jurisdiction; it would be remedied by ordering the investor to pay gains-based damages to the host state,[60] with the host state's court being left to decide what (criminal) consequences should follow for the persons associated with the investor who effected the bribery.[61] How the proposed jurisprudence applies to this case might prompt the thought of using the same method for all cases of illegal conduct performed by the investor. But as serious establishment illegality revolves around proof of harm to the host state's economy, it represents a breach of the bargain at the core of international investment law.[62] For this reason, it warrants a graver response: the arbitral tribunal's lack of jurisdiction.

2 INVESTMENT REPRISAL AND POST-ESTABLISHMENT ILLEGALITY – LEGAL CONTENT AND ATTRIBUTION

Before delving into the details of their legal content, a disclaimer needs to be issued: the following analysis assumes that investment reprisal and post-establishment illegality are creatures that have evolved from the general principles of law source, as opposed to being treaty-based concepts. If a plea is based on a treaty provision that contains a rule resembling either investment reprisal or post-establishment illegality, then its stipulations dictate the relevant legal content. But as concepts growing out of this source, investment reprisal and post-establishment illegality should be constituted by two similar legal elements: one legal element on the requisite nature of the investor's conduct and another that links this conduct to the investment dispute. The advantage that this analysis benefits from, compared to mismanagement, is the availability of a number of arbitral awards capable of informing the meaning of these legal elements.

2.1 *The Nature of the Conduct Legal Element*

2.1.1 Investment Reprisal – Affront to State Sovereignty

Much of this arbitral case law, however, inadequately qualifies these legal elements – a fact most evident with respect to the first legal element of

---

[59] See Schill, 'Illegal Investments', 290.

[60] See section 2.3.4 below for an explanation of why gains-based damages would be awarded.

[61] For this purpose, a distinction is made between the legal order that affects an investment, which is a matter for the arbitral tribunal in investment arbitration, and any other legal orders that affect the investor's directors and officers, such as criminal sanctions ordered by the host state's courts; see further section 2.3.4 below.

[62] See Salacuse and Sullivan, 'Do BITs Really Work?', 77.

investment reprisal. The relevant question is: what makes the investor's conduct wrongful? Two of the leading cases, *Yukos v. Russia*[63] and *Occidental v. Ecuador*,[64] seem to indicate that this wrongfulness is created by the investor's fault, a view which finds support in Article 39 of the ILC Articles on State Responsibility.[65] But designating fault as the proper criterion is somewhat nonsensical. Unlike mismanagement, investment reprisal, as a form of provocation, focuses on the host state's state of mind, with the result being that the main question is whether the investor's conduct reaches some minimum level of objective wrongfulness, not whether the investor foresees that that conduct will cause the host state to react in the way that it does. Without this minimum level, provocation can too readily be used as a licence to breach.

To reach that minimum level, the requisite standard might be the breach of a liability rule of the host state's domestic law. An example of such conduct can be found in *Copper Mesa v. Ecuador*. There, the arbitral tribunal found that the investor's premeditated conduct of firing guns and spraying mace[66] at those opposed to its investment had contributed 30 per cent to its final investment loss.[67] Following this precedent, breaches of domestic law might constitute the requisite wrongful conduct that activates a plea of investment reprisal, but, for the reasons that follow, this is not a conclusion that should be readily subscribed to. First, investment reprisal should only apply in circumstances where the host state has no other course of action available to it in pursuing justice for the investor's illegality.[68] In most cases where the investor has breached a rule of domestic law, the relevant rule should specify some action that the host state can implement in response to it. Second, the defence of post-establishment illegality has been developed with a view to its application in cases where the investor has breached the host state's domestic law. Third, and most significantly, considering the exceptional nature of investment reprisal as a permitted form of self-help, it should only apply in circumstances where the investor's misconduct is particularly egregious, which will not usually be the case with mere breaches of domestic law.

What this means is that the conduct forming the basis of a plea of investment reprisal must be objectively wrongful, but not necessarily illegal. The investor's misconduct in *Yukos v. Russia* met this description. In its conclusion on contributory fault, the arbitral tribunal not only described the investor's

---

[63] *Yukos v. Russia* § 1608.

[64] *Occidental v. Ecuador*, Award § 380.

[65] According to that provision, the investor's conduct must be either 'wilful' or 'negligent'; see ILC Articles on State Responsibility, Art. 39.

[66] *Copper Mesa v. Ecuador* § 6.99.

[67] Ibid. § 6.133.

[68] See section 1.1.2 above.

conduct as illegal,[69] but also emphasised that it was abusive[70] and 'questionable'.[71] There is likely to be an objection that measuring wrongfulness without reference to a predetermined standard makes this defence overly vague and, for that reason, open to misuse. Yet, as explained in the paragraph immediately below, strict parameters guide what amounts to wrongful conduct for the purpose of investment reprisal. Additionally, making this element more open-ended offers a concession to host states whose legal systems are still developing to act against (seriously) errant investors.

This introduces the next task: defining what the investor's wrongful conduct should look like. As indicated by the heading, it should amount to an 'affront to state sovereignty', a concept comprising two elements. The first of these is that the investor's conduct has to harm the host state. Ostensibly, this is not controversial, until it is compared with the conception of reprisal on which investment reprisal is based. According to Christian Wolff,[72] reprisal arose when a person (the investor) harmed either the state or its citizens. Investment reprisal, however, excludes harm to the host state's citizens because such persons should have legal recourse against the investor in the host state's courts and, potentially, other domestic courts, remembering that investment reprisal should only be available if there is no other avenue for seeking justice against the relevant wrongdoer. Additionally, it is unclear how a finding of investment reprisal could deliver justice to the affected citizens as this concept ultimately acts to reduce the host state's liability, as opposed to, for example, giving those persons a right to claim compensation.[73] Finally, it presents a risk of double recovery because, on top of the partial liability that it assumes on a finding of investment reprisal, the investor might have to pay compensation to those persons if they bring a successful claim in a domestic court.

The findings in *Yukos v. Russia* and *Occidental v. Ecuador* validate this principle. With its 'tax minimisation scheme' in the former case, the investor managed to avoid paying significant amounts of taxes to Russia. In the latter, the investor farmed out some of its obligations under a contract with Ecuador's

---

[69]   *Yukos v. Russia* § 1611.
[70]   Ibid. § 1612.
[71]   Ibid. § 1634.
[72]   Wolff, 'Jus Gentium', 302, cited from Spiegel, 'Origin and Development of Denial of Justice', 74.
[73]   A problem that the arbitral tribunal alluded to in *Urbaser S.A. and Consorcio de Aguas Bilbao Bizkaia, Bilbao Biskaia Ur Partzuergoa v. The Argentine Republic*, ICSID Case No. ARB/07/26, Award (8 December 2016) ('*Urbaser v. Argentina*') § 1220.

state-owned oil company without Ecuador's consent, which was a clear breach of Ecuadorian law, thereby:[74]

> prevent[ing] the Respondent from exercising, in a formal way, its sovereign right to vet and approve [the third person] as the transferee of those rights and, even more importantly on the facts of the present case, to vet any other unknown investor to which [the third person] could eventually transfer its rights.

This extract introduces the second principle: the investor's conduct must breach one of the host state's sovereign rights.[75] How exactly this might occur is a question that will be deliberately left open so as to allow it to be moulded to the facts of future disputes, but it should be found when the investor's conduct is an assumption of power traditionally reserved to states. For example, in *Copper Mesa v. Ecuador* the investor's employment of a private security company and its resort to violence broke the host state's monopoly on violence.[76] Equally, as indicated in the extract above, the investor's conduct in *Occidental v. Ecuador* denied Ecuador the chance to exercise its sovereign right to determine who extracted its natural resources. Establishing a breach of Russia's sovereignty on the facts of *Yukos v. Russia* is more difficult. It could be argued that the fraudulent nature[77] of the investor's misconduct breached Russia's sovereign right to collect taxes, but the evidence suggests that the investor was transparent regarding its tax minimisation strategy.[78] What this shows is that post-establishment illegality should have been pleaded in *Yukos v. Russia* – a conclusion further reinforced by the finding in section 2.2.1 below on the application of the motivation legal element to the facts of this case. One case where this legal element could not have been made out was *Bear Creek v. Peru*. There, Peru unsuccessfully (by majority) contended that the investor contributed in numerous ways, most particularly by failing to obtain a social licence from the local communities where it operated. This caused community protests and eventually Peru's breach. As explained in more detail in section 2.2.1.2 below, the investor's conduct is an example of a cause-prevention omission, a concept introduced in section 4.1.2.1 of chapter 3; in other words, the investor failed to stop the communities from protesting, which in turn prompted Peru to

---

[74] *Occidental v. Ecuador*, Award § 679.
[75] Whiteman, *Damages*, 80–81.
[76] The key ingredient of modern statehood; see Weber, *Economy and Society*, 54.
[77] This was the contention of Russia; see *Yukos v. Russia* §§ 1291 and 1307.
[78] Ibid. § 486.

breach. For the purposes of applying this legal element, the protesting is the relevant conduct that needs to be assessed because the investor merely assumes causal responsibility for this conduct, meaning that the latter remains a cause in the causal constellation for Peru's breach.[79] For this case, there is no difficulty in concluding that this protesting was not an affront to Peru because the citizens were merely exercising their right to freedom of speech.

2.1.2 Post-Establishment Illegality – Breach of a Liability Rule

As its name suggests, the conduct legal conduct for post-establishment illegality is stricter because it requires the breach of a liability rule. As opposed to investment reprisal, whose existence is predicated on the undeveloped state of international investment law, post-establishment illegality is a concept that seeks to promote the rule of law, particularly as it applies to the investor. For this reason, it is activated by a breach of an established liability rule applicable to the investor. Such liability rules can be potentially sourced from a contract between the investor and the host state, the host state's domestic law, or international law, provided that these sources are designated as applicable substantive laws in respect of the dispute. This proviso raises a potential complication, but it can be resolved if the applicable investment treaty contains a governing law clause.[80] Even where such a clause was absent, arbitral tribunals have generally been willing to apply the host state's domestic law[81] and general international law[82] in investment arbitrations.

2.1.2.1 *Liability Rules in Host State's Domestic Law*
If the liability rule originates from the host state's domestic law, the arbitral tribunal will have to confront the task of determining whether this rule is a valid one. The case of *Yukos v. Russia* aptly demonstrates this. In addition to its effective plea of investment reprisal, Russia alleged that the investor had breached the 'bad faith taxpayer' doctrine under Russian law.[83] This allegation failed to find favour with the arbitral tribunal as it reasoned that there were

---

[79] See sections 4.1.2.3 and 4.4.1 of chapter 3. In this respect, cause-prevention omissions can be compared with legal imperatives as the latter subsume the cause which they relate, meaning that they become part of the relevant causal constellation, see section 4.4.1.1 of chapter 3.
[80] See, for example, Austria-Macedonia BIT, Art. 21.
[81] Banifatemi, 'Law Applicable in Investment Treaty Arbitration', 193; Petersmann, 'Introduction and Summary', 12.
[82] McLachlan and others, *International Investment Arbitration*, § 1.63.
[83] See *Yukos v. Russia* § 288 for an overview of the relevant 'law'.

serious doubts as to the doctrine's existence and content.[84] With this finding, the arbitral tribunal effectively ruled that the doctrine was not a valid one for reasons of (lack of) legality. Scholars of legal philosophy will have noted that the arbitral tribunal's reasons for not recognising the doctrine correspond to the second ('duly promulgated')[85] and fourth ('minimally clear and intelligible')[86] principles of Lon Fuller's 'principles of legality'. This correspondence with Fuller's principles is presumably a coincidence, but they are ideally suited to the task of determining a liability rule's validity. One obvious situation when the relevant rule should be classified as invalid for this purpose is when it violates one of the applicable investment treaty's standards. For example, if the host state enacts a rule that unfairly discriminates against the investor, thereby breaching one of the discrimination-based rules in the applicable investment treaty, and the investor commits numerous breaches of this rule, those breaches should not be the basis of a plea of post-establishment illegality.

2.1.2.2 *Liability Rules from International Law*

Validity issues are also likely to arise if the relevant liability rule, which the host state alleges that the investor has breached, hails from international law, most particularly if its doctrinal foundations are grounded in the general principles of law or customary international law. The human rights norms, which form part of customary international law, usually do not suffer from this potential defect.[87] These norms should be classified as liability rules because, like all liability rules, they impose conduct obligations on their subjects, with the orthodox view being that only states can assume such obligations.[88] If this is true, human rights norms cannot provide a basis for a plea of post-establishment illegality. In the recent past, however, there has been a concerted effort to extend human rights obligations to non-state entities, including investors in international investment law,[89] which lays the foundations for the question that the following paragraphs are preoccupied with: can investors be made subject to human rights norms?

This question arose in *Urbaser v. Argentina*.[90] There, the investor held a shareholding in a company that had signed an investment contract with

---

[84] Ibid. § 292.
[85] Fuller, *Morality of Law*, 49.
[86] Ibid. 63.
[87] See, for example, the arbitral tribunal's recognition of the human right of access to clean water in *Urbaser v. Argentina* § 1205.
[88] Clapham, *Human Rights Obligations*, 25.
[89] For a list of these sources, see Dumberry and Dumas-Aubin, 'How to Impose Human Rights Obligations?', fn. 3.
[90] For the arbitral tribunal's summary of the facts, see *Urbaser v. Argentina* § 34.

the Province of Buenos Aires.[91] That contract provided that the provincial government would grant this operating company a permit to supply water and sewerage services, and in return the company would make investments to upgrade the existing infrastructure for these services. As the relationship between the investor and the provincial government began to deteriorate, the investor failed to perform. It was this failure that was said to be in breach of the human right of access to clean water.[92]

In making this counterclaim, the host state successfully navigated some complicated questions regarding the arbitral tribunal's jurisdiction to entertain it.[93] Most significantly, the arbitral tribunal agreed that investors were in principle subject to human rights norms,[94] particularly those norms taking the form of prohibitions.[95] But for norms that take the form of directives, other circumstances must exist before an investor can assume liability for them, with the arbitral tribunal noting that the human right of access to clean water is such a norm because it requires performance on the part of its obligor. What the arbitral tribunal made clear is that a similar performance obligation in the investment contract was not such a circumstance.[96] If it were otherwise, host states would be able to dress up their contract-based counterclaims in human rights clothing to avoid the shortcomings that afflict such contract-based counterclaims, such as the host state's waiver of the investor's breach.[97] The arbitral tribunal rightly refused to let the host state indulge in this fiction.

This rejection begs the question: what circumstance could transfer a host state's human rights obligation to an investor? The arbitral tribunal's reasoning indicates that if Argentina could have established that the human right of access to clean water was a 'governmental primary focus',[98] then that factor and the investor's performance obligation under the investment contract could have combined to transfer liability to the investor. Argentina's lackadaisical attitude towards the investor's non-performance and its implicit approval thereof meant that this human right could not be classified as a governmental primary focus.[99]

---

[91]   Ibid. § 63.
[92]   Ibid. § 1137.
[93]   Ibid. § 1155.
[94]   See also Reiner and Schreuer, 'Human Rights', 84.
[95]   *Urbaser v. Argentina* § 1210.
[96]   Ibid. § 1210.
[97]   Ibid. § 1212.
[98]   Ibid. § 1214.
[99]   Ibid. § 1219.

2.1.2.3 *Meaning of Post-Establishment*

The other aspect of this legal element is that the illegality must be committed 'post-establishment'. This includes any conduct not falling within the definition of establishment illegality and any non-serious establishment illegality.[100] This latter inclusion makes post-establishment slight misleading, but this should not be overdramatised because it is a cosmetic matter. It is more important to recognise that post-establishment illegality comes in two forms. The most egregious is what is called 'core illegality'. Core illegality arises where the main income-generating activity for the investment is illegal under the host state's law at the time of the performance of that activity. An example of such a case would be where the investment is a shareholding in a company that sells alcohol in a state where its consumption is criminal. Where it arises, the defence of post-establishment illegality affords the host state a complete defence, which is the main point of distinction between this form and the form that this monograph is principally concerned with, peripheral illegality. This is illegal conduct that supports the main income-generating activity. Its occurrence does not offer the host state a complete defence, but a partial defence, as detailed in section 2.3.4 below. Given the greater frequency of peripheral illegality, the analyses of this monograph assume that it is the form of post-establishment illegality in play when discussing the application of the defence of post-establishment illegality. Finally, post-establishment does not include any conduct relating to the proceedings.[101] If an investor engages in conduct that breaches the applicable procedural rules, that is a matter best dealt with through appropriate costs orders.

2.2 *The Link Legal Element*

2.2.1 Investment Reprisal – Motivation for Host State's Breach

As a form of provocation, it follows that investment reprisal's link legal element requires that the investor's affront to state sovereignty must have motivated the host state's breach. The key concept here is 'motivate'. That a natural person can be motivated to act is obvious, but the same idea with respect to a state is factually nonsensical. Overcoming this problem necessitates recourse to the doctrine on the imputation of knowledge, or, more accurately for this

---

[100] For explanations of these concepts, see sections 1.2.2.1 and 1.2.2.2 above.

[101] For an example of a case where the host state sought to argue that the investor's alleged misconduct in the arbitral proceedings was an instance of post-establishment illegality, see *Olin v. Libya*. The arbitral tribunal summarily dismissed this plea; see *Olin Holdings Ltd v. Libya*, ICC Case No. 20355/MCP, Final Award (25 May 2018) § 514.

legal element, the imputation of motivation. Compared to the voluminous amounts of jurisprudence available on this doctrine in company law, there is a dearth of jurisprudence in international law. The probable explanation for this is the general principle that the liability rules of international law by default do not contain fault legal elements.[102]

2.2.1.1 *Imputation of Motivation to Host State*

On account of this, the first question that needs to be addressed is: which person's motivation can be imputed to the host state? One ground rule guides the answer to this question: motivation consists of two elements, one being the knowledge of the investor's conduct, and the other being that this conduct must cause the host state's breach. These elements are indivisible. They must be concentrated in one person because it is illogical that a host state could be motivated where the person who pulls the levers to effect the breach acts not on knowledge that he or she has, but on another person's knowledge of the investor's conduct. This narrows the list of candidates from whom motivation can be imputed to the host state to one: the person who pulls the levers. For example, in *Occidental v. Ecuador*, it was Ecuador's Minister of Energy and Mines who cancelled the participation between the investor and Ecuador,[103] meaning that it was the minister who needed the requisite knowledge.

In most cases, there should be no controversy over who this person is. The only wrinkle involves cases where the host state's legislature, which is constituted by a parliament, effects its breach. The question is: if only some members of the parliament know of the investor's conduct and vote on the basis of it, can their motivation be imputed to the host state? The question is really in the realm of the theoretical because it would be extremely unlikely that these members would not disclose what they knew about the investor. For that reason, no analysis is dedicated to this question, but if pressed to answer it, it is submitted that the person with this knowledge would have to form part of the voting block that brings the relevant law into being for his or her motivation to be imputed.

2.2.1.2 *Proving Motivation*

After identifying the person from whom the host state's motivation can be imputed, the next task is to collect the evidence that proves this person's motivation. From a legal perspective, what is most interesting about that process is whether the investor's affront needs to be the sole reason for acting. The arbitral

---

[102] ILC Articles on State Responsibility (with commentaries), Art. 2 (cmt 10).
[103] *Occidental v. Ecuador*, Award § 199.

tribunals in both *Yukos v. Russia* and *Occidental v. Ecuador* indicate that other factors may influence the decision. In the former, the arbitral tribunal found that Russia's primary reason for acting was to neutralise the political ambitions of the investor's chief executive officer, Mikhail Khordorkovsky.[104] The investor's tax avoidance scheme was a matter of secondary importance[105] as it was merely a 'pretextual justification'.[106] This description is doctrinally troubling. Literally, it means that the investor's conduct need not have any causal connection to the host state's conduct, thereby completely devaluing this legal element. Moreover, it begins to confuse investment reprisal with post-establishment illegality.[107]

The arbitral tribunal in *Occidental v. Ecuador* fortunately respected the need for this causal connection. However, it unhelpfully added that the investor's conduct must be a 'material and significant'[108] reason for the host state's breach – an addition that was justified with reference to the commentary attaching to Article 39 of the ILC Articles on State Responsibility[109] and one that was endorsed by the arbitral tribunal in *Copper Mesa v. Ecuador*.[110] Unsurprisingly, both the arbitral tribunal and the International Law Commission made no attempt to illuminate the meaning of 'material and significant',[111] which was a telling indictment of its incurable vagueness. Rather than engaging in the illusory task of grading a cause's potency, arbitral tribunals would be better served by sticking to the principle that causality is binary: it exists or it does not.

Finally, it is worth looking at the causation issue that arose in *Bear Creek v. Peru*. In its very concise dismissal of Peru's plea, the arbitral tribunal by

---

[104] *Yukos v. Russia* § 811.

[105] That the investor's tax practices were a pretext is corroborated by evidence that, one, the host state published information to make its expropriation, on the basis of the investor's conduct, publicly acceptable and, two, the host state's attempts to fabricate evidence relating to the investor's conduct; see ibid. § 146 and § 516.

[106] Ibid. § 1614–1615.

[107] As noted by Ernest Weinrib, lack of causality is one basis on which the domestic law concept of illegality (post-establishment illegality) can be distinguished from contributory/comparative negligence (investment reprisal), as it is known in Anglo-American tort law; see Weinrib, 'Illegality as a Tort Defence', 36.

[108] *Occidental v. Ecuador*, Award § 670.

[109] ILC Articles on State Responsibility (with commentaries), Art. 39 (cmt 5). In *Occidental v. Ecuador* the arbitral tribunal referred to the decision on annulment in *MTD v. Chile* – see *Occidental v. Ecuador*, Award fn. 117 – although it later noted that the 'material and significant' requirement came from the ILC Articles on State Responsibility; see *Occidental v. Ecuador*, Award § 673.

[110] *Copper Mesa v. Ecuador* § 6.97.

[111] The main scholarly commentary on Article 39 of the ILC Articles on State Responsibility (Moutier-Lopet, 'Contribution to the Injury') is also silent on how to measure degrees of causality.

majority ruled that the investor did not contribute to its loss.[112] Unfortunately, the arbitral tribunal did not specify its reasons for this ruling, but if the theory on causation developed in chapter 3 was applied, the result might have been different. Following that theory, the investor can become causally responsible for the citizens' conduct if the investor's conduct amounts to a cause-prevention omission. As detailed in 4.1.2.1 of chapter 3, a cause-prevention omission can be established if the four elements of preventability, capacity, awareness, and special relationship are present. The issue in this case would be whether there was a special relationship between the investor and the citizens. As the investor did not acknowledge this relationship, it could have only arisen by imposition of law and considering that there were consultation obligations indirectly applicable to the investor pursuant to Article 17 of the ILO Convention 169, there is an arguable case that it implicitly arose.

2.2.2 Post-Establishment Illegality – Beneficial Relationship to the Investment

By contrast, the link legal element for post-establishment illegality merely requires that the investor's conduct benefit its investment, with this beneficial relationship being established if this conduct increases the investment's value or otherwise makes its operation easier. An example of the latter would arise where the investor bribes a governmental inspector to overlook the fact that it does not provide its employees with the required training for their work.

The difficulty that this legal element faces is that it lacks secure doctrinal foundations. None of the arbitral awards or academic commentary mentions it, although good reasons can be summoned to support its recognition. First, it ensures that the investor's conduct is properly connected to the dispute, which is the general reason for the inclusion of this legal element in the domestic law equivalents of post-establishment illegality. Second, and most significantly, it gives effect to the profit element of the general principle of law from which it originates, namely that a person should not profit from his or her own illegality.

2.3 *Investment Reprisal and Post-Establishment Illegality – Apportionment*

Unless there is core illegality as described in section 2.1.2.3 above, a finding of either investment reprisal or post-establishment illegality entails the apportionment of liability – a task that arbitral tribunals have struggled with. At

---

[112] *Bear Creek v. Peru* §568.

least with regard to investment reprisal, the percentage reduction method holds sway. The application of this method in the relevant cases follows the same rudimentary reasoning pattern, arguing as follows: that the annulment committee in *MTD v. Chile* held that arbitral tribunals enjoy much discretion when apportioning;[113] that the arbitral tribunal has 'carefully considered the facts';[114] and that the arbitral tribunal thinks that α per cent is an appropriate reduction,[115] given that the investor's conduct was a material and significance cause of its loss.[116] For *Yukos v. Russia*, *Occidental v. Ecuador*, and *Copper Mesa v. Ecuador*, these amounts were 25,[117] 30,[118] and 30 per cent,[119] respectively.[120]

It is suspected that what underlies this approach is a defeatist attitude. That attitude holds that a more scientific method cannot be developed,[121] thus justifying what this approach actually entails: guesswork.[122] This criticism does not imply that precision is expected, but merely that apportionment must be a reason-based exercise. But this point introduces an even more troubling feature of the current approach: the only principle that seemingly guides arbitral tribunals is that the investor is deserving of punishment. This is most clearly exhibited in *Occidental v. Ecuador*, where the arbitral tribunal commented that the investor 'should pay a price'[123] – an outcome that it delivered because the investor's 'punishment' of losing USD 589,875,000, the amount deducted from its final recovery, far exceeded any harm sustained by Ecuador. Similarly, in *Copper Mesa v. Ecuador*, the reduction was set at USD 4,793,398.20, an amount that bore no relationship to any harm suffered by the host state or those opposed to the investor's investment. The decision in *Yukos v. Russia* seemingly bucks the trend because the investor's reduction came to approximately

---

[113] *Yukos v. Russia* § 1636; *Occidental v. Ecuador*, Award § 686; *Copper Mesa v. Ecuador* § 6.96.

[114] *Yukos v. Russia* § 1637; *Occidental v. Ecuador*, Award § 687; *Copper Mesa v. Ecuador* § 6.102.

[115] *Yukos v. Russia* § 1637; *Occidental v. Ecuador*, Award § 687; *Copper Mesa v. Ecuador* § 6.102.

[116] *Occidental v. Ecuador*, Award § 672 and *Bear Creek v. Republic of Peru*, ICSID Case No. ARB/14/21, Partial Dissenting Opinion of Professor Philippe Sands QC (12 September 2017) § 39 ('*Bear Creek v. Peru*, Dissent').

[117] *Yukos v. Russia* § 1637.

[118] *Occidental v. Ecuador*, Award § 687. Although in her dissenting opinion, Arbitrator Stern indicated that she would have reduced Ecuador's liability by 50 per cent, see *Occidental Petroleum Corporation and Occidental Exploration and Production Company v. The Republic of Ecuador*, ICSID Case No. ARB/06/11, Dissenting Opinion (20 September 2012) § 8.

[119] *Copper Mesa v. Ecuador* § 6.102.

[120] In the dissenting opinion in *Bear Creek v. Peru*, an effective finding of investment reprisal was also made. On the basis of that finding, it was proposed that Peru's liability be reduced to 50%, see *Bear Creek v. Peru*, Dissent § 39.

[121] For a similar sentiment, see Sabahi and Duggal, 'Occidental Petroleum v. Ecuador', 289.

[122] See Cardenas Garcia, 'Era of Petroleum Arbitration Mega Cases', 583.

[123] *Occidental v. Ecuador*, Award § 680.

USD 16,673,622,000, as compared to the tax amount of approximately USD 24,000,000,000, including interest and fines, which Russia controversially[124] alleged was owed by the investor.[125]

2.3.1 Reformulating Apportionment for Investment Reprisal

The apportionments in *Occidental v. Ecuador* and *Copper Mesa v. Ecuador* effectively granted punitive damages in favour of the host states. The problem with this is that arbitral tribunals presumably lack competence to issue such orders. Investment treaties rarely specify an arbitral tribunal's competence with respect to remedies,[126] but the conventional view from the jurisprudence of general international law supports this presumption. Some objections can be marshalled against the dominance of that view, however, starting with the arbitral tribunal's dictum in *Siag v. Egypt*:[127]

> The potential availability of punitive damages, or a punitive 'enhance-ment' of compensatory damages, is a matter of some controversy in inter-national law, as indeed the Claimants acknowledged. The Tribunal notes that the prevailing view of the Iran-United States Claims Tribunal appears to have been that punitive damages are not available and *it appears that the recovery of punitive or moral damages is reserved for extreme cases of egregious behaviour.*

More substantively, the idea that underpins the exclusion of punitive damages – that any such award breaches the principle of sovereign equality – has no application to investors. In response to these objections, two counter-arguments can be raised. Primarily, some jurisdictions subscribe to the theory that ordering punishments is a privilege only enjoyed by courts, meaning that any arbitral awards making such orders are likely to be unenforceable.[128] Additionally, when compensation proves to be an inadequate response to a breach, general international law envisions that satisfaction may be awarded as a supplementary remedy.[129] Ordering satisfaction could, for example, mean that the investor has to acknowledge the wrongfulness of its conduct and apologise to the host state for it.

---

[124] The investor claimed that this amount was highly inflated; see *Yukos v. Russia* § 93.

[125] Ibid. § 92.

[126] Sabahi, *Compensation and Restitution*, 63–64.

[127] *Waguih Elie George Siag and Clorinda Vecchi v. The Arab Republic of Egypt*, ICSID Case No. ARB/05/15, Award (1 June 2009) § 545 (footnotes omitted and emphasis added).

[128] Born, *International Commercial Arbitration*, 3679–3680.

[129] ILC Articles on State Responsibility, Art. 37(1).

In such moments, the best course of action is to revert to the fundamentals and rebuild a theory for apportionment from them. The starting foundation is that the host state's response (its measure of reprisal) has to be proportionate.[130] The challenge is to ascribe the proper meaning to 'proportionate response' in this context. From the analysis immediately above, it follows that a proportionate response is not one that exacts 'an eye for an eye', an attitude which might explain arbitral tribunals' tendency to 'proportionately punish' the investor. Rather, it is proposed that a proportionate response equates to what is called 'proportionate restitution', which reflects Vattel's original conception of reprisal as a tool for gaining 'full satisfaction'.[131]

2.3.2 An Interpretation of Full Satisfaction

What 'full satisfaction' means is open to interpretation, but, with general international law's principal remedies being restitution[132] and cessation,[133] the working definition is: obliging the investor to reasonably recreate the circumstances that existed before the investor performed its affront to the host state's sovereignty[134] and/or taking reasonable steps to ensure that such conduct is not performed again. Applying this definition to *Yukos v. Russia*, the proportionate response would have been to collect the properly assessed unpaid tax obligations plus interest. For *Occidental v. Ecuador*, Ecuador should have ordered the investor to cancel the farmout contract and to deliver up any gains from this contract to the host state, thereby undoing the investor's benefit. For *Copper Mesa v. Ecuador*, proportionate restitution looks different because the investor's affront inflicted no harm on Ecuador, nor resulted in any gain for the investor. In such a case, the host state's response should be restricted to reasonable measures that aim to ensure the investor's conduct is not repeated, such as issuing an order prohibiting the use of weapons by the investor's personnel. These are apparently weak responses to the investors' misconduct in *Occidental v. Ecuador* and *Copper Mesa v. Ecuador*. In the former case, however, the investor deprived Ecuador of the opportunity to vet the investor's contracting party. Considering that the investor must have presumably still been liable under the participation contract for any malfeasance on the part

---

[130] Drawing much inspiration here from the jurisprudence on countermeasures; see Crawford, *State Responsibility*, 698.

[131] Vattel, *Law of Nations*, 228

[132] ILC Articles on State Responsibility (with commentaries), Art. 35 (cmt 3).

[133] Subscribing to the view that cessation is a remedy because its ordering follows the breach of a primary obligation; see Corten, 'Obligation of Cessation', 546.

[134] Crawford, *State Responsibility*, 510.

of its contracting party,[135] this deprivation had no legal significance. It only succeeded in creating a political storm[136] – a storm that it is feared adversely affected the arbitral tribunal's apportionment. As for the latter case, there was nothing to stop Ecuador from prosecuting the responsible persons in its criminal courts for their conduct.

For some cases, the response that achieves proportionate restitution is not readily identifiable. As an example, consider a case where a social media company sells personal information on its users, with their consent, to other companies, which then use that information to tailor their advertisements. For some time, a state hostile to the host state has had access to this information by hacking those other companies' databases. This hostile state uses this information to undermine the integrity of the host state's elections, with one favoured method being to flood the news feeds of users with disinformation that, considering their personal bias, they are likely to believe. The host state vows to take action against the social media company, which is bad news for the investor who has a substantial shareholding in this company. Rightly dismissing the idea of prohibiting social media as a disproportionate response, the host state proposes two possible responses: requiring that the social media company sell personal information only to companies that have robust security systems or generally prohibiting such sales. As the second response would deal a mortal blow to the value of the investor's shareholding, the first response might be preferred. But given the questionable effectiveness of this first response, the host state could legitimately opt for the second response because it is certain to achieve the intended outcome, which is preventing the nefarious use of users' personal information. The point is that host states should be accorded some latitude on how they recreate the circumstances that existed prior to the investor's affront.[137] This stance not only recognises that the host state can favour those responses that have a higher chance of recreating these circumstances, but also acknowledges that international investment law should not unduly restrict its sovereign autonomy.

---

[135] The investor argued that it alone remained liable under the participation contract, although the arbitral tribunal found that it was unnecessary to decide on the matter; see *Occidental v. Ecuador*, Award § 333.

[136] For further details of the political pressure exerted on Ecuador's government to act against the investor, see *Occidental v. Ecuador*, Award §§ 176–199.

[137] For an overview of the jurisprudence implicitly endorsing this approach, see Henckels, *Proportionality and Deference in Investor-State Arbitration* 140–142.

2.3.3 Excessive Reprisals

In the rare cases where the host state achieves proportionate restitution with its response, investment reprisal should act as a complete defence. But in most investment arbitrations, the host state's response will typically exceed proportionate restitution as an investment arbitration is unlikely to be initiated if the host state achieves proportionate restitution. In such cases the host state's notional liability starts at 100 per cent, in recognition of the fact that investment reprisal is a form of self-help that should not bestow any special benefits on the host state. This notional liability is subject to a reduction on account of the investor's affront. Considering that this reduction must not punish the investor, the factors that remain relevant to this reduction are, one, the gains that accrue to the investment on account of the investor's misconduct or, two, the losses that this misconduct inflicts on the host state. For example, if the investor had earned gains of USD 50,000,000 through its farmout contract in *Occidental v. Ecuador*, then the host state would have been liable for the investment loss in the amount of USD 2,309,500,000, as compared to the amount for which it was actually held liable, USD 1,769,625,000.[138]

As regards the losses that can form part of this reduction, it is worth emphasising that they must be losses for the host state. Accordingly, the injuries that the investor caused those persons opposed to their investment in *Copper Mesa v. Ecuador* cannot be considered in the apportionment of liability.[139] This exclusion is likely to incense host states, but sound doctrine supports it. First, by including such losses, the claims that the affected persons have against the investor are effectively assigned to the host state. If these claims are subsequently entertained by a court in the host state, the risk of double recovery arises. Additionally, the legal basis for assigning these claims to the host state is unclear. Second, arbitral tribunals in investment arbitrations should focus their remedial orders on the investment at the centre of the dispute, as opposed to seeking to render justice in other disputes.

2.3.4 Apportionment for Post-Establishment Illegality

Somewhat similar to cases of investment reprisal, apportioning liability in cases of post-establishment illegality involves the designation of a legal consequence for the investor's breach and setting that consequence off

---

[138] Ibid. § 876.

[139] This is a point on which investment reprisal differs from the original conception of reprisal in international law; see Vattel, *Law of Nations*, 228.

against the host state's liability. In cases where the relevant rule speci-
fies that a certain legal consequence must mandatorily follow its breach,
that designation is unproblematic. Importantly, this legal consequence
must be one that affects the investment, as opposed to the person who
actually committed the breach. With reference to the example in section
2.2.2 above where a governmental inspector is bribed, a legal consequence
affecting the investment would be the payment of a fine by the company in
which the investor has its shareholding (the investment), while a prosecution and subsequent criminal punishment for that company's chief executive officer is not.

2.3.4.1 *Disproportionate Legal Consequences for Breaches of International Law and Domestic Law*

The objection that this approach will likely encounter is that it will visit unfairness on the investor when the mandatorily applicable legal consequence
is disproportionate as measured against the wrongfulness of the investor's
misconduct. Yet, given that the rule of law requires congruence between a
breach and the legal consequence that follows it,[140] this objection should not
be entertained. This assumes that the rule is sourced from the host state's
domestic law, but the same conclusion holds true in respect of rules derived
from treaties. While both Grotius and Vattel advocated that the unfairness of a
treaty provision could render it invalid,[141] the consensus is that no unfair treaty
provision doctrine exists in general international law.[142]

   This objection holds more water if the legal consequence affecting the
investment applies at the host state's discretion. The source of the support
for this view is *Occidental v. Ecuador*. There, after finding that Ecuador
enjoyed some discretion as to what response it could adopt to the investor's
misconduct,[143] the arbitral tribunal ruled that ordering the investor to for-
feit its investment was a disproportionate legal consequence.[144] In cases
involving disproportionate legal consequences, post-establishment illegality
should act as a partial defence and the arbitral tribunal should apply the
principles outlined in section 2.3.3 above to apportion liability between the
disputants.

---

[140] See generally Fuller, *Morality of Law*, 81.
[141] Caflisch, 'Unequal Treaties', 52.
[142] Ibid., 80.
[143] *Occidental v. Ecuador*, Award § 424.
[144] Ibid. § 452.

2.3.4.2 *Disproportionate Legal Consequences for*
Investor-State Contract Breaches
Another troubling problem is the question of whether arbitral tribunals should give effect to disproportionate legal consequences that arise from a minor breach by the investor of a contract between it and the host state. Again, the assumption is that such legal consequence mandatorily applies and affects the investment. For example, suppose that a considerable portion of the host state's populace is gripped by a 'migrant crisis'. As part of a series measures aimed to alleviate this crisis, the host state announces that all contracts between it and foreign investors will include a 'local employment requirement'. This requirement provides that the investor must only employ local workers or engage local consultants, unless a foreign consultant/employee visa (difficult to obtain) is granted to it. If this provision is breached, a very substantial performance bond payable by the investor's parent company becomes due, which is a valid legal consequence under the contract's governing law (the host state's law). In a subsequent dispute between the investor and the host state it emerges that the investor breached this provision on multiple occasions by flying in a consultant from its head office for high-level advice on the investment.

The host state implores the arbitral tribunal to order that the investor's parent company, which is also a party to the investment arbitration, pay the performance bond. It supports this claim by constantly emphasising that freedom of contract demands that the contract's clear terms be respected. Furthermore, as the investor forms part of a large corporate group, it cannot plead that it is an unsophisticated party, thereby deserving some relief from the dictates of freedom of contract. This is a powerful argument and it raises a difficult question: what is the role of freedom of contract in international investment law?

This monograph cannot comprehensively answer this question, although the working assumption is that freedom of contract is generally applicable. What the following analysis focuses on is a potential exception to its general application: the investor's lack of consent on account of the host state's coercion. This is not a case where one of the investor's directors signed the contract while a governmental officer held a gun to his or her head, but rather a case where the investor unfairly had to agree to include the local consultant/ employee provision. In reality, there are few cases where a person had to agree because there is usually the simple alternative not to contract. That alternative is discounted, however, if it will likely lead to some negative outcome, relative to any consequences of contracting, for the affected person. For example,[145] a

---

[145] Example taken from Trebilcock, *Limits of Freedom of Contract*, 87.

person is on a sinking boat in the middle of an ocean. By chance, a ship full of pirates sails close by and they propose the following contract: a passage to safety in exchange for USD 5,000,000. After initially balking, the deal is agreed to as this person reasons that losing USD 5,000,000 is better than losing one's life.

The difficulty for the investor is that the negative consequence it faces is losing out on the (substantial) revenue stream that the contract with the host state would have created – a consequence that seemingly pales in comparison to loss of life. For a company, however, revenue flow is its lifeblood, which serves as the first plank for the conclusion that the investor was coerced into including the local consultant/employee provision. What stands most prominently in the way of that conclusion is the objection that, following this reasoning, all contracts that any company signs are the result of coercion. Two reasons militate against that objection.

First, assuming that the investment is a large-scale piece of transport infrastructure, such as an airport, the investor will only have a limited market for its services. Accordingly, if the host state proposes terms on the airport's construction that the investor finds unacceptable, it will rarely have the option of expediently finding another willing buyer of its services or using that potential buyer's terms to resist these unacceptable terms. But a limited market alone is insufficient. A finding of constrained volition should only be made with respect to non-core terms because disrespecting the dictates of the core terms, such as price, has overtones of command economy theory. More significantly, after the core terms have been agreed to and the non-core terms are being negotiated, the investor is practically committed to the contract with the host state because of the transaction costs that it has incurred. At this juncture, it would be irrational to sacrifice the efforts that have gone towards agreeing to the core terms on account of a non-core terms.

The other militating reason is the relevance of the other part of coercion: the unfairness of the local consultant/employee provision. This characterisation follows if a provision's imposition is a product of any circumstance other than its promoter's (host state's) labour or skills. For example, a popular musician does not coerce an audience member to pay a very high ticket price – even though this musician naturally enjoys a monopoly position vis-à-vis this audience member – because his or her music is the product of his or her unique skills.[146] By contrast, in the sinking boat case the pirates profit from the occurrence of a violent storm to extort USD 5,000,000 from the affected person, and this is the factor that explains why courts have held such contracts

---

[146] Ibid., 87–88.

to be void. Similarly, in the investment dispute under consideration, the host state benefits from another fortuitous circumstance in imposing the local consultant/employee provision on the investor: the migrant crisis. Combining this conclusion with the earlier finding of constrained volition on the investor's part, it follows that the investor's consent with respect to this provision has been vitiated. This does not entail its general invalidity, but only that the remedy for its breach be proportionate to the gravity of the harm caused.

2.3.4.3 *Apportionment after Host State's Response*
This analysis of apportionment has assumed that the host state's conduct in breach of the applicable investment treaty is divorced from the investor's misconduct. This will be the case when the host state discovers such misconduct in the context of devising a strategy to combat the investor's claim in an investment arbitration, and then introduces this finding as the fundamental circumstance for its plea of post-establishment illegality. But in many cases it can be expected that the host state's conduct in breach will be its response to the investor's misconduct, as was the case in *Occidental v. Ecuador*. An example would be where the host state imposes numerous fines on the company in which the investment is held on account of the investor's misconduct, with such fines rendering the company insolvent. The investor subsequently claims for compensation on the basis of a breach of the applicable investment treaty, which the host state seeks to answer with the plea of post-establishment illegality – a plea that essentially argues that its breach is excused on the ground that its conduct was provided for under its domestic law.

In the example above, the host state's plea looks more like one of investment reprisal, but this appearance is deceptive. Most particularly, the investor's misconduct has not motivated the host state's conduct (the imposition of fines), as is required to raise a successful plea of investment reprisal.[147] Rather, it is an application of the relevant rule's dictates – a process governed by the rule of law, not any causal notions, because there is no causality between a breach of a rule and the subsequent legal consequence. This distinction might seem artificial, but it reflects a deeper truth about investment reprisal and post-establishment illegality. Investment reprisal concerns conscious responses to misconduct that compromise the host state's sovereignty, whereas post-establishment illegality is more concerned with notions of legality.

How investment reprisal differs from post-establishment illegality, however, is a distraction from the question that this section needs to answer: in circumstances where the host state's conduct in breach of the applicable

---

[147] See section 2.2.1 above.

investment treaty is also the conduct that should follow under its domestic law for the investor's misconduct, can post-establishment illegality be pleaded as a defence? The short answer is yes, but the extent of the protection that this defence can offer varies according to the rules on apportionment of liability detailed in sections 2.3.4 and 2.3.4.1 above. Accordingly, if the host state's conduct is the mandatory response under its domestic law to the investor's misconduct, then post-establishment illegality will operate as a complete defence. If, however, the host state enjoys some discretion as to its response, the principle of proportionality will be applicable and, because of that, post-establishment illegality will only partially excuse the host state's breach if the conduct constituting that breach is disproportionate.

2.3.5 Conclusions on Apportionment for Investment Reprisals and Post-Establishment Illegality

Tying all these strands together, apportionment for cases of investment reprisal and post-establishment illegality will usually be the same. The fact that there is a dispute in a case where investment reprisal is pleaded will usually mean that the host state's response has exceeded the bounds of proportionate restitution. In that circumstance, the investor's gains and the host state's losses are deducted from the host state's liability – a method that should usually be followed for cases of post-establishment illegality. This usual approach can be ousted in favour of setting off the host state's liability against the legal consequence that should be ordered upon the investor's breach of the relevant liability rule. Yet even assuming that that rule provides for a legal consequence, its application may be thwarted if the investor proves that the arbitral tribunal lacks the jurisdiction to order it or it is disproportionate relative to the wrongfulness of the investor's misconduct.

2.4 *Investment Reprisal and Post-Establishment Illegality – Attribution*

Attribution is another topic on which the rules for investment reprisal and post-establishment illegality converge. This is a topic that has received scant attention given the infrequency with which it arises.[148] It did arise, however, in *Yukos v. Russia* and *Churchill Mining v. Indonesia*. The relevant facts of the former have been summarised in section 2.2.1.2 above. What needs to be added to that account is that the investor acquired its shareholding from

---

[148] See, for example, Diel-Gilgor and Hennecke, 'Investment in Accordance with the Law', §§ 26–27.

other persons, who in turn had acquired it from Russia in a public auction. The significance of those circumstances is that there were various red flags signalling that this auction was compromised by corruption.[149] Accordingly, the investor's ownership was potentially tainted with illegality. This is not an instance of investment reprisal or post-establishment illegality, because the investor's ownership is a circumstance relevant to the arbitral tribunal's jurisdiction,[150] but lessons can be drawn from the arbitral tribunal's reasoning to inform the rules for answering the question: when can a former owner's misconduct be attributed to the investor?

The facts of *Churchill Mining v. Indonesia* are similar to those in *Yukos v. Russia*. There, the relevant third person forged a collection of mining exploration permits,[151] managed to register the interests they created with the relevant governmental authorities,[152] and then upgraded them to exploitation permits,[153] notwithstanding the fact that another company had been granted permits over the same permit area. Later, the investor executed contracts with this third person that let the investor work those permits in exchange for 75 per cent of the generated revenue.[154] The arbitral tribunal concluded that this misconduct should be attributed to the investor.[155] Its deciding reasons are difficult to decipher, but it appears that the most important factor was the investor's constructive knowledge of this misconduct,[156] which introduces the next question: what is constructive knowledge?

2.4.1 The Meaning of Constructive Knowledge

What is apparent from the arbitral tribunal's reasoning in *Churchill Mining v. Indonesia* is that constructive knowledge consists of two prongs, the first of which might be called potential knowledge. The investor has potential

---

[149] This is a contentious issue. Initially, it was thought that the shareholdings were auctioned at a price significantly below market value; see Black and others, 'Russian Privatization and Corporate Governance', 1736. For a contrary view, see Treisman, '"Loans for Shares" Revisited', 210–215.

[150] See section 2.1 of chapter 1.

[151] *Churchill Mining v. Indonesia* § 510.

[152] Although the third person probably had the assistance of a government insider for this purpose; ibid. § 528.

[153] Ibid. § 511.

[154] *Churchill Mining Plc v. Republic of Indonesia*, ICSID Case Nos. ARB/12/14 and ARB/12/40, Decision on Jurisdiction (24 February 2014) § 25.

[155] *Churchill Mining Plc v. Republic of Indonesia*, ICSID Case Nos. ARB/12/14 and ARB/12/40, Decision on Jurisdiction (24 February 2014) § 528.

[156] The arbitral tribunal often referred to the investor's lack of due diligence to justify its decision; see ibid. §§ 516–527, in particular.

knowledge of the third person's misconduct if it could have become aware of it by conducting its own investigations. In assessing this element, the arbitral tribunal in *Churchill Mining v. Indonesia* dismissed the investor's contention[157] that it engaged in 'exhaustive due diligence',[158] as the investor had failed to verify the assurances that its mining permits were valid.[159] This obligation to verify arose because the investor's sources on the mining permits' validity were persons who had an interest in their validity.

The second prong asks: were the investigations identified in the first prong reasonable to undertake? As the arbitral tribunal's reasoning in *Churchill Mining v. Indonesia* indicates, this inquiry ultimately involves weighing the benefits and detriments of performing the investigations. The arbitral tribunal specifically pointed to the facts that the investor knew of: one, the problems that plagued the host state's administration of mining permits; two, the lack of coordination between governmental agencies; three, the frequency of overlapping permit areas; and four, endemic corruption.[160] These four factors significantly increased the chance that the permits had been forged,[161] a chance which in turn increased the value of the benefit of discovering this forgery. As the notional value of this benefit was affixed at this high level, this necessarily meant that the investor should have pursued its investigations.

Although not addressed by either of the arbitral tribunals in *Yukos v. Russia* and *Churchill Mining v. Indonesia*, another pertinent issue is: when should the investor acquire this constructive knowledge? From the investor's perspective, the preferred answer is only during the period before it gained ownership of its investment. The investor could support this restriction by arguing that at any juncture before gaining ownership it has the chance to disassociate itself from the investment, a chance that might not be practicable postownership. But the better view is that the timing of the investor's knowledge is irrelevant because misconduct retains its wrongful nature regardless of when the investor knows of it. Additionally, the doctrine pronounced below on the requirement of taking ownership gives the investor the opportunity to wash its hands clean of the third person's misconduct. This is a convenient point to launch into the question: what is the requirement of taking ownership and what is its purpose?

---

[157] *Churchill Mining v. Indonesia* § 518.
[158] Ibid. § 485.
[159] Ibid. § 525.
[160] Ibid. § 517.
[161] Ibid. § 519.

2.4.2 The Requirement of Taking Ownership

Addressing the second part of that question, it must be appreciated that attributing this misconduct to the investor will effectively harm it. This harm can be potentially equal to the value of its investment loss because if the arbitral tribunal finds that it lacks jurisdiction on account of the misconduct, the investor will usually have no other means of pursuing its claim. There are few examples where the law inflicts this gravity of harm on the basis of mere knowledge, thereby explaining the inclusion of a requirement that the investor take ownership. Moreover, the commentary attaching to Article 11 of the ILC Articles on State Responsibility, which is the main article containing the rules on attributing the conduct of third persons to states, clarifies that mere acknowledgement of conduct is an insufficient basis for attribution and there must be an act that takes ownership.[162]

2.4.2.1 *Potential Modes of Taking Ownership*

That act could take three possible forms: endorsement, continuation, or accepting the benefit. The first possibility can readily be dismissed. Primarily, mere endorsement is unlikely to exacerbate the harm that the illegal conduct has already caused, invoking the Kantian idea that punishment, which is the practical outcome of attribution to the investor, should follow harm.[163] Additionally, punishing a person for a speech act is unusual because it constitutes a restriction on freedom of speech. If, for example, the investor wants to condone the previous owner's practice of avoiding what the investor thinks is an unfair tax, the investor should be at liberty to do so. A wise investor, however, would be mindful of the potential degradation of its goodwill for any such endorsement.

Continuation of the misconduct is a well-recognised act of taking ownership in general international law.[164] An example of its occurrence would be where the investor adopts the same methods as the former owner, both of which pollute a nearby waterway. But notwithstanding its sound doctrinal grounding, continuation should not be recognised as an act of taking ownership for the purposes of international investment law. The reason for this exclusion is that the former owner and the investor are related by nothing

---

[162] '[A]rticle 11 makes it clear that what is required is something more than a general acknowledgement of a factual situation, but rather that the State identifies the conduct in question and *makes it its own*'; ILC Articles on State Responsibility (with commentaries), Art. 11 (cmt 6) (emphasis added).

[163] Hall, *General Principles of Criminal Law*, 221.

[164] ILC Articles on State Responsibility (with commentaries), Art. 11 (cmt 6).

more than their ownership of the same investment. Further, their misconduct can be distinguished – a fact that stands in contrast to the instances of
continuation in general international law. The main case is *US v. Iran*.[165]
There, a group of students took American diplomats in Tehran hostage. The
state's act of continuation was to keep these diplomats hostage.[166] In this way,
the third persons' act was a necessary precursor to Iran's act of continuation.
Additionally, these acts are united by a common political purpose, whereas in
the pollution example the former owner and the investor act for two separate
purposes: their own profit.

What this analysis reveals is that the act of taking ownership must link the
investor to the third person's misconduct. That link must be of such a nature
that the investor becomes culpable, considering that a determination of attribution will make the investor liable for this misconduct. An act that would satisfy
this criterion of some minimal culpability is accepting the benefit. The investor
accepts the benefits of a third person's misconduct if, one, that misconduct
runs with the investment and, two, the investor fails to disown this misconduct.
As regards the first element, the misconduct must create some benefit for the
investment that the investor continues to profit from. An example would be
where the former owner builds a residential complex with inexpensive, but fire
hazardous, materials, which in turn passes on a benefit to the investor because
it pays a lower amount for this investment compared to what it would have paid
for it if the former owner had built it with the proper materials. For the second
element, the investor fails to disown if it does not take action to remedy the
harm resulting from the former owner's misconduct. What form this remedial
action will take depends on the nature of the misconduct. If, for example, it is
criminal conduct, the investor should inform the host state for it to potentially
prosecute the former owner; while for tortious conduct, the investor should
proceed to take appropriate remedial action itself. The costs that it incurs for
such action might later be recovered from the former owner.

2.4.2.2 *Objections to Disownership Element*
Aside from culpably linking the investor to the third person's misconduct,
the disownership element is also designed to give the investor an escape
route. But in cases where the misconduct relates to the ownership or legality
requirements for jurisdiction, disowning the former owner's misconduct will
usually hurt the investor rather than help. Take the facts from *Churchill*

---

[165] Crawford, *State Responsibility*, 183.
[166] *Case concerning United States Diplomatic and Consular Staff in Tehran (United States of America v. Iran)*, [1980] ICJ Reports 3, Judgment (24 May 1980) § 74.

Mining v. Indonesia.[167] In this case, the investor could have disowned the misconduct by reporting the suspicions of the forgery relating to its production permit to Indonesia, but if it had done so, the permit would almost certainly have been declared invalid. Not that there should be any profound sense of sympathy for the investor, however. First, as the investor must have constructive knowledge of the misconduct before it can be attributed, then the fallout from the decision on attribution should land on it, as opposed to subjecting the host state to the task of defending itself from a tainted claim. Second, the investor has the option of pursuing a claim against the third person. Third, in some cases, the investor might be able to negotiate a settlement with the host state, again with the option of subsequently claiming the costs of such settlement from the third person.

A final objection is that a legal fiction lies at the core of accepting the benefit: it assumes that the investor has actual knowledge of the former owner's misconduct. The difficulty with that assumption is that attribution for this purpose requires mere constructive knowledge. In most cases, however, a finding of constructive knowledge will necessarily imply the existence of actual knowledge. The preference for constructive knowledge over actual knowledge is for reasons of procedural expediency because proof of constructive knowledge can rely entirely on objective evidence.

3 INVESTMENT REPRISAL AND POST-ESTABLISHMENT ILLEGALITY – JURISDICTION AND ADMISSIBILITY

3.1 *Consent of the Investor*

As is the case with any cause of action, a plea of investment reprisal or post-establishment illegality can only be adjudicated if, one, the arbitral tribunal has jurisdiction to entertain it and, two, it is admissible. Most particularly for pleas of post-establishment illegality, one jurisdictional requirement ostensibly poses a considerable hurdle: the existence of the investor's consent. There is a pervasive theory that the investor must explicitly consent to the host state's plea, as the investor did in *Burlington v. Ecuador*.[168] The arbitral tribunals that have applied this theory do not refer to the investor's plea as one of post-establishment illegality, but rather designate it as a counterclaim.[169] This is the

---

[167] See section 2.4 above.

[168] *Burlington v. Ecuador*, Decision on Ecuador's Counterclaims § 60.

[169] These cases include: *Saluka Investments B.V. v. The Czech Republic*, Ad Hoc Arbitration (UNCITRAL Arbitration Rules), Decision on Jurisdiction over the Czech Republic's

first, albeit minor, error. As explained in section 4.1 below, a counterclaim is a claim advanced by the host state, acting as a respondent, that alleges some form of investor misconduct relating to another investment belonging to the investor. A plea of post-establishment illegality makes the same allegation, but with the difference that the investor's misconduct must relate to the same investment as that which it claims the host state has harmed.

3.1.1 Deriving the Investor's Consent from the Investor-State Dispute Resolution Clause

But this is ultimately a matter of terminology. The basic problem remains that arbitral tribunals usually[170] insist on explicit consent.[171] The default reasoning to support this conclusion is exemplified by the following extract from *Karkey v. Pakistan*:[172]

> The Tribunal finds that the text of the BIT is decisive in determining its jurisdiction over the counterclaims. In the present case, however, there is no provision in the BIT that contemplates the possibility of counterclaims.

Following this, the arbitral tribunal proceeded to highlight how the investor-state dispute resolution clause in the Pakistan-Turkey bilateral investment treaty contemplates a claim in arbitration being made only by the investor.[173] This is not surprising. What would be surprising is if the states that are party to the applicable investment treaty used this clause to declare the investor's consent to arbitrate causes of action or defences that the former initiate, which is what the arbitral tribunal's decision in *Karkey v. Pakistan* effectively requires. Investor-state dispute resolution clauses should be recognised for what they are: unilateral expressions of consent by the host state for the investor to bring a claim against it via arbitration.[174] Whether for arbitration or any other purpose, it is not the place of one person to give consent for another.

Counterclaim (7 May 2004); *Limited Liability Company Amto v. Ukraine*, SCC Case No. 080/2005, Final Award (26 March 2008); *Antoine Goetz and others and S.A. Affinage des Metaux v. Republic of Burundi*, ICSID Case No. ARB/01/2, Award (21 June 2012) ('*Goetz v. Burundi*'); *Occidental v. Ecuador*, Award; *Hesham T. M. Al Warraq v. Republic of Indonesia*, Ad Hoc Arbitration (UNCITRAL Arbitration Rules), Final Award (15 December 2014); *Urbaser v. Argentina*; *Burlington v. Ecuador*, Decision on Ecuador's Counterclaims; *Karkey Karadeniz Elektrik Uretim A.S. v. Islamic Republic of Pakistan*, ICSID Case No. ARB/13/1, Award (22 August 2017) ('*Karkey v. Pakistan*').

[170] For an exception, at least in arbitration conducted under the ICSID Convention, see *Goetz v. Burundi* §§ 279–280.
[171] See, for example, Reiner and Schreuer, 'Human Rights', 89.
[172] *Karkey v. Pakistan* § 1012.
[173] Ibid. §§ 1013–1014.
[174] See generally Paulsson, 'Arbitration Without Privity', 240–241.

There is another objection against this conventional wisdom. Strictly applied, it would deny the arbitral tribunal jurisdiction over pleas of investment reprisal because the investor does not consent to the arbitral tribunal's jurisdiction with respect to the misconduct that founds such pleas. But thinking back to the cases where investment reprisal was successfully pleaded,[175] could the investor have credibly pleaded that it did not consent to the arbitral tribunal's jurisdiction over those pleas? Patently not, because they formed an integral part of the dispute. On this basis, it is submitted that when an investor makes an investment in the host state and initiates investment arbitration against the host state, it implicitly consents to all pleas of defences that are founded on facts that form part of the dispute. For one, judicial economy supports this interpretation, because if the arbitral tribunal lacks jurisdiction, then the host state will be forced to turn to the courts to seek redress for the investor's misconduct. To this end, the most likely destination will be the host state's courts.[176] Yet the principal reason for giving the investor the option to pursue investment arbitration is to avoid this outcome,[177] most particularly because investors perceive that these courts are biased against them – a perception that is more likely to reflect reality if the host state's claim against the investor is filed after the investor is successful in investment arbitration. Accordingly, it is in investors' interests that they implicitly consent to the arbitral tribunal's jurisdiction over any pleas of defence based on investor misconduct advanced by host states.

3.1.2 Vitiation of the Investor's Consent by Arbitration Agreements or Exclusive Jurisdiction Clauses

A better argument that the investor has not consented to the arbitral tribunal's jurisdiction can be made if the host state's plea is based on a breach of contract and disputes arising from that contract are subject to an arbitration agreement or an exclusive jurisdiction clause. The same argument has been deployed by host states to thwart investors' 'treaty claims' – typically based on the rules on fair and equitable treatment or observance of undertakings – that are more accurately classified as contract claims, with the relevant contract containing an arbitration agreement or an exclusive jurisdiction clause.[178] This issue,

---

[175] For a list, see fn. 3 above.
[176] Reinisch and Malintoppi, 'Methods of Dispute Resolution', 694.
[177] Dolzer and Schreuer, *Principles of International Investment Law*, 232.
[178] See, for example, *SGS Société Générale de Surveillance S.A. v. Republic of the Philippines*, ICSID Case No. ARB/02/6, Decision of the Tribunal on Objections to Jurisdiction (29 January 2004) §§ 136–155. For an overview of the historical foundations of the relevant jurisprudence, see Ho, *State Responsibility of Breaches of Investment Contracts* 39–41.

however, is one of the most vexed in international investment law[179] because some arbitral tribunals have ruled that such contract breaches can transform into treaty breaches,[180] which begs the question: could the host state recast its contract claims against the investor as treaty breaches? As international investment law currently stands, a negative answer must follow. Unlike investors, host states do not have the luxury of arguing that the investor's contractual conduct reaches the standard of a treaty breach because, as international investment law stands, there are almost universally no obligations on investors in investment treaties.

3.2 *Jurisdictional Requirement of Relation to Investment*

One jurisdictional requirement that might prove problematic for a plea of investment reprisal or post-establishment illegality is the condition stipulating that the investor's conduct must relate to the investment. How this standard applies can be exemplified by the case of *Gemplus v. Mexico*. There, the investor was contracted by Mexico to establish a car registration scheme.[181] During the establishment of the scheme, it came to light that one of the investor's directors, Ricardo Cavallo, had previously been involved in large-scale car theft, as well as being responsible for torturing political prisoners in Argentina during the military dictatorship.[182] After this information came to light, the investor's contract was terminated.[183] Mexico unsuccessfully[184] pleaded contributory fault,[185] although the plea is better viewed as one of investment reprisal.

Considering that Mexico's own investigations did not reveal Cavallo's past, it was held that the investor could not have had potential knowledge of it.[186] Although the arbitral tribunal decided this matter assuming that it formed part of the legal content of investment reprisal, the investor's knowledge is better viewed as a circumstance relevant to the question of attribution of

---

[179] Causing a leading commentator to describe the jurisprudence as a 'crazy quilt rather than a Persian rug'; see Crawford, 'Treaty and Contract', 353.

[180] For an overview of these decisions, see Dolzer and Schreuer, *Principles of International Investment Law*, 190.

[181] *Gemplus S.A., SLP S.A., Gemplus Industrial S.A. de C.V. v. The United Mexican States*, ICSID Case No. ARB(AF)/04/3, Award (16 June 2010) § 4.38.

[182] Ibid. § 4.95.

[183] Although there are other reasons explaining this termination; see ibid. § 4.184.

[184] Ibid. § 11.15.

[185] Ibid. § 11.6.

[186] Ibid. § 11.14.

Cavallo's conduct to the investor.[187] This introduces a salient, but important, question: what is this 'conduct'? There are two candidates: the conduct of hiring Cavallo, or his prior criminal conduct. Although the arbitral tribunal indicates that the first candidate is the relevant conduct, the second candidate is the more doctrinally sound selection. This is because it is this conduct that is the foundational circumstance for a plea of investment reprisal – a conclusion that can be proven by asking: was the act of hiring the conduct that provoked Mexico? Patently not. What actually provoked Mexico was the fact that Cavallo had previously engaged in egregious criminal conduct.

With this conclusion, the relevant question is: does the conduct of previous involvement in large-scale car theft or the torturing of political prisoners specifically relate to an investment for the creation of a national car registry? For each form of conduct, the answers should be 'yes' and 'no'. A negative answer for the torturing of political prisoners might be surprising given the particularly egregious nature of this conduct, but it should not mask the fact that it has no relation to efficiently carrying on a business of registering cars.[188]

3.3 Admissibility – Prior Prosecution of Corrupted Governmental Officers

The jurisdictional issues potentially affecting a plea of investment reprisal or post-establishment illegality pale in comparison to the questions of admissibility that they raise, most particularly if the investor's misconduct takes the form of corruption of a state official. How to fairly deal with cases involving corruption has been a conundrum that the jurisprudence of international investment law has struggled with. The impulse reaction of arbitral tribunals has been to effectively punish the investor, most typically by ruling that they lack jurisdiction on account of the corruption.[189] But in those few cases where it has been found, arbitral tribunals have had to grapple with the fact that by punishing the investor, they are also rewarding the host state.[190] The problem with that approach is that with corruption, it takes two to tango.

---

[187] As discussed in section 2.1.1 above, investment reprisal does not focus on the investor's state of mind, but the host state's. Moreover, a principal's (investor's) knowledge of an agent's (another person's) conduct is treated as a requirement for the equivalent of attribution under domestic law; see, for example, Restatement (Third) of Agency § 4.06 (Knowledge Requisite to Ratification).

[188] This line of argument was also put forward by one of the investor's witnesses; see *Gemplus v. Mexico*, Award § 7-43.

[189] Menaker, 'Determinative Impact of Fraud and Corruption', 69.

[190] Llamzon, *Corruption*, 1–2.

The challenge is how to adequately respond to the investor's misconduct but not reward the host state for what is sometimes an equal role in the corruption. One proposed solution is to create a rule to the effect that, before a plea based on corruption is admitted, the host state must prosecute those individuals who were involved. By addressing its part in the corruption, the host state clears the way for its subsequent plea in investment arbitration.[191] A couple of problems afflict this approach, however. First, there may be legitimate reasons why the state should not prosecute the relevant persons; for example, it agrees not to prosecute in exchange for a person offering evidence in relation to a more serious matter. Second, if the host state does not prosecute, for whatever reason, the investor then becomes unaccountable for its part in the wrongdoing. On account of these reasons, it is considered that prior prosecution should not be a prerequisite for a plea based on corruption, although a successful prosecution could serve as cogent evidence that the alleged corruption has occurred.[192]

3.4 Admissibility – Initiation of Corruption by Host State

Another approach to resolving the corruption conundrum comes from *Gavrilovic v. Croatia*. The facts were highly contentious in this case,[193] but what is not disputed is that the investor purchased a state-owned company from Croatia in a public auction.[194] The investor lacked the requisite funds to finance this purchase. Contrary to Croatian law, the Croatian ministry of finance loaned these funds to the investor to complete the purchase.[195] Importantly, the arbitral tribunal found that granting this loan was part of a larger transaction. In that transaction, Croatia's consideration was to help the investor secure his investment, a company formerly owned by his family before being expropriated by the communist government of Yugoslavia after the Second World War. In exchange, the investor would assist Croatia in skirting an arms embargo that was detrimentally affecting its efforts in the Croatian War of Independence.[196]

---

[191] Kulick and Wendler, 'Corrupt Way to Handle Corruption?', 68.
[192] *Georg Gavrilovic and Gavrilovic d.o.o. v. Republic of Croatia*, ICSID Case No. ARB/12/39, Award (25 July 2018) § 345.
[193] Ibid. § 82.
[194] Ibid. § 95.
[195] Ibid. § 386.
[196] Ibid. § 349.

In rejecting Croatia's plea that the alleged corruption was a ground on which the arbitral tribunal should refuse to entertain the investor's claim, the arbitral tribunal held:[197]

> The Tribunal notes that its decision has been based on the evidence before it and on the legal conclusion that under international law the State cannot oppose a claim on grounds of illegality where the evidence shows that the State was involved with such illegality (including where, as here, it is likely on a balance of probabilities that *the State orchestrated the potentially illegal scheme*).

By extrapolation, this principle could form the basis of an admissibility rule for pleas of either investment reprisal or post-establishment illegality founded on corruption: such a plea is inadmissible if the host state initiates the misconduct. Morally, it is most appealing because, in this circumstance where both parties are at fault, the burden falls most heavily on the person who acts as the initiator.

3.5 Admissibility – Binding Adjudication of Investor Misconduct and Waiver

What is not controversial is the applicability of admissibility rules that bar pleas of investment reprisal or post-establishment illegality based on misconduct that either has already been adjudicated[198] or is the subject of a waiver by the host state. As regards the meaning of 'adjudicated', what must be emphasised is that the investment must have been at the centre of the relevant adjudicative proceedings. Accordingly, prosecuting a director of the investor for a criminal offence does not equate to adjudication. By contrast, if the host state prosecutes a company in which the investor has a shareholding for breaches of its competition law with the result that the company has to pay damages, any decision from the relevant court would amount to adjudication.

Sometimes referred to as 'approval', 'endorsement', or 'estoppel', waiver arises when the host state, in full knowledge of the surrounding circumstances, acts against the investor in a manner that is inconsistent with the legal rights accruing to it on account of the investor's misconduct.[199] This admissibility rule has only been recognised in respect of pleas claiming that the arbitral

---

[197] Ibid. § 398 (emphasis added).
[198] Prior adjudication is recognised as a general principle of law; see Griffith and Seif, 'Work in Progress', § 8.01.
[199] Feichtner, 'Waiver', § 5.

tribunal lacks jurisdiction because of the investor's misconduct,[200] although there is no reason why it cannot be extended to pleas of investment reprisal and post-establishment illegality which is seemingly what happened in *Bear Creek v. Peru*. In its reasoning, the arbitral tribunal noted that Peru continuously approved and supported the investor's conduct which it complained about via an effective plea of investment reprisal, meaning that it could not invoke it later to hold the investor to account.[201]

4 INVESTMENT REPRISAL, POST-ESTABLISHMENT ILLEGALITY, AND OTHER RELATED LEGAL CONCEPTS

This chapter began by distinguishing investment reprisal from post-establishment illegality. In the course of elucidating those concepts, it has become apparent that they also need to be distinguished from other similar legal concepts. This is the concern of the following sections, starting with a distinction that has already briefly been touched upon, that between post-establishment illegality and counterclaims.

4.1 *Post-Establishment Illegality and Counterclaims*

In section 3.1 above, it was posited that a plea of post-establishment illegality is distinguishable from a counterclaim as the latter relates to an investment other the one that stands at the centre of the investment arbitration.[202] As such, the facts on which a counterclaim is founded do not form part of the dispute, which means that the investor's consent to investment arbitration does not extend to it; in other words, the investor implicitly consents to the adjudication of pleas of post-establishment illegality by the submission of its claim, but no such implicit consent exists for counterclaims. The distinction between pleas of post-establishment illegality and counterclaims would therefore appear to hang solely on the interpretation given to the investor's consent. This interpretation is properly held up by reasons of judicial economy and the investor's probable preference for the adjudication of any of the host state's claims in investment arbitration. Yet if those reasons are accepted, then they might also be invoked to further extend the investor's consent to the host state's 'counterclaims', as this monograph conceives them. With this extension,

---

[200] Kalicki and others, 'Legality of Investment', 139.
[201] *Bear Creek v. Peru* § 567.
[202] See *Urbaser v. Argentina* § 1151. In this paragraph, the arbitral tribunal notes that a 'counterclaim', or what this monograph would call a plea of post-establishment illegality', must relate to the 'same investment' as the investor's cause of action.

the proposed distinction between pleas of post-establishment illegality and counterclaims becomes illusory.

But there must be boundaries on the scope of the investor's consent and the most logical boundary is that the host state's plea relate to the same dispute from which the investor's claim originates. This introduces the question: what facts make up the dispute for this purpose? More than merely relating to the investment, they must be connected to that investment's value because that is the factor that lies at the core of any investment arbitration.

4.2 *Investment Reprisal, Post-Establishment Illegality, and Unclean Hands*

The other concept that has to be distinguished from investment reprisal and post-establishment illegality is unclean hands. When allegations of misconduct on the part of the claimant are made in a case before an adjudicative body applying international law, they are frequently part of a broader argument that such claimant has unclean hands. Upon proof of unclean hands, the usual result is that the claimant's claim becomes inadmissible.[203] Assuming this to be true,[204] this is the first point on which investment reprisal and post-establishment illegality differ from unclean hands because, as defences, the former relate to the respondent (host state's) liability. It is considered, however, that unclean hands cannot be a rule relating to a claim's admissibility. The usual explanation for this relation is that permitting a claimant to claim in circumstances where it has unclean hands would amount to an abuse of process.[205] The exact meaning of abuse of process is contentious,[206] but, as explained above,[207] the relevant conduct must use the adjudicative process for a purpose other than that for which it was set up[208] (the abusive element[209]). Adjudicating a claim tainted by unclean hands cannot breach this principle because an adjudicative body's core purpose is to decide on the rights and

---

[203] See Douglas, 'Plea of Illegality', 186 (although only certain forms of misconduct make a claim inadmissible according to Douglas's theory); Llamzon, 'Yukos Universal ', 317; Newcombe, 'Investor Misconduct', 189 (although less serious forms of misconduct should be classified as relating to the liability question).

[204] For a summary of the cases in which it has allegedly been implicitly recognised, see Llamzon, 'Yukos Universal', 318.

[205] See, for example, *Churchill Mining v. Indonesia* § 492.

[206] Gaillard, 'Abuse of Process', 2.

[207] See section 1.2.1 above.

[208] Examples include submitting the same claim to multiple fora or filing a claim to attract media attention; see Gaillard, 'Abuse of Process', 7–10.

[209] Fukunaga, 'Abuse of Process', 183. See also the Anglo-American law cause of action 'abuse of process' as found in Restatement (Second) of Torts(1977) § 682.

wrongs of the disputants' conduct,[210] which is what any plea founded on
the claimant's misconduct asks the adjudicative body to do. Moreover, as
explained in section 3 of chapter 1, admissibility is fundamentally concerned
with a claim's readiness for adjudication, not with passing judgment on the
rights and wrongs of the conduct underlying the claim.

It follows that unclean hands can only be classified as a defence. But this
is where the similarities with investment reprisal and post-establishment
illegality end. Unlike investment reprisal and post-establishment illegality, the
doctrinal foundations of unclean hands have been seriously compromised[211] in
recent jurisprudence. In dismissing Russia's plea of unclean hands in *Yukos
v. Russia*, the arbitral tribunal[212] commented that:[213]

> The Tribunal is not persuaded that there exists a 'general principle of law
> recognized by civilized nations' within the meaning of Article 38(1)(c) of the
> ICJ Statute that would bar an investor from making a claim before an arbi-
> tral tribunal under an investment treaty because it has so-called 'unclean
> hands'.

A symptom of this lack of recognition is the uncertainty of unclean hand's
legal content. Hopefully by virtue of this chapter, the legal content of investment reprisal and post-establishment illegality is sufficiently defined to make
them amenable to application by arbitral tribunals.

---

[210] Finnis, 'Adjudication and Legal Change', 399. For an illuminating example of how procedural misconduct should be distinguished from substantive misconduct, reference can be
made to *Equatorial Guinea v. France*. There, it was held that Equatorial Guinea's rebranding
of a luxury apartment in Paris from a private residence to an embassy, for the purpose of
avoiding its forfeiture under French criminal law, could only amount to, if proven, an abuse
of rights. This was classified as a matter for the merits as, following the principle stated
above, it concerned the rights and wrongs of Equatorial Guinea's conduct that formed part
of the dispute. See *Equatorial Guinea v. France*, Preliminary Objections § 151. By contrast,
France's objection that Equatorial Guinea submitted its claim with a view to halting criminal proceedings in France was a matter for this claim's admissibility – an application of the
principle that a form of abuse of process is submitting a claim for an illegitimate reason; see
ibid. § 143.
[211] For a contrarian view, see Dumberry, 'State of Confusion', 243.
[212] This arbitral tribunal also included Stephen Schwebel, who had previously vouched for
the existence of unclean hands in international law; see *Military and Paramilitary Activities
in and against Nicaragua (Nicaragua v. United States of America)* [1986] ICJ Reports 259
(Dissenting Opinion of Judge Schwebel) § 268. See generally Schwebel, 'Cleans Hands,
Principle', (2013).
[213] *Yukos v. Russia* § 1358. This reflects the position in general international law; see Crawford,
Second Report on State Responsibility § 334, citing Rousseau, *Droit international public*, vol.
5, § 170.

5 CONCLUSION

This chapter completes the process, which began in chapter 4, of eluci-dating three similar but conceptually distinct defences. Investment reprisal and post-establishment illegality stand apart from mismanagement because they are based on investor misconduct. For investment reprisal, that mis-conduct is open textured because it need only amount to an affront to the host state's sovereignty, while post-establishment illegality requires illegal conduct under the applicable investment treaty, the host state's law, or a contract between the investor and the host state. What links the miscon-duct for post-establishment illegality to the investment is the benefit that the investment derives from it, whereas the link legal element for invest-ment reprisal is the misconduct's provocation of the host state, with this cause legal element also making investment reprisal a form of contributory fault. Technically, investment reprisal can operate as a complete defence if the host state's measure of reprisal achieves proportionate restitution. If a dispute proceeds to investment arbitration, however, it is likely that that standard has been exceeded, in which case the default option applies: the investor's gains and the host state's losses connected to the investor's miscon-duct are subtracted from the host state's liability. That same default option applies to the apportionment of liability on a finding of post-establishment illegality if the host state's response to the investor's illegality is dispropor-tionate, although this option only applies in so far as the liability rule that has been breached provides for a discretionary legal consequence, as opposed to a mandatory legal consequence. If there is a specification of a mandatory legal consequence, then the arbitral tribunal should reduce the host state's liability by an amount reflecting that legal consequence. This means that in cases where the application of a mandatory legal consequence gives rise to the host state's liability, post-establishment liability will act as a complete defence. This will also be the case when the host state applies a discretionary legal consequence in response to the investor's illegality and that legal con-sequence is proportionate.

6

A Restatement of Contributory Fault and Investor Misconduct in International Investment Law

1 A CHRONICLE OF CONTRIBUTORY FAULT AND INVESTOR MISCONDUCT

The remaining task is to deliver on the promise, set forth in chapter 1, to restate the rules on contributory fault and investor misconduct. To give that restatement its proper context, it is worth chronicling where this monograph has taken these concepts. Although contributory fault started life as a defence under the ILC Articles on State Responsibility,[1] Roberto Ago's assumption of the position of Special Rapporteur saw it reclassified as a remedy rule.[2] This new classification mirrored how the concepts equivalent to contributory fault in domestic law are viewed, and it has been accepted into the jurisprudence of international investment law. The practice of arbitral tribunals in investment arbitrations, however, has been to apply contributory fault as a defence – a position that it was submitted reflected contributory fault's true legal function. Rather than substantiating that position by citing the practice of arbitral tribunals, an attempt has been made to put the classification on firmer theoretical foundations, beginning by showing that defences are rules distinguishable from other types of rules. From there, a definition of defence was proposed to highlight what attributes it should have in comparison to other types of rules. The application of that definition entailed the original proposition that contributory fault was a defence, thereby bringing contributory fault back to where it began its life in international law.

The proper classification of contributory fault was only part of the story. The other part looked at its legal content. According to its original conception, contributory fault was made up of two legal elements: a causal contribution

---

[1] See United Nations, *Yearbook*, 50–55.
[2] Jagota, 'State Responsibility', 253–254.

by the claimant to its loss and the wrongful nature of the conduct constituting that cause. This conception was basically correct, but the vagueness of these legal elements was such that they obscured the adjudicative reasoning on contributory fault. The clarification process began with the cause legal element. After concluding that the current approach to causal questions was inadequate and inapplicable for international investment law, a new theory was proposed. Among other things, this theory mandated that direct causes be rigorously distinguished from indirect causes. What this meant was that there could not be one form of contributory fault, but two forms, depending on the causal directness of the investor's conduct. For the purposes of international investment law, these forms were called mismanagement (direct contribution) and investment reprisal (indirect contribution).

The significance of this distinction lay in the fault elements that attached to them; in other words, what made mismanagement wrongful was different from what made investment reprisal wrongful. For mismanagement, wrongfulness was established by the investor's foresight of the political risk that would subsequently crystallise into the host state's breach. This conduct will not be inherently objectionable in itself because it will usually be the act of making an investment, which is something that benefits the host state. By contrast, an indirect causal contribution for a finding of investment reprisal must be inherently wrong, and wrongful to such an extent that the host state should be provoked by it. Recognising that not all wrongful conduct will provoke the host state, but is nonetheless part of the fabric of the dispute because the relevant investment benefits from it, a third defence was introduced: post-establishment illegality.

By carefully dissecting the legal content of these defences, the first leg on the path towards making the adjudication of contributory fault and investor misconduct more transparent was completed. The next leg examined how a finding of any of these defences impacted on the host state's liability. As all of them would typically operate as partial defences, theories for apportioning liability were required. Again, the distinctive nature of the investor's fault for each defence means that apportionment for each differs. For mismanagement, the jurisprudence indicated that apportionment was a matter of guessing the disputants' fault or the causal potency of their contributions. But that approach assumes that the investor's conduct is of no value to the host state, which is usually not the case in investment arbitrations. On account of this, a new theory on apportionment was proposed, where each compensable loss was identified and liability for that loss was pinned to either the investor or the host state according to the rules developed for that purpose. As regards the apportionment of findings of investment reprisal, it was submitted that this task served as the arbitral tribunal's chance to punish the investor. This approach was problematic on two fronts, thus laying the platform for an alternative approach that saw the investor's gains and the host state's losses flowing from the investor's misconduct transferred to the host state as a representative figure of the investor's liability. This same set-off approach could also be used for apportioning liability on a finding of post-establishment illegality. By adopting these approaches, the default practice of intuitively picking a percentage can be a thing of the past. Apportionment can be a rational exercise, and a failure to provide reasons to support how liability should be divided is potentially a ground for challenging an arbitral award.

2   THE RULES OF MISMANAGEMENT, INVESTMENT REPRISAL, AND POST-ESTABLISHMENT ILLEGALITY

Against the background of all this theory, the restatement of the rules on contributory fault and investor misconduct can begin. At the beginning of this monograph, contributory fault in international investment was sourced to Article 39 of the ILC Articles on State Responsibility, which reads as follows:

> In the determination of reparation, account shall be taken of the contribution to the injury by wilful or negligent action or omission of the injured State or any person or entity in relation to whom reparation is sought.

From this provision, two defences emerged, the first of which was mismanagement:

Rule 1 – Mismanagement
It is a defence to any breach of an investment treaty by, excluding breaches involving corruption on the part of state officials, the host state if the investor directly caused its main investment loss.

Rule 2(a) – Mismanagement
In apportioning liability, the host state is:

  (i) fully liable for:
      1) the investor's direct contributions; and
      2) any tax payments made to the host state on the investor's indirect contributions
  (ii) partially liable, after deducting the degree of the investor's foresight of the political risk that materialises into its breach, for:
      1) the net income to its economy from the investor's indirect contributions
      2) any remaining amount likely to be injected into its economy that forms part of this loss ('qualifying remaining amount'); and

3) any profit component of the loss of an investment established by the investor.

Rule 2(b) – Mismanagement

In apportioning liability, the investor is:

(i) fully liable for any amount that is not a direct contribution, indirect contribution, or qualifying remaining amount; and
(ii) partially liable, to the extent of the degree of its foresight of the political risk that materialises into the host state's breach, for the net income from its indirect contributions and any profit component of the loss of an investment established by it.

This defence is a form of contributory fault, as is investment reprisal:

Rule – Investment Reprisal

It is a defence to any breach of an investment treaty by the host state if such breach is motivated by conduct of the investor that amounts to an affront to the host state's sovereignty.

Rule 2 – Investment Reprisal

If the host state's conduct which constitutes its breach:

(i) achieves proportionate restitution, then its liability is eliminated; or
(ii) exceeds proportionate restitution, then its liability is reduced by an amount that reflects any gains that the investor made and any losses that the host state incurred on account of the affront to its sovereignty.

Investment reprisal is an example of a defence whose foundational circumstance is investor misconduct, as is post-establishment illegality:

Rule 1 – Post-Establishment Illegality

It is a defence to any breach of an investment treaty if the investor performs post-establishment illegal conduct and such conduct benefits the investment that is the subject of the dispute between the host state and it.

Rule 2 – Post-Establishment Illegality (core illegality)

If the investor's main income-generating activity is illegal under the host state's domestic law, at the time that the investor first performs that conduct, then the defence in Rule 1 operates as a complete defence.

Rule 3 – Post-Establishment Illegality (peripheral illegality)

If the investor's conduct supports its main income-generating activity and is illegal under:

(i) a contract between the host state and it, then any proportionate legal consequence provided for under the contract for such conduct is set off against the host state's liability;

(ii)   the host state's domestic law and the relevant rule provides for a mandatory legal consequence, then that legal consequence is set off against the host state's liability;

(iii)   the host state's domestic law and the relevant rule provides for a discretionary legal consequence, then that legal consequence is set off against the host state's liability to an extent that is proportionate having regard to the gravity of the investor's misconduct; or

(iv)   the investment treaty, then any legal consequence provided for under this treaty for such conduct is set off against the host state's liability.

Rule 4 – Post-Establishment Illegality (no consequence for breach)

If the relevant liability rule does not stipulate a legal consequence for its breach, then the host state's liability is reduced by an amount that reflects any gains that the investor made and any losses that the host state incurred on account of the investor's conduct.

Rule 5 – Post-Establishment Illegality (response to investor's misconduct)

If the host state's conduct in breach of the investment treaty is also the conduct in response to the investor's breach of the relevant liability rule, then post-establishment illegality operates as a:

(i)   complete defence if that response is proportionate; or

(ii)   partial defence, applying the stipulations of Rule 4 to apportion liability, if that response is disproportionate, as measured against the standards in Rule 3.

This transformation takes the concepts of contributory fault and investor misconduct from a state of primitivism to one of development. The guesswork that arbitral tribunals have previously engaged in when applying these concepts, starting with whether they are relevant to jurisdiction, admissibility, liability, or remedies and ending with the apportionment of liability, should become a thing of the past. In the future, if arbitral tribunals wrongly classify an instance of investor misconduct as a circumstance relevant to their jurisdiction and decline jurisdiction on that basis, the investor will be on firmer doctrinal grounds in challenging that decision. Similarly, if arbitral tribunals fail to provide reasons for their apportionment of liability, this should also constitute a ground for appealing the arbitral award. What this ultimately means is that the adjudicative reasoning on contributory fault and investor misconduct will become more transparent, and that in turn will contribute to a bigger project: establishing the legitimacy of investment arbitration and international investment law.

Bibliography

Aaken, Anne van, 'Primary and Secondary Remedies in International Investment Law and National State Liability: A Functional and Comparative View' in Stephan Schill (ed.), *International Investment Law and Comparative Public Law* (2010)

Arria, Amelia and others, 'Trajectories of Energy Drink Consumption and Subsequent Drug Use during Young Adulthood', 179 *Drug and Alcohol Dependence* (2017)

Artigot i Golobardes, Mireia and Gomez Pomar, Fernando, 'Contributory and Comparative Negligence in the Law and Economics Literature' in Michael Faure (ed.), *Tort Law and Economics* (2009)

Austin, John, 'A Plea for Excuses: The Presidential Address', 57 *Proceedings of the Aristotelian Society* (1956–1957)

The Province of Jurisprudence Determined, vol. 1 (2nd ed., 1861)

Baker, Lynne, 'Folk Psychology' in Rob Wilson and Frank Keil (eds.), *The MIT Encyclopedia of the Cognitive Science* (1999)

Banifatemi, Yas, 'The Law Applicable in Investment Treaty Arbitration' in Katia Yannaca-Small (ed.), *Arbitration under International Investment Agreements: A Guide to the Key Issues* (2010)

Bar, Christian von, *Non-Contractual Liability Arising Out of Damage Caused to Another* (2009)

The Common European Law of Torts, vol. 2 (2000)

Bar, Christian von, Clive, Eric, and Schulte-Nölke, Hans (eds.), *Principles, Definitions and Model Rules of European Private Law* (2008)

Bederman, David, 'Contributory Fault and State Responsibility', 30 *Virginia Journal of International Law* (1990)

Beebee, Helen, 'Causing and Nothingness' in John Collins and others (eds.), *Causation and Counterfactuals* (2004)

Beebee, Helen and others, 'Introduction' in Helen Beebee and others (eds.), *Oxford Handbook on Causation* (2009)

Birmingham, Robert, 'Folk Psychology and Legal Understanding', 32 *Connecticut Law Review* (2000)

Bishop, Doak and others, *Foreign Investment Disputes: Cases, Materials, and Commentary* (2nd ed., 2014)

Bjorklund, Andrea, 'Emergency Exceptions: State of Necessity and *Force Majeure*' in Peter Muchlinski and others (eds.), *The Oxford Handbook of International Investment Law* (2008)

Black, Bernard and others, 'Russian Privatization and Corporate Governance: What Went Wrong?', 52 *Stanford Law Review* (2000)

Blackstone, William, *Commentaries on the Laws of England: Book the Fourth* (1769)

Bollecker-Stern, Brigitte, *Le préjudice dans la théorie de la responsabilité internationale* (1973)

Born, Gary, *International Commercial Arbitration* (2nd ed., 2014)

Brady, James, 'Recklessness, Negligence, Indifference, and Awareness', 43 *Modern Law Review* (1980)

Briggs, Ray, 'Normative Theories of Rational Choice: Expected Utility' in *Stanford Encyclopedia of Philosophy* (2014)

Brown, Chester, *A Common Law of International Adjudication* (2007)

'The Regulation of Foreign Direct Investment by Admission Requirements and the Duty on Investors to Comply with Host State Law', 21 *New Zealand Business Law Quarterly* (2015)

Buffett, Warren, *1992 Letter to Shareholders of Berkshire Hathaway Inc.* (1993)

Burgstaller, Markus and Ketcheson, Jonathan, 'Should Expropriation Risk Be Taken into Account in the Assessment of Damages?', 32 *ICSID Review* (2017)

Burr Williams, John, *The Theory of Investment Value* (1938)

Caflisch, Lucius, 'Unequal Treaties', 35 *German Yearbook of International Law* (1992)

Campbell, Kenneth, 'Offence and Defence' in Ian Dennis (ed.), *Criminal Law and Justice* (1987)

Canadian Paediatric Society, 'Needle Stick Injuries in the Community', 13 *Paediatrics Child Health* (2008)

Cardenas Garcia, Julian, 'The Era of Petroleum Arbitration Mega Cases', 25 *Houston Journal of International Law* (2013)

Chinkin, Christine, *Third Parties in International Law* (1993)

Christakis, Théodore, 'Les circonstances excluant l'illicéité: illusion optique?' in Jean Salmon (ed.), *Droit du pouvoir, pouvoir du droit: Mélanges offerts à Jean Salmon* (2007)

Churchland, Paul, 'Folk Psychology' in Paul Churchland and Patricia Churchland (eds.), *On the Contrary: Critical Essays 1987–1997* (1998)

Clapham, Andrew, *Human Rights Obligations of Non-State Actors* (2006)

Clermont, Kevin, 'Res Judicata as Requisite for Justice', 68 *Rutgers University Law Review* (2016)

Collins, Lawrence and others (eds.), *Dicey, Morris and Collins on the Conflict of Laws* (15th ed., 2012)

Colvin, Eric, 'Exculpatory Defences in Criminal Law', 10 *Oxford Journal of Legal Studies* (1990)

Condorelli, Luigi and Kress, Claus, 'The Rules of Attribution: General Considerations' in James Crawford and others (eds.), *The Law of International Responsibility* (2010)

Corton, Olivier, 'The Obligation of Cessation' in James Crawford and others (eds.), *The Law of International Responsibility* (2010)

Crawford, James, *Brownlie's Principles of International Law* (8th ed., 2012)

First Report on State Responsibility (1998)

Second Report on State Responsibility (1999)

State Responsibility (2013)

'Treaty and Contract in Investment Arbitration', 24 *Arbitration International* (2008)

Crawford, James and Olleson, Simon, 'The Application of the Rules of State Responsibility' in Mark Bungenberg and others (eds.), *International Investment Law: A Handbook* (2015)

Dam, Cees van, *European Tort Law* (2nd ed., 2013)

Damodaran, Aswath, *Investment Valuation: Tools and Techniques for Determining the Value of Any Asset* (2002)

Deakin, Simon and others, *Markesinis and Deakin's Tort Law* (5th ed., 2003)

Diel-Gligor, Katharina and Hennecke, Rudolf, 'Investment in Accordance with the Law' in Mark Bungenberg and others (eds.), *International Investment Law: A Handbook* (2015)

Dobbs, Dan, *Law on Remedies: Damages-Equity-Restitution* (1993)

Dodge, William, 'Res Judicata' in *Max Planck Encyclopedia of Public International Law* (updated January 2006)

Dolzer, Rudolf and Schreuer, Christoph, *Principles of International Investment Law* (2nd ed., 2012)

Douglas, Zachary, *The International Law of Investment Claims* (2009)

'The Plea of Illegality in Investment Treaty Arbitration', 29 *ICSID Review* (2014)

Dowe, Phil, 'Causal Processes' in *Stanford Encyclopedia of Philosophy* (2007)

Duarte d'Almeida, Luis, 'Defining "Defences"' in Andrew Dyson and others (eds.), *Defences in Tort* (2015)

Duff, Antony, *Answering for Crime: Responsibility and Liability in the Criminal Law* (2009)

Dugan, Christopher and others, *Investor-State Arbitration* (2011)

Dumberry, Patrick, 'State of Confusion: The Doctrine of "Clean Hands" in Investment Arbitration after the Yukos Award', 17 *The Journal of World Investment & Trade* (2016)

Dumberry, Patrick and Dumas-Aubin, Gabrielle, 'How to Impose Human Rights Obligations on Corporations under Investment Treaties?', 4 *Yearbook on International Investment Law and Policy* (2011–2012)

Dworkin, Ronald, *Taking Rights Seriously* (1978)

Dye, Frank (ed.), *Dictionary of Stem Cells, Regenerative Medicine, and Translational Medicine* (2017)

Dyson, Andrew and others, 'Thinking in Terms of Contract Defences' in Andrew Dyson and others (eds.), *Defences in Contract* (2017)

Edgerton, Henry, 'Legal Cause II', 72 *University of Pennsylvania Law Review* (1924)

Fair, David, 'Causation and the Flow of Energy', 14 *Erkenntnis* (1979)

Feichtner, Isabel, 'Waiver' in *Max Planck Encyclopedia of Public International Law* (2006)

Feldthusen, Bruce, *Economic Negligence: The Recovery of Pure Economic Loss* (4th ed., 2000)

Fernández-Armesto, Felipe, *Columbus* (1992)

Finnis, John, 'Adjudication and Legal Change' in John Finnis (ed.), *Philosophy of Law: Collected Essays Volume IV* (2011)

Fitzmaurice, Gerald, *The General Principles of International Law Considered from the Standpoint of the Rule of Law* (1957)
  The Law and Procedure of the International Court of Justice (1986)
Fletcher, George, *Rethinking Criminal Law* (2000)
Fodor, Jerry, *Psychosemantics: The Problem of Meaning in the Philosophy of Mind* (1987)
  'The Persistence of the Attitudes' in Scott Christensen and Dale Turner (eds.), *Folk Psychology and the Philosophy of Mind* (1993)
Frouville, Olivier de, 'Attribution of Conduct to the State: Private Individuals' in James Crawford and others (eds.), *The Law of International Responsibility* (2010)
Fukunaga, Yuka, 'Abuse of Process under International Law and Investment Arbitration', 33 *ICSID Review* (2018)
Fuller, Lon, *The Morality of Law* (revised ed., 1969)
Gaillard, Emmanuel, 'Abuse of Process in International Arbitration', 32 *ICSID Review* (2017)
Gardner, John, 'Fletcher on Offences and Defences', 39 *Tulsa Law Review* (2003)
  Offences and Defences: Selected Essays in the Philosophy of Criminal Law (2007)
Gardiner, Richard, *Treaty Interpretation* (2008)
Gilles, Stephen, 'On Determining Negligence: Hand Formula Balancing, the Reasonable Person Standard, and the Jury', 54 *Vanderbilt Law Review* (2001)
Goudkamp, James, *Tort Law Defences* (2013)
Gray, Belinda and others, 'Cardiovascular Effects of Energy Drinks in Familial Long QT Syndrome: A Randomized Cross-Over Study', 231 *International Journal of Cardiology* (2017)
Gray, Christine, *Judicial Remedies in International Law* (2nd ed., 1990)
Green, Leon, 'Foreseeability in Negligence Law', 61 *Columbia Law Review* (1961)
  The Rationale of Proximate Cause (1927)
Greenawalt, Kent, 'The Perplexing Borders of Justification and Excuse', 84 *Columbia Law Review* (1984)
Griffith, Gavan and Seif, Isabella, 'Work in Progress: Res Judicata and Issue Estoppel in Investment Arbitration' in Neil Kaplan and Michael Moser (eds.), *Jurisdiction, Admissibility and Choice of Law in International Arbitration: Liber Amicorum Michael Pryles* (2018)
Hall, Jerome, *General Principles of Criminal Law* (1960)
Hart, Herbert, 'Definition and Theory in Jurisprudence' in Herbert Hart (ed.), *Essays in Jurisprudence and Philosophy* (1983)
  Punishment and Responsibility: Essays in the Philosophy of Law (2008)
Hart, Herbert and Honoré, Tony, *Causation in the Law* (2nd ed., 1985)
Harten, Gus van, 'Perceived Bias in Investment Treaty Arbitration' in Michael Waibel and others (eds.), *The Backlash against Investment Arbitration* (2010)
Henckels, Caroline, *Proportionality and Deference in Investor-State Arbitration* (2015)
Hepburn, Jarrod, 'In Accordance with Which Host State Laws? Restoring the "Defence" of Investor Illegality in Investment Arbitration', 5 *Journal of International Dispute Settlement* (2014)
Hertsgaard, Mark, 'If It's Good Enough for Big Oil', *Bloomberg Business Week* (15 November 2014)
Hirschleifer, Jack, 'Investment Decision under Uncertainty: Choice Theoretic Approaches', 79 *Quarterly Journal of Economics* (1965)

Ho, Jean, *State Responsibility for Breaches of Investment Contracts* (2018)

Hoffmeister, Frank, 'Article 15: Consent to be bound by a treaty expressed by accession' in Oliver Dörr and Kirsten Schmalenbach (eds.), *Vienna Convention on the Law of Treaties: A Commentary* (2nd ed., 2018)

Honoré, Tony, 'Causation in the Law' in *Stanford Encyclopedia of Philosophy* (updated November 2010)

'Necessary and Sufficient Conditions in Tort Law' in David Owen (ed.), *Philosophical Foundations of Tort Law* (1995)

Horder, Jeremy, *Excusing Crime* (2007)

Horgan, Terence and Woodward, James, 'Folk Psychology is Here to Stay' in Scott Christensen and Dale Turner (eds.), *Folk Psychology and the Philosophy of Mind* (1993)

Howse, Rob, 'Designing a Multilateral Investment Court: Issues and Options', 36 *Yearbook of European Law* (2017)

Hume, David, *A Treatise of Human Nature* (1978 (reprint))

Hurd, Heidi, 'The Moral Magic of Consent', 2 *Legal Theory* (1996)

International Law Commission, *Draft Articles on Responsibility of States for Internationally Wrongful Acts, with Commentaries* (2001)

Jagota, S.P., 'State Responsibility: Circumstances Precluding Wrongfulness', 16 *Netherlands Yearbook of International Law* (1985)

James Jr., Fleming and Perry, Roger, 'Legal Cause', 60 *The Yale Law Journal* (1951)

Jansen, Nils, 'Developing Legal Doctrine: Fault in the German Law of Delict' in Nils Jansen (ed.), *The Development and Making of Legal Doctrine, Volume 6* (2010)

Jeffries Jr., John and Stephan III, Paul, 'Defenses, Presumptions, and Burden of Proof in the Criminal Law', 88 *The Yale Law Journal* (1979)

Jones, Michael (ed.), *Clerk and Lindsell on Torts* (20th ed., 2010)

Junker, Abbo, *Internationales Privatrecht* (2nd ed., 2017)

Kalicki, Jean and others, 'Legality of Investment' in Meg Kinnear and others (eds.), *Building International Investment Law: The First 50 Years of ICSID* (2015)

others, 'What Are the Appropriate Remedies for Findings of Illegality in Investment Arbitration?' in Andrea Menaker (ed.), *International Arbitration and the Rule of Law: Contribution and Conformity* (2017)

Kantor, Mark, 'The Impact of Contributory Investor Conduct: Only with Difficulty Commensurable' in Meg Kinnear and others (eds.), *Building International Investment Law: The First 50 Years of ICSID* (2015)

Mark, *Valuation in International Arbitration* (2008)

Kaushal, Asha, 'Revisiting History: How the Past Matters', 50 *Harvard International Law Journal* (2009)

Kaveny, Cathleen, 'Inferring Intention from Foresight', 120 *Law Quarterly Review* (2004)

Keating, Gregory, 'The Idea of Fairness in the Law of Enterprise Liability', 95 *Michigan Law Review* (1997)

Keeton, Robert, *Legal Cause in the Law of Torts* (1963)

Keeton, Werdner and others, *Prosser and Keeton on the Law of Torts* (5th ed., 1984)

Kelsen, Hans, *Principles of International Law* (2nd ed. (by Robert Tucker), 1967)

Kennedy, John, *JFK Address at U.N. General Assembly* (1961)

Kerr, John and others, 'Apoptosis: A Basic Biological Phenomenon with Wide-Ranging Implications in Tissue Kinetics', 26 *British Journal of Cancer* (1972)

Kingsbury, Benedict and Schill, Stephan, 'Public Law Concepts to Balance Investors' Rights with State Regulatory Actions in the Public Interest: The Concept of Proportionality' in Stephan Schill (ed.), *International Investment Law and Comparative Public Law* (2010)

Kruschwitz, Lutz and Löffler, Andreas, *Discounted Cash Flow: A Theory of the Valuation of Firms* (2006)

Kulick, Andreas and Wendler, Carsten, 'A Corrupt Way to Handle Corruption? Thoughts on the Recent ICSID Case Law on Corruption', 37 *Legal Issues of Economic Integration* (2010)

Lapradelle, Albert and Politis, Nicolas, *Recueil des arbitrages internationaux (volume I)* (1905)

Lehmann, Heinrich, *Recht der Schuldverhältnisse: Ein Lehrbuch von Ludwig Enneccerus* (1958)

Lengwiler, Yvan, 'The Origins of Expected Utility Theory' in Wolfgang Hafner and Heinz Zimmermann (eds.), *Vinzenz Bronzin's Option Pricing: Models, Expositions, and Appraisals* (2009)

Llamzon, Aloysius, *Corruption in International Investment Arbitration* (2014)

　'Yukos Universal Limited (Isle of Man) v The Russian Federation: The State of the "Unclean Hands" Doctrine in International Investment Law: Yukos as both Omega and Alpha', 30 *ICSID Review* (2015)

Locke, John, *An Essay Concerning Human Understanding, Book III* (1690)

Lowe, Vaughan, 'Precluding Wrongfulness or Responsibility: A Plea for Excuses', 10 *European Journal of International Law* (1999)

MacCormick, Neil, *Rhetoric and The Rule of Law: A Theory of Legal Reasoning* (2005)

Machina, Mark, 'Expected Utility Hypothesis' in *The New Palgrave Dictionary of Economics* (3rd ed., 2018)

Mackie, John, *The Cement of the Universe: A Study of Causation* (1974)

Malone, Wex, 'Ruminations on Cause-in-Fact', 9 *Stanford Law Review* (1956)

Mansour, Affef Ben, 'Circumstances Precluding Wrongfulness in the ILC Articles on State Responsibility: Consent' in James Crawford and others (eds.), *The Law of International Responsibility* (2010)

Marboe, Irmgard, *Calculation of Compensation and Damages in International Investment Law* (2nd ed., 2017)

Markesinis, Basil and Unberath, Hannes, *The German Law of Torts: A Comparative Treatise* (4th ed., 2002)

Matsumoto, David (ed.), *The Cambridge Dictionary of Psychology* (2009)

Maupin, Julie, 'Transparency in International Investment Law: The Good, the Bad and the Murky' in Andrea Bianchi and Anne Peters (eds.), *Transparency in International Law* (2013)

McLachlan, Campbell and others, *International Investment Arbitration: Substantive Principles* (2nd ed., 2017)

Menaker, Andrea, 'The Determinative Impact of Fraud and Corruption on Investment Arbitration', 25 *ICSID Review* (2010)

Merizalde, Juan Felipe, 'Proportionality, Contributory Negligence and Other Equity Considerations in Investment Arbitration', 8 *Investment Treaty Arbitration and International Law* (2015)

Meyer, Susan, *Aristotle on Moral Responsibility: Character and Cause* (2011)

Mill, John Stuart, *A System of Logic, Ratiocinative and Inductive*, vol. I (1843)

Minow, Martha, 'Archetypal Legal Scholarship: A Field Guide', 63 *Journal of Legal Education* (2013)

Moore, Michael, *Act and Crime: The Philosophy of Action and Its Implications for Criminal Law* (2nd ed., 2010)

    Causation and Responsibility: An Essay in Law, Morals, and Metaphysics (2009)

Morse, Stephen, 'Determinism and the Death of Folk Psychology: Two Challenges to Responsibility from Neuroscience', 9 *Minnesota Journal of Law, Science & Technology* (2008)

Moutier-Lopet, Anaïs, 'Contribution to the Injury' in James Crawford and others (eds.), *The Law of International Responsibility* (2010)

Murray, Peter and Stürner, Rolf, *German Civil Justice* (2004)

Newcombe, Andrew, 'General Exceptions in International Investment Agreements' in Marie-Claire Cordonier Segger and others (eds.), *Sustainable Development in World Investment Law* (2011)

    'Investor Misconduct: Jurisdiction, Admissibility or Merits?' in Chester Brown and Kate Miles (eds.), *Evolution in Investment Treaty Law and Arbitration* (2011)

Neyers, Jason, 'A Theory of Vicarious Liability', 43 *Alberta Law Review* (2005)

Nolan, Brett, 'Are Railroads Liable When Lightning Strikes?', 79 *The University of Chicago Law Review* (2012)

Olleson, Simon, 'Attribution in Investment Treaty Arbitration', 31 *ICSID Review* (2016)

Orwell, George, *Nineteen Eighty-Four* (1987 ed.)

Paddeu, Federica, 'Clarifying the Concept of Circumstances Precluding Wrongfulness (Justifications) in International Law' in Lorand Bartels and Federica Paddeu (eds.), *Exceptions and Defences in International Law* (forthcoming)

    Justification and Excuse in International Law: Concept and Theory of General Defences (2018)

Palandt, Otto, *Bürgerliches Gesetzbuch* (77th ed., 2018)

Parlett, Kate, 'Diplomatic Protection and the International Court of Justice' in Christian Tams and James Sloan (eds.), *The Development of International Law by the International Court of Justice* (2013)

Parra, Antonio, *The History of ICSID* (2012)

Paulsson, Jan, 'Arbitration Without Privity', 10 *ICSID Review* (1995)

    'Jurisdiction and Admissibility' in Gerald Aksen and others (eds.), *Global Reflections on International Law, Commerce and Dispute Resolution: Liber Amicorum in Honour of Robert Briner* (2005)

Pauwelyn, Joost, 'Defenses and the Burden of Proof in International Law' in Lorand Bartels and Federica Paddeu (eds.), *Exceptions and Defences in International Law* (forthcoming)

Pearson, Richard, 'Apportionment of Losses under Comparative Fault: An Analysis of the Alternatives', 40 *Louisiana Law Review* (1980)

Perry, Stephen, 'Protected Interests and Undertakings in the Law of Negligence', 42 *University of Toronto Law Journal* (1992)

Petersmann, Ernst Ulrich, 'Introduction and Summary: "Administration of Justice" in International Investment Law and Adjudication?' in Pierre-Marie Dupuy and others (eds.), *Human Rights in International Investment Law and Arbitration* (2009)

Pfeil, Julia, 'Naulilaa Arbitration (Portugal v Germany)' in *Max Planck Encyclopedia of Public International Law* (updated March 2007)

Phelps, Kerryn and Hassed, Craig, *Genetic Conditions – General Practice: The Integrative Approach Series* (2012)

Phelps, Shirelle and Lehman, Jeffrey (eds.), *West's Encyclopedia of American Law* (2nd ed., 2005)

Phillips, Jerry, 'Product Misrepresentation and the Doctrine of Causation', 2 *Hofstra Law Review* (1974)

Plakokefalos, Ilias, 'Causation in the Law of State Responsibility and the Problem of Overdetermination: In Search of Clarity', 26 *European Journal of International Law* (2015)

Pollock, Frederick, *Essays in Jurisprudence and Ethics* (1882)

Price, John, *The Conscious Investor: Profiting from the Timeless Value Approach* (2011)

Proelss, Alexander, 'Article 34: General rule regarding third States' in Oliver Dörr and Kirsten Schmalenbach (eds.), *Vienna Convention on the Law of Treaties: A Commentary* (2nd ed., 2018)

Prosser, William, 'Comparative Negligence', 51 *Michigan Law Review* (1953)

Puppe, Ingeborg, 'The Concept of Causation in the Law' in Benedict Kahmen and Markus Stepanians (eds.), *Critical Essays on 'Causation and Responsibility'* (2013)

Radcliffe, Matthew, 'From Folk Psychology to Commonsense' in Daniel Hutto and Matthew Ratcliffe (eds.), *Folk Psychology Re-Assessed* (2007)

Rapp, Geoffrey, 'The Wreckage of Recklessness', 86 *Washington University Law Review* (2008)

Reiner, Clara and Schreuer, Christoph, 'Human Rights and International Investment Arbitration' in Pierre-Marie Dupuy and others (eds.), *Human Rights in International Investment Law and Arbitration* (2009)

Reinisch, August, 'Jurisdiction and Admissibility in International Investment Law', 16 *The Law & Practice of International Courts and Tribunals* (2017)

'The Proliferation of International Dispute Settlement Mechanisms' in Isabelle Buffard and Gerhard Hafner (eds.), *International Law between Universalism and Fragmentation: Festschrift in Honour of Gerhard Hafner* (2008)

Reinisch, August and Malintoppi, Loretta, 'Methods of Dispute Resolution' in Peter Muchlinski and others (eds.), *The Oxford Handbook of International Investment Law* (2008)

Ripinsky, Sergey and Williams, Kevin, *Damages in International Investment Law* (2008)

Robb, David and Heil, John, 'Mental Causation' in *Stanford Encyclopedia of Philosophy* (updated 14 January 2013)

Roberts, Anthea, 'Power and Persuasion in Investment Treaty Interpretation: The Dual Role of States', 104 *Australian Journal of International Law* (2010)

Robinson, Paul, 'Criminal Law Defenses: A Systematic Analysis', 82 *Columbia Law Review* (1982)

Rousseau, Charles, *Droit international public*, vol. 5, *Les rapports conflictuels* (5th ed., 1983)

Ruffert, Matthias, 'Reprisals' in *Max Planck Encyclopedia of Public International Law* (2015)

Russell, Bertrand, 'On the Notion of Cause', 13 *Proceedings of the Aristotelian Society* (1912–1913)

Sabahi, Borzu, *Compensation and Restitution in Investor-State Arbitration: Principles and Practice* (2011)

Sabahi, Borzu and Duggal, Kabir, 'Occidental Petroleum v Ecuador (2012): Observations on Proportionality, Assessment of Damages and Contributory Fault', 28 *ICSID Review* (2013)

Säcker, Franz and others (eds.), *Münchener Kommentar zum Bürgerlichen Gesetzbuch*, Book 6 (7th ed., 2017)

Salacuse, Jeswald and Sullivan, Nicholas, 'Do BITs Really Work?: An Examination of Bilateral Investment Treaties and Their Grand Bargain', 46 *Harvard International Law Journal* (2005)

Salomon, Claudia, 'Prescription Periods for Investment Treaty Claims: A Brief Comment', 3 *Transnational Dispute Management* (2004)

Sattorova, Mavluda, *The Impact of Investment Treaty Law on Host States: Enabling Good Governance?* (2018)

Scalia, Antonin and Garner, Bryan, *Reading Law* (2012)

Schill, Stephan, 'Illegal Investments in Investment Treaty Arbitration', 11 *The Law & Practice of International Courts and Tribunals* (2012)

Schlemmer, Engela, 'Investment, Investor, Shareholders' in Peter Muchlinski and others (eds.), *The Oxford Handbook of International Investment Law* (2008)

Schneiderman, David, *Constitutionalizing Economic Globalization: Investment Rules and Democracy's Promise* (2008)

Schreuer, Christoph, 'Consent to Arbitration' in Peter Muchlinski and others (eds.), *The Oxford Handbook of International Investment Law* (2008)

Schreuer, Christoph and others, *The ICSID Convention: A Commentary* (2nd ed., 2009)

Schroeder, Tim, 'Desire' in *Stanford Encyclopedia of Philosophy* (2015)

Schultz, Thomas and Dupont, Cédric, 'Investment Arbitration: Promoting the Rule of Law or Over-Empowering Investors? A Quantitative Empirical Study', 25 *European Journal of International Law* (2014)

Schultz, Wolfram, 'Neuronal Reward and Decision Signals: From Theories to Data', 95 *Physiological Reviews* (2015)

Schwebel, Stephen, 'Clean Hands, Principle' in *Max Planck Encyclopedia of Public International Law* (2013)

Schwitzgebel, Eric, 'Belief' in *Stanford Encyclopedia of Philosophy* (updated March 2015)

Scott, Austin, 'Collateral Estoppel by Judgment', 56 *Harvard Law Review* (1942)

Seavey, Warren, 'Reliance upon Gratuitous Promises or Other Conduct', 64 *Harvard Law Review* (1951)

Sebok, Anthony, 'Purpose, Belief, and Recklessness: Pruning the Restatement (Third)'s Definition of Intent', 54 *Vanderbilt Law Review* (2001)

Shakespeare, William, *King Lear*

Silberman, Linda and others, *Civil Procedure: Theory and Practice* (4th ed., 2013)

Simons, Kenneth, 'Exploring the Relationship between Consent, Assumption of Risk, and Victim Negligence' in John Oberdiek (ed.), *Philosophical Foundations of the Law of Torts* (2014)

'The Puzzling Doctrine of Contributory Negligence', 16 *Cardozo Law Review* (1995)

Sinai, Yuval, 'Reconsidering *Res Judicata*: A Comparative Perspective', 21 *Duke Journal of Comparative & International Law* (2011)

Sorabji, Richard, *Necessity, Cause, and Blame: Perspectives on Aristotle's Theory* (1980)

Sourgens, Frederic and others, *Evidence in International Investment Arbitration* (2018)

Spiegel, Hans, 'Origin and Development of Denial of Justice', 32 *The American Journal of International Law* (1938)

Stapleton, Jane, 'Causation in the Law' in Helen Beebee and others (eds.), *The Oxford Handbook of Causation* (2009)

'Factual Causation', 38 *Federal Law Review* (2010)

'Legal Cause: Cause-in-Fact and the Scope of Liability for Consequences', 54 *Vanderbilt Law Review* (2001)

Steel, Sandy, 'Defining Causal Counterfactuals in Negligence', 130 *Law Quarterly Review* (2014)

Proof of Causation in Tort Law (2015)

Stern, Brigitte, 'The Obligation to Make Reparation' in James Crawford and others (eds.), *The Law of International Responsibility* (2010)

Stich, Stephen, *From Folk Psychology to Cognitive Science: The Case Against Belief* (1983)

Stretton, Dean, 'The Birth Torts: Damages for Wrongful Birth and Wrongful Life', 10(1) *Deakin Law Review* (2005)

Szurek, Sandra, 'The Notion of Circumstances Precluding Wrongfulness' in James Crawford and others (eds.), *The Law of International Responsibility* (2010)

Tomuschat, Christian, 'International Organizations as Third Parties under the Law of International Treaties' in Enzo Cannizzaro (ed.), *The Law of Treaties Beyond the Vienna Convention* (2011)

Trebilcock, Michael, *The Limits of Freedom of Contract* (1993)

Treisman, Daniel, '"Loans for Shares" Revisited', 26 *Post-Soviet Affairs* (2010)

United Nations, *Yearbook of the International Law Commission 1958*, vol. II (1958)

Vandevelde, Kenneth, 'Rebalancing through Exceptions', 17 *Lewis & Clark Law Review* (2013)

Vattel, Emmerich de, *The Law of Nations or the Principles of Natural Law*, trans. Charles Fenwick (1916)

Viñuales, Jorge E., 'Seven Ways of Escaping a Rule: Of Exceptions and Their Avatars in International Law' in Lorand Bartels and Federica Paddeu (eds.), *Exceptions and Defences in International Law* (forthcoming)

Virgo, Graham, 'Justifying Necessity as a Defence in Tort Law' in Andrew Dyson and others (eds.), *Defences in Tort* (2015)

Vrey, Rogier de, *Towards a European Unfair Competition Law: A Clash Between Legal Families* (2005)

Wade, John, 'The Place of Assumption of Risk in the Law of Negligence', 22 *Louisiana Law Review* (1961)

Waibel, Michael, 'Investment Arbitration: Jurisdiction and Admissibility' in August Reinisch and others (eds.), *International Investment Law: A Handbook* (2015)

Walton, Christopher and others (eds.), *Charlesworth & Percy on Negligence* (12th ed., 2010)

Wasserstrom, Richard, *The Judicial Decision: Towards a Theory of Legal Justification* (1961)

Weber, Max, *Economy and Society: An Outline of Interpretive Sociology*, vol. 1 (1968)

Weinrib, Ernest, 'Illegality as a Tort Defence', 26 *University of Toronto Law Journal* (1976)

Wells, Louis, 'Backlash to Investment Arbitration: Three Causes' in Michael Waibel and others (eds.), *The Backlash against Investment Arbitration* (2010)

Whiteman, Marjorie, *Damages in International Law*, vol. I (1937)

Wigmore, John, 'Tripartite Division of Torts', 8 *Harvard Law Review* (1894)

Williams, Glanville, *Joint Torts and Contributory Negligence: A Study of Concurrent Fault in Great Britain, Ireland and the Common-Law Dominions* (1951)

'Offences and Defences', 2 *Legal Studies* (1982)

'The Logic of "Exceptions"', 47 *Cambridge Law Journal* (1988)

'The Unresolved Problem of Recklessness', 8 *Legal Studies* (1988)

Wolff, Christian, 'Jus Gentium Methodo Scientifica Pertractatum' in James Scott (ed.), *The Classics of International Law*, vol. II, trans. Joseph Drake (1934)

Wouters, Jan and Verhoeven, Sten, 'Prescription' in *Max Planck Encyclopedia of Public International Law* (updated November 2008)

Wright, Richard, 'Causation in Tort Law', 73 *California Law Review* (1985)

'Causation, Responsibility, Risk, Probability, Naked Statistics, and Proof: Pruning the Bramble Bush by Clarifying the Concepts', 73 *Iowa Law Review* (1988)

'Duty, Causal Contribution, and the Extent of Legal Responsibility', 54 *Vanderbilt Law Review* (2001)

Wright, Richard and Puppe, Ingeborg, 'Causation: Linguistic, Philosophical, Legal and Economic', 91 *Chicago-Kent Law Review* (2016)

York, Kenneth and Bauman, John, *Remedies: Cases and Materials* (3rd ed., 1979)

Youngs, Raymond, *English, French & German Comparative Law* (2nd ed., 2007)

Zipursky, Benjamin, 'Reasonableness In and Out of Negligence Law', 163 *University of Pennsylvania Law Review* (2015)

Zuckerman, Adrian, *Zuckerman on Civil Procedure: Principles of Practice* (3rd ed., 2013)

Index